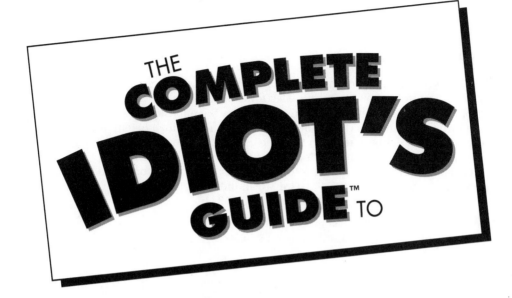

THE COMPLETE IDIOT'S GUIDE™ TO

Windows® 95
Second Edition

by Paul McFedries

A Division of Macmillan Publishing
201 W.103rd Street, Indianapolis, IN 46290 USA

To Karen, of course.

©1997 Que® Corporation

International Standard Book Number: 0-7897-1161-3
Library of Congress Catalog Card Number: 97-65009

99 98 97   8 7 6 5 4 3 2 1

Interpretation of the printing code: the rightmost number of the first series of numbers is the year of the book's printing; the rightmost number of the second series of numbers is the number of the book's printing. For example, a printing code of 97-1 shows that the first printing of the book occurred in 1997.

Screen reproductions in this book were created by means of the program Collage Complete from Inner Media, Inc., Hollis, NH.

Printed in the United States of America

Publisher
Roland Elgey

Editorial Services Director
Elizabeth Keaffaber

Publishing Director
Lynn E. Zingraf

Acquistions Editor
Martha O'Sullivan

Acquistions Coordinator
Michelle R. Newcomb

Managing Editor
Michael Cunningham

Product Development Specialist
Henly Wolin

Production Editor
Mark Enochs

Director of Marketing
Lynn E. Zingraf

Cover Designers
Dan Armstrong
Barbara Kordesh

Book Designer
Kim Scott

Illustrations
Judd Winick

Technical Specialist
Nadeem Muhammed

Production Team
Mary Hunt, Tricia Flodder,
Daniela Raderstorf, Beth Rago

Indexer
Becky Hornyak

Thanks to Tim Schubach and Rick Brown for ensuring
the technical accuracy of this book.

We'd Like to Hear from You!

As part of our continuing effort to produce books of the highest possible quality, Que would like to hear your comments. To stay competitive, we *really* want you, as a computer book reader and user, to let us know what you like or dislike most about this book or other Que products.

You can mail comments, ideas, or suggestions for improving future editions to the address below, or send us a fax at (317) 581-4663. For the on-line inclined, Macmillan Computer Publishing has a forum on CompuServe (type **GO QUEBOOKS** at any prompt) through which our staff and authors are available for questions and comments. The address of our Internet site is **http://www.mcp.com** (World Wide Web).

In addition to exploring our forum, please feel free to contact me personally to discuss your opinions of this book: on America Online, I'm at **HWolin**, and on the Internet, I'm **hwolin@que.mcp.com**.

Thanks in advance—your comments will help us to continue publishing the best books available on computer topics in today's market.

Henly Wolin
Product Development Specialist
Que Corporation
201 W. 103rd Street
Indianapolis, Indiana 46290
USA

Contents at a Glance

Contents

Introduction

These days, there's no shortage of ways Windows users are made to feel like complete idiots. Armies of alleged "Windows experts" and "Windows consultants"—their pockets appropriately protected—charge exorbitant fees for prattling on in some techno-language that bears only the faintest resemblance to English. Magazines spout Windows "tips" and "tricks" that give a whole new meaning to the word "esoteric." The shelves in bookstore computer sections groan under the weight of more bloated and incomprehensible Windows volumes than you can shake a stick at. (If you plan to check this out, be careful: I think public stick shaking is illegal in some states.) And, of course, the worst offender is Windows itself, with its genius for turning routine tasks into heart-stopping adventures.

Well, a pox on all their houses! We are definitely *not* complete idiots. (*Partial* idiots? Well, okay, maybe sometimes; but *complete* idiots? No, never.) In fact, we're smart enough to know a thing or two ourselves:

➤ We're smart enough to know that, despite the claims of those geek-speaking gurus, Windows isn't brain surgery or even rocket science. So it shouldn't take a Ph.D. to figure out how to use it.

➤ We're smart enough to know that the only truly useful tips are those that either make Windows easier to use or make it easier for us to get our work done.

➤ We're smart enough to know that life's too short to read five kazillion pages of arcane and mostly useless information about a computer program. We have lives to lead, after all.

➤ And we're smart enough to know that there *has* to be an easier way to work with Windows.

A Book for Smart Windows Idiots

If you're no fool, but Windows makes you feel like one, welcome to *The Complete Idiot's Guide to Windows 95, Second Edition*! This is a book for those of you who aren't (and don't even want to be) computer wizards. This is a book for those of you who have a job to do (a job that includes working with Windows 95) and just want to get it done as quickly and painlessly as possible. This isn't one of those absurdly serious, put-a-crease-in-your-brow-and-we'll-begin books. On the contrary, you'll even have a little fun at Windows 95's expense as you go along. (I do, however, feel compelled to apologize for some of the jokes in advance.)

You'll also be happy to know that this book doesn't assume you have any previous experience with Windows 95. I'll begin each topic at the beginning and build your knowledge from there. However, if you have used a previous version of Windows, I'll be pointing out the differences in Windows 95 so you can get productive posthaste.

With *The Complete Idiot's Guide to Windows 95, Second Edition*, you get just the facts you need—not everything there is to know. This means I'll be avoiding long-winded discussions of boring, technical details. Instead, I'll present all the information in short, easy-to-digest chunks that you can quickly skim through to find just the information you want.

What to Expect

With Windows, *anything* can happen (and often does). So my best advice as you cross over into Windows 95 territory is to expect (you guessed it) the unexpected. However, the last thing you need is to be thrown a few curve balls by the book that's supposed to be your trusted guide in this newfound land. So, to get you better prepared for the journey to come, let's bone up on some of the flora and fauna you'll be seeing along the way.

First, the itinerary. The *Complete Idiot's Guide to Windows 95, Second Edition* is organized into seven reasonably sensible sections. To help you locate what you need fast, here's a summary of what you'll find in each section.

Part 1: An Introduction to Windows 95

The book leads with its chin by presenting two chapters designed to help you get your Windows travels off on the right foot. Chapter 1 gives you some general Windows 95 tidbits and answers a few common questions. Chapter 2 tells you about the all-important chore of installing Windows 95.

Part 2: Workaday Windows 95

Ninety percent of learning Windows 95 involves learning a few simple techniques that you can apply to almost any Windows 95 program. These universal skills are the ones you'll use day in and day out, and they're the subject of Part 2. You'll learn how to start Windows 95, how to use the mouse and keyboard, how to crank up programs and commands, and how to get through fundamental tasks such as opening and closing files, printing stuff, and resetting a stuck computer with a well-aimed kick.

Part 3: Navigating Your Computer with Windows 95

My Computer and *Explorer* are the Windows 95 tools that give you an easy, graphical way to work with your computer's files, folders, and floppy disks. The three chapters in this section explain the basic features of both My Computer and Explorer and tell you just enough about files and folders to mess you up for the rest of your life.

Part 4: Okay, Enough Gawking. It's Time to Get Some Work Done!

This section of the book covers a hodgepodge of topics to help you get the most out of your Windows 95 investment. The first few chapters concentrate on the various freebie programs that are part of the Windows 95 package. I'll discuss WordPad (a word processor), Paint (a drawing and painting program), and lots more. Then I'll show you how to share info between applications, use Windows 95's multimedia programs, work with fonts, and more. There's also a chapter that tackles Windows' most common problems and gives you easy, nontechnical sulutions.

Part 5: Remaking Windows 95 in Your Own Image

The chapters in Part 5 prove that, yes, you *can* have Windows 95 your way. The program comes with a fistful of customization options that allow you to give Windows 95 a complete makeover. In particular, I'll show you how to change the colors and background pattern of the Windows screen, how to set up a screen saver, how to customize the mouse, and how to add new hardware and software to your system.

Part 6: Modems and More: Communicating with Windows 95

We live in a wired world, so it's not surprising the Windows 95 would include lots of features for the modem hounds in the crowd. Part 6 presents five chapters that take you through all the basic communications doodads in Windows 95. I'll begin by showing you how to set up your modem. From there, I'll tell you how to use your modem to dial your phone, call bulletin boards, connect with online services, and other geeky things. I'll then show you how to use Windows 95 to connect to both your network and that Internet thing everyone's talking about. From there, I'll take you on a tour of the Microsoft Exchange program's e-mail capabilities.

To make the instructions easier to read, *The Complete Idiot's Guide to Windows 95, Second Edition* uses the following conventions:

➤ Text that you type, items you select, and text that you see on your screen appear in **bold**.

➤ As you'll see, Windows 95 uses quite a few keyboard shortcuts. These shortcuts almost invariably require you to hold down one key and press another. For example, one shortcut you may use a lot requires you to hold down the **Ctrl** key, press the **Esc** key, and then release Ctrl. To avoid writing out a mouthful like that over and over, we needed an easier way to express these *key combinations* (a sort of "shortcut shorthand," if you will). So key combinations appear with a plus sign (+) in the middle, as in **Ctrl+Esc**.

➤ The names of dialog box controls appear in a special font like this: Select the **Create from File** option button and then click the **Display As Icon** check box.

Also, look for the following features that point out important information.

Check This Out

These boxes contain notes, tips, warnings, and asides about Windows 95 that are interesting and useful (at least theoretically!).

Transitional State

I realize that many of you aren't new to Windows, just to Windows 95. So, to make the transition a little smoother and a little more manageable, these icons point out major differences between Windows 3.1 and Windows 95.

Techno Talk

These "geek boxes" contain technical information you can use to impress your friends (and then forget five minutes later). But really, you may find these fascinating if you're a closet geek wannabe, or if you're interested in background information and technical details that will help you feel more like an "insider" in the computer world.

What's New in the Second Edition?

Sending a book out to market is a little like watching your kids leave home. Will they be okay? Will other people accept them? Will they be successful in their chosen field? Will they be displayed prominently at the front of the store? I'm happy to report that *The Complete Idiot's Guide to Windows 95* has been a phenomenal success in its first venture into the cold, cruel world. It has literally helped hundreds of thousands of people make the leap from complete Windows 95 idiot to competent Windows 95 user.

So why put out a second edition? Well, a slightly different version of Windows 95 (called Windows 95B) slipped quietly into the new-computer market in the fall of 1996, so I wanted to cover its new features. Also, I wanted to beef up the coverage of the Internet and networking. You'll find all this in the second edition, as well as extra coverage of many Windows 95's basics. Best of all, everything's written in the same easy-to-digest format that people the world over have come to know and love. (Now if we could just do something about my lack of modesty!)

Acknowledgments and Other Assorted Tips o' the Propeller Beanie

Although a small army of dedicated men and women had a hand in making this book (you'll find a complete list near the front), there are a few I'd like to point out in particular. Martha O'Sullivan asked me to write it (she is, therefore, the one to blame for the whole thing); the tag-team of Melanie Palaisa and Henly Wolin ensured the layout made sense and provided many valuable ideas about structure and content; San Dee Phillips made sure that I crossed my i's and dotted my t's and expunged all traces of the dreaded passive voice; and Mark Enochs shepherded the project expertly through the production process. Thanks to all of you for a job well done.

Trademarks

Terms suspected of being trademarks or service marks have been appropriately capitalized. Que Corporation cannot attest to the accuracy of this information. Use of a term in this book should not be regarded as affecting the validity of any trademark or service mark.

Part 1
An Introduction to
Windows 95

Okay, you have a computer, you have Windows 95, you have your favorite accessories (coffee, relaxing background music, and so on). Hey, you're ready to go! However, just to build the suspense, this section presents some "look before you leap" stuff. (But if you're a dedicated leaper, don't let me stop you; feel free to head right into Part 2.)

Chapter 1

Walking in a Windows Wonderland

In This Chapter

➤ What Windows is and what you can use it for

➤ How Windows makes your life easier

➤ Why you can still keep your old DOS programs

➤ What's new with Windows 95

➤ A leisurely amble through the Windows landscape

As strange as it may sound, I was actually at a baseball game when I first realized Windows was a Big Thing. Where I live, we have one of those state-of-the-art baseball stadiums with all the modern-day amenities: artificial turf, a McDonald's, and the main attraction: a huge 110-foot TV screen (the biggest in the world, I hear) that tells everyone when they're having fun.

Of course, with tens of thousands of people as a captive audience, you'd better believe this monster TV is going to show commercials. So there I was, shelling peanuts and waiting to root root root for the home team in the next inning, when on comes a commercial for (wait for it) Windows. Whoa! Here I am sitting with 50,000 of the faithful, and we're all watching a Windows ad. The specifics of the ad have faded from memory (although I *do* remember some slinky blonde getting unrealistically hot and bothered in front of a PC), but I recall thinking that if Microsoft (the publisher of Windows) was willing to shell out megabucks to peddle this new software at a major league baseball game, something BIG was happening.

Actually, with Windows now selling over a million copies a month, "humongous" might be a better word. Windows is, truly, a phenomenon unlike any other in the world of personal computers. This chapter explores the Windows mystique and attempts to answer no fewer than five questions:

➤ What's with all this Windows hoopla?

➤ Is Windows really as easy to use as everyone says?

➤ I have Windows; now what the heck do I do with it?

➤ Do I have to toss my DOS programs?

➤ What's new and improved in Windows 95?

What's with All the Windows Hoopla?

Windows ads don't appear only on 110-foot TVs. You see them on normal-sized TVs, inside newspapers, and on billboards, sandwich boards, bulletin boards, and ironing boards. (Yeah, I made up that last one; but hey, with Microsoft, you never know.) You name it, Windows is there. Computer magazines (and even some real magazines) are stuffed full of articles with titles such as "57 Cool New Ways to Make Windows Bark Like a Dog!" and "He's Hot and You're Not—How Windows Can Help!" Everywhere you go, people are talking about Windows. So why all the fuss?

Well, in a nutshell, Windows represents an entirely new way to get things done with a computer. The old way (that is, the DOS way) involved typing commands on your keyboard and waiting (or more likely, praying) for the computer to respond. There are two major drawbacks to this approach:

➤ Most of us are pathetic typists.

➤ Most of the things you have to type bear only the slightest resemblance to the English language. I mean, imagine having to type—or even *remember*—a command like this:

xcopy c:*.* a: /d:04/15/95 /v

Gag me! Using DOS is like going to a fancy French restaurant where you have to write down your order. If you get anything wrong—like spelling crème as créme (or is it the other way around?)—you don't eat.

Windows changes all that because it works the way human beings work: visually. Your programs and all the commands or options you need to choose are represented visually on the screen (or they're a few mouse clicks or keystrokes away). Just think: no more convoluted commands and snaggled syntax to remember. In fact, Windows may be the first computer application that doesn't require you to remember anything!

Well, When I Was a Kid...

Although using the keyboard may not be the best way to operate a computer, things used to be worse. In the old days, intrepid users had to enter information through a series of toggle switches on the front of the machine. I think it took about three days just to enter your name.

Is Windows Really as Easy to Use as Everyone Says?

Well, yes and no. I mean it's not like you're boiling water or anything (yes, bachelors, boiling water *is* easy). On the other hand, it's not exactly brain surgery, either.

When you get right down to it, Windows, like just about anything else, is as easy or as hard as you make it. This is a fully loaded piece of software that comes with a veritable cornucopia of bells and whistles. It's possible to sink into its mired depths and never be heard from again (except possibly as a story on "Unsolved Mysteries"). If that's what you want, you're reading the wrong book. My goal is to show you just how easy Windows is to both learn and use. The secret, as you'll soon see, is to learn just what you need to know—not what everyone else thinks you should know.

How does Windows make it easier to use a computer? Well, as I said before, images are the key. When you start up a Windows application, most of what you can do with the program is laid out visually in front of you. Carrying on with the French restaurant example, using Windows would be like ordering from a menu that has nice pictures of each of the dishes. You point to the selection you want, and voilà: your meal is served up piping hot. Windows 95 even maps out your entire computer (floppy disks, hard drives, CD-ROMs, printers, and all) in a nice, neat visual display like the one shown on the following page. (The program you see is called My Computer. I'll tell you all about it in Part 3, "Navigating Your Computer with Windows 95.")

This box gives you a visual representation of all the components of your computer.

Of course, cute little pictures are only part of the story. Another feature that makes Windows easy to use is the *dialog box* concept. Although you'll learn about these in detail in Chapter 6, a brief introduction here won't hurt. As the name implies, a dialog box is simply a means by which you and Windows communicate. Now don't expect long philosophical discussions that last into the wee hours of the morning. Windows is good, but not *that* good. No, you'll see a dialog box anytime Windows needs more information from you or needs you to confirm that what you asked it to do is what you actually want it to do. Here's an example of a confirmation dialog box.

This Windows 95 dialog box asks you to confirm a file deletion.

It's a What?

Windows is an example of what computer nerds call a GUI—a *Graphical User Interface*—which is pronounced "*GOO-ey.*" (No, I did not make that up.) Personally, I think PUI—*Pictorial User Interface*—would have been better, but I suppose the pronunciation "*POO-ey*" would turn people off.

The third key to Windows' ease-of-use is consistency. Certain operations such as opening and saving files are implemented the same way in almost all Windows applications, and most Windows applications look more or less the same. These consistencies from pro-gram to program mean that you have much less to learn with each new program you use. (This is a real benefit to those of us whose brain cells are the innocent victims of our misspent youth.) Check out Part 2, "Workaday Windows 95," to find out about many of these consistencies.

Okay, I Have Windows; Now What the Heck Do I Do with It?

I'm not here to be an evangelist for Windows, so I'm not going to tell you that Windows can do everything except wax the cat. And I'm certainly not going to tell you that the only limit to Windows is your imagination. This is bunk. Computers and the programs that run on them (including Windows 95) are big, dumb galoots that exist only to do your bidding. They are pack animals—mere beasts of burden born only to handle the grunt work that the rest of us don't want to bother with. If you're new to computers, please tape this statement to your forehead now: *you are infinitely smarter than your computer will ever be*. This, of course, does not mean you've just wasted several thousand dollars; it just means there's a limit to what one can reasonably expect from a machine.

However, donkeys live useful, productive lives, and so can Windows. For one thing, Windows will still allow you to do what people have been doing with personal computers for years: write letters, mess around with numbers, draw pictures, and play cool games. Windows, though, brings a number of advantages to the table:

➤ Once you're comfortable with the Windows way of doing things (which won't take you very long), you can do all those normal computer tasks more easily and quickly.

➤ Your finished product is, generally speaking, more professional-looking.

➤ Windows lets you work on multiple projects at once (called *multitasking*). For example, while a letter or report prints, you're free to muck about with a completely different program. (So you can, for example, reward yourself with a couple of rounds of FreeCell—one of the games that comes with Windows 95.)

Check This Out...

Geekspeak: Multitasking

The capability to run several programs at the same time (more on this seemingly amazing feat in Chapter 4).

Windows by itself is easily worth the price of admission (especially if it came bundled with your new computer), but there's actually a lot more fun stuff lurking in the Windows box. The Windows programmers—bless their nerdy hearts—have included, at no extra charge, a hatful of small programs (they're called *accessories*). With these programs, you can do all of the following things:

➤ Write letters, memos, résumés, or even your latest Great American Novel.

➤ Draw and paint pictures, logos, cartoons, and whatever else your inner child feels like doing.

➤ Make quick calculations (so you'll know if that check is going to bounce before you write it).

➤ Make backup copies of your important files (just in case disaster strikes).

➤ Play cool games (all work and no play…).

See Part 4, "Okay, Enough Gawking. It's Time to Get Some Work Done!" for information on these and other Windows tricks.

Do I Have to Toss My DOS Programs?

In a word, no. The creators of Windows looked at the tens of millions of people using DOS programs and figured they'd better keep these people happy. So they made sure that DOS applications would work reasonably well under Windows. They'll run a bit slower, and some of the more misbehaved programs might give Windows a little gas, but they will run.

What's New and Improved in Windows 95?

In the time from its inception in 1993 to its release in 1995, Windows 95 reached new heights of marketing hype (or new lows, depending on your tolerance for hyperbole and puffery). But for every "Gee, whiz" type who insisted that Windows 95 was the greatest thing since the Veg-O-Matic, there was a skeptic who insisted equally vehemently that the program was nothing but the "same old, same old" dressed in a shiny new suit.

Who's right? Well, as usual, the answer lies somewhere in the middle. Windows 95 certainly isn't the Second Coming, but it's definitely not just a warmed-over version of Windows 3.1. It boasts a boatload of improvements, big and small, that are sure to make the time you spend each day hunkered down in front of your monitor—whether it's a few minutes or a few hours—a little less drudging. I'll be giving you the details on many of these improvements as we go along, but just to whet your appetite, here's a list of the major ones to watch out for:

Keep it simple, stupid.   The overall design of Windows 95 is simpler and cleaner than that of Windows 3.1. For example, Program Manager is history; to crank up a program or accessory, you simply click the **Start** button and then select what you want from the Start menu that appears.

Belly up to the taskbar.   All the programs you have running appear in a special area at the bottom of the screen called the *taskbar*. Using the taskbar, you always know which programs are loaded, and you can switch to any of the programs with a simple click of the mouse.

Examine your computer with Explorer.   Windows Explorer is easier to use and more ergonomically sound than its predecessor, File Manager. For example, Explorer treats your computer as a whole, letting you work easily with all your floppy drives, hard drives, CD-ROMs, printers, and whatever else you have glued to your machine. And you may as well remove the word "directory" from your Windows vocabulary. Directories are now called "folders" in Windows 95, and you better get used to them because they're everywhere.

A Mecca for mouse mavens.   Although Windows 3.1 was designed with the mouse in mind, most people eventually found they preferred the keyboard for the majority of tasks. Windows 95 may change all that, because, while it too is made for the mouse, it's smart about it. Lots of tasks take only a single mouse click; you can drag things hither and thither; and there are toolbars to beat the band. (A *toolbar* is a strip of buttons that gives you one-click access to common functions.)

At last! The right mouse button becomes useful.   Speaking of the mouse, did you ever wonder what the heck the right button was supposed to be for? True, some programs made use of it, but not Windows itself. With Windows 95, however, you use the right mouse button to display *shortcut menus* that give you quick access to frequently used commands and features. This often saves you from having to hunt through endless pull-down menus to find what you want.

Hallelujah: longer file names!   For my money, Windows 95's Most Valuable Feature award definitely goes to its support of longer file names. That's right: no more trying to shoehorn a meaningful name into a measly eight characters. Now you can go crazy because the limit has been bumped up to a positively verbose 255 characters! (One word of warning, though: only programs designed for Windows 95 can understand these long-winded names.)

Wizards: the Windows 95 pit crew.   With Windows 3.1, you were on your own when it came to performing tasks such as setting up a new printer. With Windows 95, however, you're never alone because the program comes with a whole crew of so-called wizards. These helpers take you through common Windows tasks (such as installing a printer) by asking the right questions and recording your answers.

Helmets off: Windows becomes crash-proof (well, almost).   By far the most annoying thing about Windows 3.1 was its perverse tendency to go up in flames whenever an important deadline or meeting was looming large. Windows 95 was

9

designed from the ground up to be more stable and not to give up the ghost as easily as Windows 3.1 did. (Again, however, you'll need to use programs created specifically for Windows 95 to get semi-bullet-proof operations.)

Less dirty DOS dancing.   Many of the things you used to have to do in DOS are now built right into Windows 95. For example, DriveSpace (the program that creates more room on your hard drive) is now a seamless part of Windows 95.

Help for hardware headaches.   Windows 95 has built-in support for something called *Plug and Play* (PnP). This means that if you add PnP-compatible hardware to your system, Windows 95 will recognize it and configure the device for you automatically.

Where's the beef? Check out the new accessories.   Many of the no-charge programs that come with Windows 95 have been beefed up from their Windows 3.1 versions. For example, WordPad (the word processor) has quite a few more features than Write, its anemic Windows 3.1 cousin. There's also a bunch of brand new accessories that are making their debuts in Windows 95. These rookies include Phone Dialer (which dials your phone for you), CD Player (which plays music CDs on your CD-ROM drive), and Microsoft Fax (which enables you to send and receive faxes right from your computer).

Get online with the Microsoft Network.   If you have a modem, Windows 95 includes an easy link to the new Microsoft Network. This online service boasts electronic mail, programs, lots of info, and even links to the Internet.

Windows and DOS: now a happy couple.   Before Windows 95, DOS and Windows were, at best, acquaintances. They got along reasonably well most of the time, but their spats could be nasty ones. Now, however, DOS and Windows have shacked up and are living happily together under one Windows 95 roof. This, combined with the new Windows 95 versions of some important DOS programs, should mean that most of us can say good-bye to the old DOS world.

The Transition from Windows 3.1 to Windows 95

Lots of people will be heading into Windows 95 having already struggled with the intricacies of Windows 3.1. While Windows 95 isn't completely different from Windows 3.1, it's different enough that you'll have a bit of a learning curve ahead of you.

To help you get through, I'll be pointing out the significant differences between the two products throughout this book. To give you a bit of an idea what to expect, though, the following table summarizes what became of the Windows 3.1 programs (and some DOS 6 ones, too) in the move to Windows 95.

Windows 3.1 Programs and Their Windows 95 Counterparts

Windows 3.1/DOS 6	Windows 95
Program Manager	Start menu
File Manager	Windows Explorer
Calculator	Calculator (new version)
Calendar	Same
Cardfile	Same
Character Map	Character Map (new version)
Clipboard Viewer	Clipboard Viewer (new version)
Clock	On the taskbar
DEFRAG (DOS 6)	Disk Defragmenter
DriveSpace (DOS 6)	DriveSpace
Media Player	Media Player (new version)
MS-DOS Prompt	MS-DOS Prompt (new version)
Notepad	Notepad (new version)
Object Packager	Object Packager (new version)
Paintbrush	Paint
Print Manager	Control of individual printers
Recorder	Gone
ScanDisk (DOS 6)	ScanDisk
Solitaire	Same
Terminal	HyperTerminal
Undelete	The Recycle Bin
Write	WordPad

The Least You Need to Know

This chapter gave you a brief introduction to the world of Windows and showed you how it can make your computing life easier. From here, you have two choices. If Windows 95 isn't yet installed on your computer, move on to Chapter 2 where I'll take you through the installation process. If Windows is already installed, skip ahead to Chapter 3 to get a tour of the Windows 95 screen and learn some mouse and keyboard basics.

SHUCKA
SHUCKA

From Floppy Disk to Hard Disk: Installing Windows 95

In This Chapter

➤ Preparing to install Windows 95

➤ The installation steps

➤ Some post-installation chores

➤ Everything you need to know, from go to whoa

My favorite thing about having a computer (except possibly switching the unruly beast off at night) is probably the moment a new software package arrives. It sits there gleaming in its shrink wrap, full of nothing but possibilities and great expectations, innocent as a baby in the womb. Awwww. But, alas, this blissful state soon ends. The wrapper gets torn off, the box gets mangled, the contents (the manuals, the disks, and the registration card that I always forget to fill out) get spilled and scattered. And then, just as you must slap a baby to induce breathing, so, too, must you install your software to bring it alive on your computer. (Okay, so that last metaphor was a bit of a stretch. Whaddya want, Hemingway?)

If you've just purchased Windows 95, this chapter leads you gently out of the age of innocence and shows you how to install the program on your computer.

Is This Installation Rigmarole Necessary?

Before diving into the deep end of the Windows 95 installation process, you should dip a toe into the waters to see if you even have to bother. Why? Well, most new computers come with Windows 95 preinstalled by the manufacturer, so the legwork may have already been done. If you're not sure, turn on your computer and see if it loads Windows 95. If you see a screen that looks something like the one shown here, you're in luck: Windows 95 is ready to go. In this case, you can safely bail out of this chapter and head for Chapter 3.

If you see this screen a minute or two after you fire up your computer, Windows 95 is installed on your computer.

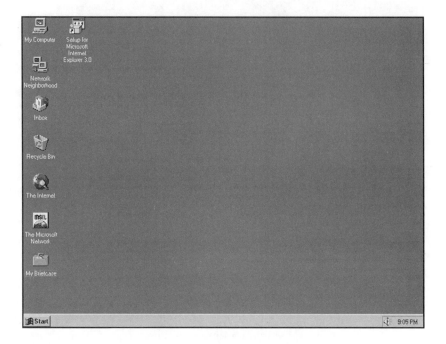

Getting the Installation Show on the Road

When I was a kid, I used to get nervous when I received Christmas presents that said "Some assembly required" on the box. I *knew* what that meant. First of all, it meant I couldn't play with the toy right away—a major bummer. Second, it meant that someone (usually my father or a slightly inebriated uncle) would have to do the assembling. Several hours and several missing parts later, the poor thing would have been relegated to a corner somewhere, half-assembled and sad-looking.

Installing computer software fills me with the same apprehension. Most installation programs are written by people who assume that everybody will know what they mean when they say, "Change the BUFFERS setting in your CONFIG.SYS file to 50" or some such nonsense. What this world needs is a simple installation program that you don't need a Ph.D. to figure out.

Well, I'm happy to report that the Windows 95 installation program (called Setup) comes pretty close. Setup handles all the installation dirty work behind the scenes. All you have to do is answer a few simple questions and shuffle the installation disks in and out when Setup tells you to. (And you can avoid all that disk swapping if you install Windows 95 from a CD-ROM.) Sound simple? It is, so let's get to it.

Step 1: Get the Installation Disks Ready

If you're installing Windows 95 from the floppy disks, liberate them from their plastic wrapper and look for the one that says "Disk 1/Setup" on its label (it should be on top of the pile). Keep the others nearby.

If you're installing Windows 95 from the CD-ROM, pluck the Windows 95 compact disc from its jewel case.

Step 2: Insert the Setup Disk

For the floppy disk installation, place Disk 1 in the appropriate drive (the one that matches the size of disk you have). To insert a floppy disk, hold it so the label faces up and away from you. Then insert the disk into the drive as far as it will go. The 3 ½ inch disks will snap into place with a satisfying clunk.

If you're installing from a CD-ROM, insert the disc into your CD-ROM drive.

Step 3: Start the Installation Program

How you start Setup depends on whether you're upgrading to Windows 95 from an earlier version of Windows or installing Windows for the first time.

If you're upgrading from an earlier Windows version, you need to crank things up from within Windows. Here are the steps to follow:

1. Start Windows (if it isn't started already) by typing **WIN** at the DOS prompt and pressing **Enter.**

2. Pull down the **File** menu and select the **Run** command. Program Manager displays the Run dialog box.

3. In the **Command Line** text box, type the letter of the drive where you inserted the Setup disk or CD-ROM, followed by a colon (:), followed by **\setup.exe**. For example, if the disk is in drive D, type **d:\setup.exe**.

4. Select **OK**. The Windows 95 Setup screen appears.

If you're installing Windows for the first time (that is, you're a newcomer to the world of Windows), you need to install Windows 95 from the DOS prompt.

Your first order of business is to make sure you're at the DOS prompt. You should see one of the following four things on your screen:

➤ **The DOS prompt.** The DOS prompt looks something like this:

C:\>

You may see a letter other than C, or you may see something like C> or C:\DOS. In any case, your computer is ready for the Windows 95 installation.

➤ **The MS-DOS Shell program.** If you see **MS-DOS Shell** at the top of your screen, hold down the **Alt** key, press the **F4** key, and then release Alt. This will return you to the DOS prompt.

➤ **Some kind of menu system.** Many computers are set up with a menu system that gives the user a list of programs to run. Look for an option called **Exit to DOS**, **Quit**, or something similar. You can also try pressing the **Esc** key.

➤ **Some other program.** If you're in another program, exit the program to get to the DOS prompt.

Now that you're at the DOS prompt, type the letter of the drive where you inserted the Setup disk or Windows CD, type a colon (:), and press **Enter**. For example, if the Setup disk is in drive D, type **D:** and press **Enter**. In this case, you'll see a D:\> prompt.

You're in Trouble!

After you type **A:** (or whatever) and press **Enter**, DOS may report this ominous message:

> **Not ready reading drive A**
> **Abort, Retry, Fail?**

Yikes! Most likely, the problem is that there's no disk in drive A, which means the Windows disk must be in drive B, instead. In this case, press **F** (for "Fail"), type **B:** and press **Enter**. This should give you the B prompt (B:\> or something similar).

Now type **setup** and press **Enter**. Setup chugs away for a few seconds and then lets you know it's going to "perform a routine check on your system." Sounds harmless enough, so press **Enter** to set things in motion, and then just follow the prompts on the screen. You'll eventually see the Windows 95 Setup screen.

Step 4: Continuing the Installation

From the Windows 95 Setup screen, either click the **Continue** button or press **Enter** to proceed with the installation. Setup takes a few minutes to rummage around in your system while it's "preparing the Setup Wizard." (Which conjures up images of some elderly gent hurriedly donning his robes, searching frantically for his wand, and saying "My hat! I can't go on without my hat!")

If you're installing from floppy disks, you'll eventually be asked to insert Disk 2. Remove Disk 1, plop Disk 2 into the same drive, and then click **OK** or press **Enter**. (CD-ROM installers can smile to themselves, smug in the knowledge that this disk shuffling rigmarole is beneath them.)

Setup continues chugging along until, eventually, the Software License Agreement dialog box appears. Click **Yes** or press **Enter** to continue (although you can read the legalese if you're feeling brave enough). Next, you'll see the Windows 95 Setup Wizard dialog box, shown in the next figure.

The Windows 95 Setup Wizard guides you through the installation process.

This is your first contact with one of those wizards I told you about in Chapter 1. This dialog box sports the following three buttons:

< Back	Select this button to return to the previous step in the Setup process. (You can't select this button yet because this is the first Setup Wizard dialog box.)
Next >	Select this button when you complete the current step and want to move on to the next one. In most cases, you can choose this button just by pressing **Enter**.
Cancel	Select this button to bail out of the Setup process altogether.

The first Setup Wizard screen just gives you an outline of the steps to come. Once you read it, select **Next >** to move on.

Step 5: Finishing the Installation

The rest of the installation procedure involves nothing more than answering some simple questions and feeding disks into your computer when prompted by the Setup Wizard (unless, of course, you're installing via the handy CD-ROM). Just so you know what to expect, here's a rundown of some of the screens the Setup Wizard may send your way:

Choose Directory From this screen, you can select a storage location on your hard drive for Windows 95. In most cases, you'll choose the default choice provided by the Setup Wizard (usually C:\WINDOWS).

Are You Upgrading?

If you're upgrading to Windows 95, you might want to keep your existing version of Windows intact and install Windows 95 to a separate directory. The advantage of doing this is that you can always go back to your old Windows setup if you have problems with Windows 95. The disadvantage is that you have to reinstall all your Windows applications and re-create your program groups. If you want to try it, select **Other Directory**, select **Next >**, and then type in the new directory you want to use (say, C:\WIN95).

Setup Options From this screen (see the following figure), you pick out the type of installation that suits your needs. Most people select Typical, and that's the one you should probably use. However, you can also select Portable (if you're installing Windows 95 on a notebook computer), **Compact** (if you don't have enough hard disk real estate for the Typical installation), or Custom (if you really know what you're doing).

User Information Enter your name and company name here. (If you use Windows at home, you can leave the Company field blank. Or even better, you can make up a silly name such as "Buy-or-Dye Gift Shop and Hair Salon" or "Profane Gas Company." Why not? Believe me, Windows won't mind.)

Analyzing Your Computer Use this screen to tell Windows 95 what kind of hardware you have. In the list of devices that appears, click the ones you know are installed on your system.

Windows Components In this screen, choose which pieces of Windows 95 you want installed on your machine. To make your life easier, though, I'd recommend accepting the default option (namely, Install the most common components).

Startup Disk If your computer gives up the ghost and you can't start Windows 95, you (or a nearby computer guru) needs to do some troubleshooting. Your first task, however, is to regain control of your wayward computer, and the best way to do that is with a "startup disk." In the Startup Disk screen, select the **Yes, I want a startup disk** option to get Windows 95 to create a startup disk for you. I highly recommend that you do this.

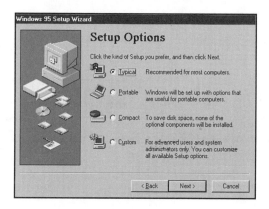

Use the Setup Options screen to tell Windows 95 what kind of installation suits your fancy.

A Few Post-Installation Chores

Once the Setup Wizard finishes copying all the files, it displays the Finishing Setup screen. Floppy disk installers must remove the last disk from the drive and then select the **Finish** button. Setup restarts your computer and heads directly into Windows 95. After the program ruminates for a minute or two, it takes you through a few more tasks to make sure Windows 95 is ready to roll. The next few sections fill you in on the details.

To Password or Not to Password?

When Windows 95 starts for the first time, you may eventually see a dialog box asking you to enter your **User name** and **Password** for logging on to Windows. (You'll see this only if your computer is part of a network.) Should you enter a password or not? Good question. The good thing about a password, of course, is that it prevents busybodies from snooping around your system. The bad thing about a password is that it's an extra step to go through every time you start Windows 95. Unless you have some truly sensitive data on your computer, you're probably better off without a password. (Anyway, you can always add one later if you decide you need it.)

Once you make your choice, you can proceed in one of two ways:

➤ If you don't care about a password, just type your name in the **User name** field and press **Enter**.

➤ If you think a password is a good idea, fill in both the **User name** field and the **Password** field. (When choosing a password, use a word that's easy to remember, but not easy for someone else to guess.)

Can't Figure Out the Dialog Box?

If you're new to Windows and not comfortable with these dialog box things, you might want to pay a visit to Chapter 7.

In either case, click **OK** or press **Enter** to continue. Windows 95 will ask you to confirm your password. (Yes, it does this even if you didn't give a password.) Retype your password in the **Confirm new password** field (or leave it blank if you're avoiding the password thing), and then select **OK**.

Setting the Time Zone

The next dialog box that appears is called Date/Time Properties, and it's shown in the following figure. In this dialog box, you choose your time zone, as well as the current date and time. I'll show you how to set the time in the section in Chapter 17 titled "Doing Time with Date/Time." For now, just choose the appropriate time zone using one of the following methods:

➤ With your mouse, click your location on the map.

➤ With the keyboard, use the arrow keys to select your time zone. (The left arrow and up arrow keys move west; the right arrow and down arrow keys move east.)

When you finish, select **OK**.

Are you wondering why the heck Windows 95 wants to know your time zone, anyway? Well, one of Windows 95's nice little touches is that it automatically adjusts your computer's clock for things like Daylight Savings Time. To do this, however, it needs to know your time zone.

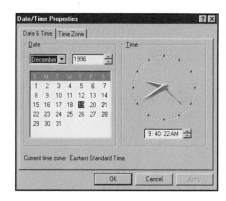

Use the Date/Time Properties dialog box to select your time zone.

That's All She Wrote!

Well, that just about does it. You'll eventually see a Welcome screen that gives you three options:

What's New   Select this button to get help on some of the new features of Windows 95.

Online Registration   Select this button to register your copy of Windows 95 with Microsoft.

Close   Select this button to close the dialog box.

The Least You Need to Know

This chapter showed you how to get Windows 95 out of the box and onto your computer. Now with Windows settled cozily onto your hard disk, it's time to get to know your system's new tenant. The chapters in Part 2 give you a rundown on most of the basic Windows chores. Chapter 3 begins with a tour of the Windows 95 screen.

Part 2
Workaday Windows 95

One of the great things about Windows 95 is what technoid types refer to as its "consistent interface." In English, this just means you can use a lot of the techniques you learn in a Windows application today in a different Windows application tomorrow. These techniques are things you'll use day in and day out, and the seven chapters in this section cover just that.

The Lay of the Windows 95 Land

As a stranger in the strange land of Windows 95, you'll want to get your bearings before lighting out for parts unknown. Well, you've come to the right place because that's exactly what this chapter's all about. Here you'll be taking in the big Windows 95 picture: the forest instead of the trees; the mountains and canyons instead of the hills and valleys. You'll also learn some valuable mouse and keyboard survival skills that'll stand you in good stead in the chapters to come. So, if you're ready (a few deep breaths might help at this point), let's get under way....

Cranking Up Windows 95

The term "no-brainer" doesn't apply to very many computer-related tasks, but it certainly applies to starting Windows 95. Why? Because there is, quite literally, nothing to it. Once Windows 95 is installed, it'll start itself up automatically each and every time you turn on your machine. (What's that? Windows 95 isn't installed on your computer? You must have skipped Chapter 2. Just flip back a few pages to see what you need to do.)

While Windows 95 is pulling itself up by its own bootstraps, you may see all kinds of strange hieroglyphics on your screen. You can safely ignore this gobbledygook. (You can, if you'd like, give thanks to the deity of your choice that a happy life in no way depends on knowing what all that junk means.)

Techno Talk

Why It's Called "Booting" and Other Semi-Interesting Trivia

You've probably heard computer types talk about *booting* (or *rebooting*) a computer. Although you might think this has something to do with punting the recalcitrant beast across the room, it's really geek-speak for starting up a computer. I didn't just conjure up the image of Windows 95 pulling itself up by its own bootstraps out of thin air. I used it because that's precisely where the term *boot* comes from. You see, Windows 95 is an *operating system*, and one of the main chores of an operating system is to load programs into your computer's memory. When you first fire up your computer, however, Windows 95 has to perform the slick trick of loading *itself* into memory. So, in a sense, it really is pulling itself up by its own proverbial bootstraps.

If you set up Windows 95 with a password (see Chapter 2 for more info), a box eventually appears on-screen asking you to enter your password. Type it in the **Password** field (for extra security, Windows 95 shows your typing as asterisks, instead of showing your actual password). If you make a mistake, press the **Backspace** key to wipe out the offending letters. When you finish, press **Enter**.

When Windows 95 Finally Loads

When Windows 95 is finally ready, the Welcome to Windows 95 box appears, as the following figure shows. Read the handy little tip (which, understandably, may not mean anything to you at this early stage of your Windows 95 career), and press **Enter** or click the **Close** button to get rid of the box. (The Welcome to Windows 95 box is an example of a *dialog box*. You'll be seeing plenty of them in your Windows 95 lifetime, so I've devoted an entire chapter—Chapter 6—to the ins and outs of using them.)

Windows' welcome mat: The Welcome to Windows 95 box appears when you first start Windows 95.

The screen you're left with (see following figure) is the basic Windows 95 screen. It's actually kind of disappointing, isn't it? Heck, all that hoopla, all those installation disks, and *this* is all you get? Spartan doesn't even begin to describe it. However, this screen represents part of the Windows 95 philosophy: keep things simple and uncluttered to make it easier for people to figure out what they're supposed to do next.

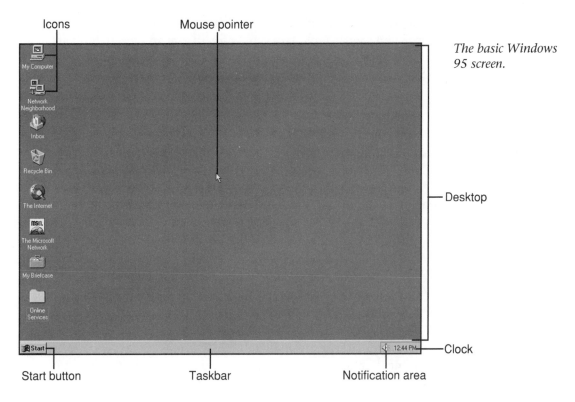

The basic Windows 95 screen.

However, the Windows 95 screen isn't completely barren; it does have a few knickknacks kicking around. The next couple of sections give you a quick rundown of the few things you *can* see.

A Sea of Green: The Desktop

Ivory tower computer types like to invent metaphors for the way the rest of us use a computer. The idea is that more people will use a computer if using a computer is more like the way we do things in real life.

For Windows 95, the metaphor of choice is the humble *desktop*. The idea is that the Windows 95 screen is comparable to the top of a real desk in a real office or den. Starting a program is like taking a folder full of papers out of storage and placing it on the desk. To do some work, of course, you need to pull papers out of a folder and place them on the desk. This is just like opening a file within the program (it could be a letter, a spreadsheet, a drawing, or whatever). To extend the metaphor a little, most programs also come with *tools* such as a ruler, a calculator, and a calendar, which are the electronic equivalents of the tools you use at your desk.

So, officially, the vast green expanse that takes up most of the screen real estate is the Windows 95 *desktop*, and it's where you'll do your work. (If you and green don't get along very well, changing to a different color or to a psychedelic pattern is no sweat. I'll tell you how in Chapter 22 in the "Doing Windows 95's Colors" section.)

Missing Program Manager?

Are you Windows 3.1 users wondering what the heck happened to Program Manager? Sorry, but it's outta there, history, done like dinner, toast. With Windows 95, you do the vast majority of your program launching via the Start button (as explained in Chapter 4).

To get you going, the Windows 95 desktop starts off with a few items already visible. These are called *icons*, and they represent either folders (which, as you'll learn in Chapter 12, are just storage areas) or programs. The number of icons you see depends on which components of Windows 95 were installed on your computer. At the very least, you see the following two:

My Computer   This folder contains visual representations of the various pieces of your computer: the floppy drives, the hard drives, the printer, and anything else attached to your machine. You'll check it out in more detail in Chapter 10.

Recycle Bin This folder is, literally, the Windows 95 garbage can. (You can make your own jokes about having a garbage can on top of your desk.) When you delete things from your computer, Windows 95 tosses them in the Recycle Bin. I'll take you through the full Recycling Bin rigmarole in Chapter 11 (see the section titled, "Tossing Files in the Recycle Bin").

Storage—In the Trash?

Now wait just a cotton-picking minute! You said a folder was a storage area. Why the heck would Windows 95 store something I'm trying to get rid of? Good question. The answer is that it's not called the "Recycle" Bin for nothing. Suppose, for example, that you change your mind about the last thing you trashed, or that you accidentally toss out something important. In the old days (unless you had special software installed), the file was toast and you were out of luck. But with Windows 95's Recycling Bin, it's easy to just pluck the errant deletion out of the folder and restore it safely to its rightful place. (Check out Chapter 11 to get the details on all this.)

Welcome to the Taskbar

The *taskbar* is the horizontal strip that runs along the bottom of the screen. It includes the Start button on the left, the notification area and clock on the right, and a blank area in between.

The *Start* button looks harmless enough, but it's actually a sort of "ignition switch" that gives you access to almost all of Windows 95. You use it to do everything from launching programs to shutting down Windows 95 for the night. I'll talk more about the Start button in Chapter 4, in "The Start Menu: Your Windows 95 Launchpad" section (although you'll also use it later on in this chapter when I show you how to quit Windows 95).

The *notification area* (it's also known as the system tray) displays little pictures that tell you what's happening with your computer. When you're printing, for example, a picture of a printer appears in the notification area. If you have a sound card installed on your computer, a picture of a speaker appears (as you can see in the figure shown earlier).

The clock is obvious enough: it just tells you the current time. For more about the clock (such as how to display the date and how to set the time), head for Chapter 17 and read the "Doing Time with Date/Time" section.

The rest of the taskbar is blank right now, but it won't be for long. Once you start running programs (which I'll show you how to do in the next chapter), Windows 95 uses the taskbar to display a button for each loaded program. You can then use these buttons to quickly navigate between the programs.

What's with This Mouse Thing?

Learning how to use a mouse just might be your most important Windows 95 survival skill. Why? Because Microsoft designed most of Windows 95 with the mouse in mind, and you'll find that using the mouse, you can accomplish most everyday tasks more quickly and easily. Does it require some superhuman level of dexterity? Nah. If you can use a fork without poking yourself in the eye, you'll have no trouble wielding a mouse.

The basic idea is simple: you move the mouse on its pad or on your desk, and a small arrow (the mouse pointer you saw earlier) moves correspondingly on the screen. By positioning the arrow on strategic screen areas and pressing the buttons, you can select objects, run programs, and alter the shape and size of windows. Not bad for a tiny, plastic mammal!

Basic Rodent Wrestling

Using a mouse is straightforward, but it does take some getting used to. Here's the basic technique:

1. Turn the mouse so its cable extends away from you.

2. Place your hand over the mouse in such a way that:

   ➤ The part of the mouse nearest you nestles snugly in the palm of your hand.

   ➤ Your index and middle fingers rest lightly on the two mouse buttons.

   ➤ Your thumb and ring finger hold the mouse gently on either side.

3. Move the mouse around on its pad or on your desk. Notice that the mouse pointer on the screen moves in the same direction as the mouse itself.

Geekspeak: Mouse Potato

A person who spends too much time in front of his video screen. (This is, of course, the computer equivalent of a couch potato.)

The Hard Part: Controlling the Darn Thing!

While moving the mouse pointer is simple enough, controlling the pesky little critter is another matter. New mouse users often complain that the pointer seems to move erratically, or that they run out of room to maneuver. To help out, here are a few tips that will get you well on your way to becoming a mouse expert:

➤ Don't grab the mouse as if you were going to throw it across the room (although there will be times when you'll be sorely tempted to do just that). A light touch is all that's needed.

➤ The distance the mouse pointer travels on the screen is proportional to, but not the same as, the distance you move the mouse. For example, depending on the size of your screen, you may only have to move the mouse a few inches to make the pointer travel from one side of the screen to the other.

➤ If you find yourself at the edge of the mouse pad but the pointer isn't where you want it to be, simply pick up the mouse and move it to the middle of the pad. This doesn't affect the position of the pointer, but it does allow you to continue on your way.

A Symphony of Mouse Movements

As you wend your way through this book, you'll find me constantly telling you to use your mouse to "point" at this, "drag" that, or "click" something else. (If you get sick of all these instructions, you're well within your rights to say "Yeah, well click *this*, buddy!) These are all run-of-the-mill mouse actions that'll soon become second nature to you. For now, though, they're probably not even third or fourth nature (or even in the top ten, for that matter), so let's see what they're all about:

Point means you move the mouse pointer so it rests on a specific screen location. For practice, point at the **Start** button in the lower-left corner of the screen. After a second or two, you'll see a little yellow banner that says **Click here to begin**.

Click means you press and release the left mouse button. Note that you generally have to point at something before you can click on it. For example, if I say "click on the green and purple doodad," it means you should first point at the green and purple doodad and then click the button. Go ahead and click the **Start** button. A whole menu appears on your screen. (This is the Start menu, and you'll be checking it out in the next chapter. To send it back whence it came, click an empty part of the desktop.)

Double-click, as you might expect, means to press and release the left mouse button twice quickly. This can be a bit tricky until you get the rhythm of it, so don't worry if Windows seems to be ignoring you. Again, you'll always point at something before you double-click

31

it. Itching to try an example? Try double-clicking the time in the lower-right corner of the screen. If you do it right, a box titled Date/Time Properties appears. To get the goods on this box, light out for Chapter 17 and head for the "Doing Time with Date/Time" section. For now, click the **Cancel** button (or press the **Esc** key) to get rid of it.

The Enlightened Double-Click

When I talk about the "rhythm" of a double-click, I'm talking about two distinct factors. First, there's the speed: the second click has to follow hot on the heels of the first, or Windows will think you're just doing two separate clicks. Second, there's the movement or, more accurately, the lack of movement: try your best not to jiggle the mouse between clicks. A properly executed double-click is a Zen-like combination of speed and stillness that requires patience and practice. Now here's the good news: the best Windows 95 program for practicing double-clicking (as well as most other mouse actions) happens to be a very addictive game called FreeCell. I'll tell you how to play it in Chapter 17 (look for the "Filling Your Free Time with FreeCell" section).

A *right-click* is similar to a regular click, except you quickly press and release the *right* mouse button. (If your mouse has three buttons, use the one on the far right.) As you'll see, when you right-click in Windows 95, a *shortcut menu* appears, giving you quick access to common commands. For example, right-click anywhere on the desktop to display one of these menus. Then click (the left button this time) on an empty part of the desktop to remove the menu.

Dragging the mouse has, fortunately, nothing to do with dressing funny. Instead, to drag means to point the mouse at a particular object, press and *hold down* the left mouse button, and then move the mouse. In most cases, the object you point at moves right along with the mouse pointer, so you'll generally use dragging to shift things from one spot and drop them on another (this is the *drag-and-drop* feature you may have heard about). It all sounds a bit vague, I know, but you'll get plenty of practice, believe me. In particular, you'll drag 'til you drop in Chapters 9 and 11.

Windows Keyboarding for Non-Typists

Although a mouse is handy for many Windows 95 tasks, it's by no means essential. In fact, many Windows 95 commands have built-in keyboard shortcuts that are big timesavers. Does this mean you have to become an expert typist to use Windows 95? Hardly. I've been using computer keyboards for years, and I wouldn't know what touch typing was if it bit me in the face.

Although there are a number of keyboard styles available, they all share a few common features. In the next few sections, I'll discuss a few of the keyboard's parts and explain how they relate specifically to Windows 95.

Ctrl, Alt, and Those Strange Key Combinations

All keyboards also include Ctrl (it's pronounced *control*) and Alt keys (some newer keyboards have two of each). In Windows, you don't use these keys by themselves, but as part of *key combinations*. The Shift key often gets into the key combination act, as well.

For example, try pressing and holding down the **Ctrl** key, pressing the **Esc** key, and then releasing Ctrl. A menu of options sprouts from the Start button. (You'll learn about this menu in the next chapter.) This method of holding down one key while pressing another is called a *key combination,* and is used extensively in Windows 95. (By the way, to remove the menu, just press **Esc** by itself.)

A Shortcut for Keyboard Shortcuts

It's going to be a real mouthful to say something like "hold down the Ctrl key, press the Esc key, and then release Ctrl" every time I tell you about a key combination. Instead, throughout this book, I'll simply write key combinations in the format key1+key2 (as in **Ctrl+Esc**).

The Esc Key

As you saw in the previous section, you can get rid of the Start menu by pressing the **Esc** key. In general, if you find yourself in some strange neck of the Windows woods and you're not sure what to do next, you can usually get back on more familiar turf by pressing the **Esc** key. (If that doesn't work, you can also try pressing the **Alt+F4** key combination.)

The Numeric Keypad

On each type of keyboard, the numeric keypad serves two functions. When the **Num Lock** key is on (there is usually a light on the keyboard that indicates when it's on), you can use the numeric keypad to enter numbers. If Num Lock is off, the keypad arrow keys (and other keys such as Home, End, Page Up, and Page Down) are enabled, and you can use them to navigate a document. Some keyboards (called *extended* keyboards) have a separate arrow keypad so you can keep Num Lock on all the time.

Shutting Down Your Computer

When you finish working with Windows 95 and want to turn off your machine for the night, you first need to exit Windows. Possibly the single most important thing to know about quitting Windows 95 is this: **never, I repeat,** *never* **turn off your computer while Windows 95 is still running**. Doing so can result in lost data, damage to important files, and accelerated hair loss. Having properly scared you into compliance, here are the steps to follow to shut down your computer:

1. Click the **Start** button. Windows 95's Start menu appears.

2. Click the **Shut Down** option, or else press the **up arrow** key once to highlight the **Shut Down** option, and then press **Enter**. (You can also use the shortcut key combination **Alt+F4** to shut your computer down.) The Shut Down Windows dialog box appears, as shown in the following figure.

When you shut down Windows 95, this dialog box appears to ask if you're sure.

3. If you're sure you want to go through with it, click the button that says **Yes**, or press **Enter**. (If you get cold feet at the last moment, you can abandon the shut down procedure either by clicking the **No** button or by pressing the **Esc** key.) Windows 95 takes a few seconds to prepare itself for bed, and then it displays a screen telling you it's okay to shut off your computer.

4. Turn off the computer and monitor.

The Least You Need to Know

This chapter got you started with Windows 95. You learned how to get Windows 95 up and running, what the various parts of the screen are all about, how to use the mouse and keyboard, and how to exit the program. You might want to take five before moving on because the next chapter is where you start to make things happen in Windows 95.

Chapter 4

Making Things Happen in Windows 95

As you might expect from that near-empty wasteland of a screen you see at startup, you have to do some digging to make Windows 95 do something. But where do you dig, how far down do you go, and how do you avoid the Windows equivalent of power lines, large rocks, and icky earthworms? What you need is a map that tells you how to get to all the good stuff in Windows 95, and that's just what this chapter is all about. I'll show you how to start programs and navigate between running programs, and I'll explain what this taskbar thing is all about.

The Start Menu: Your Windows 95 Launchpad

Okay, Windows 95 is up and running, you've surveyed the landscape, and you're even learning to love that little plastic rodent. So far so good, but now what happens? Well, now it's time to shake Windows 95 from its slumbers and start making it earn its keep.

Start For starters (literally), let's check out the most obvious point of attack: the Start button. Go ahead and click it to display the Start menu shown in the following figure. (Keyboardists can display the Start menu by pressing **Ctrl+Esc**. If you're using the crazy new Microsoft Keyboard—the one with the alphanumeric keys split down the middle and the postmodern, curvaceous, left-the-darn-thing-too-long-in-the-micro-wave-again look, you can also display the Start menu by pressing the key with the Windows logo on it. Note, too, that lots of regular—boringly rectangular—keyboards also sport the Windows logo key these days.)

Click the Start button to display the Start menu.

The Start menu ——

The Start button ——

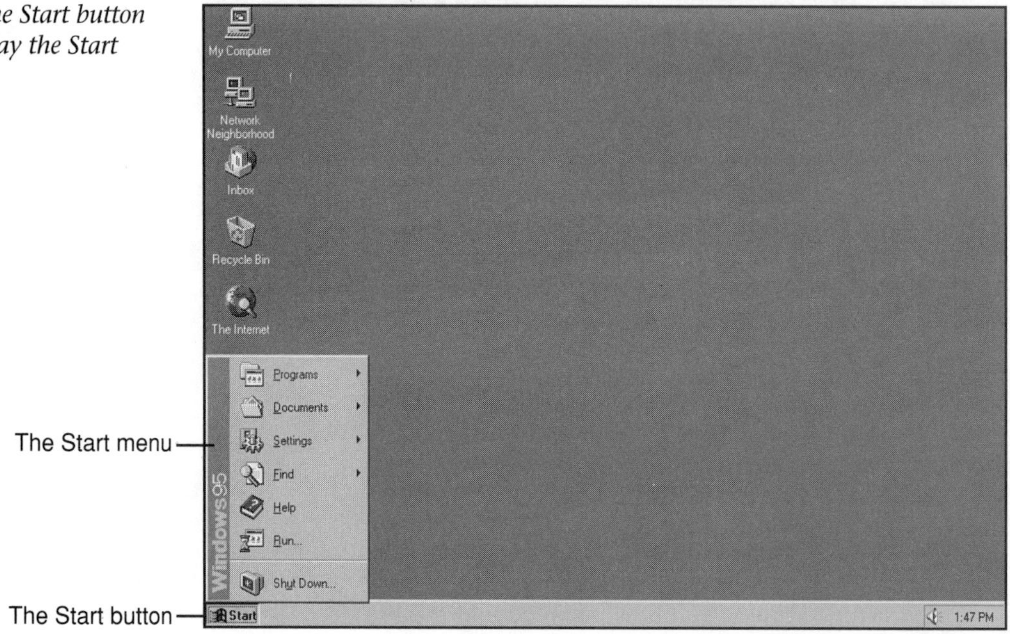

The idea behind the Start menu is simple: it's a list of various things you can do with Windows 95. These "things" fall into three categories:

Commands This is a feature that's built right into Windows 95. For example, as you saw in Chapter 3, to quit Windows 95, you select the Start menu's **Shut Down** command.

Accessories These are small programs that come as part of the Windows 95 package (some folks call these programs *applets*). As you'll see throughout this book, Windows 95 is loaded for bear with dozens of accessories for everything from word processing to dialing your phone.

Applications This is a program sold separately that you have to install on your computer. In most cases, the installation procedure thoughtfully adds the name of the application to the Start menu. (However, if the name of one of your favorite applications doesn't appear on the Start menu, don't sweat it; I'll show you how to add it by hand in Chapter 22, in the "Adding Items to the Start Menu" section.)

Selecting Start Menu Items

To select an item from the Start menu, use either of the following techniques:

➤ With your mouse, click the item you want to execute.

➤ With your keyboard, use the up and down arrow keys to highlight the item you want, and then press **Enter**. (As a shortcut, you can press the underlined letter in the item's name. For example, the **u** in the Shut Down command is underlined, so you can select Shut Down just by pressing **u**.)

Notice that the top four Start menu items (Programs, Documents, Settings, and Find) have little arrows on the right? That means these items are *folders* that contain other items. For example, click the **Programs** folder. Windows 95 opens the Programs folder and displays its contents in another menu that looks something like the one shown in the following figure. (Your menu may be different, depending on which Windows 95 options you installed.) You can then select items from the new menu using the same techniques I just outlined. (You'll work through a concrete example in a sec.)

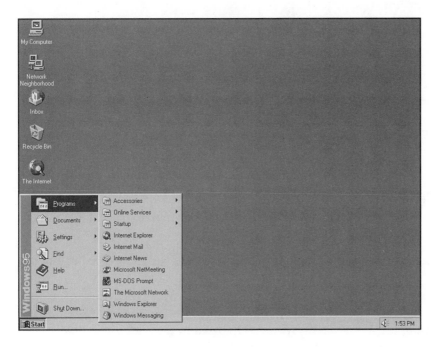

The Programs item is a folder; when you click it, Windows opens the folder and displays what's inside.

A Point's as Good as a Click

Here's a tip that can save some wear-and-tear on your clicking finger: you don't have to click a folder to open it. Instead, just point your mouse at the folder's name, and it opens automatically after a second or two. The only time you really have to click is when you select a program to run.

Here's a summary of the items on the main Start menu:

Programs   Holds the various programs (accessories *and* applications) you can run from Windows 95.

Documents   Contains a menu of the last 15 documents you worked with in any of your applications. (In this sense, a *document* is any file you work with in a program. It can be a spreadsheet, a drawing, a letter, or whatever.) When you select a document from this folder, Windows launches the appropriate program and loads the document automatically. I'll talk more about this in Chapter 7 in the "Opening a Document from the Start Menu" section.

Where, Oh Where, Have My Groups Gone?

Windows 3.1's Program Manager is history, so you may wonder what happened to your program groups and all their icons. They're still around, but Windows 95 converted the groups into folders and stuck them inside the Programs folder.

Settings   Contains a few programs you can use to play around with various Windows 95 settings. You'll check out most of these settings later in the book.

Find   Contains tools that help you find things on your computer. I'll give you the details in Chapter 11, in the "Finding File Needles in Hard Disk Haystacks" section.

Help   This command cranks up the Windows 95 Help system (which I'll talk about later on in this chapter).

Run   Use this command if the program you want to play with isn't listed in any of the Start menu folders. This isn't for the faint of heart, however. After selecting the command, you have to enter the disk drive where the program resides (for example, **C:**), its folder (such as **\WP51**), and then the name of the file that starts the program (for example, **WP51.EXE**). Whew! Compared to the Start menu, that's some true, calluses-on-the-fingertips, manual labor.

Shut Down   As you saw in Chapter 3, this command tells Windows 95 that you've had enough for one day and want to return to the real world.

Starting a Program: An Example

Let's add some flesh to all these Start menu bones by trudging through an example. The following steps show you how to launch WordPad, the word processing accessory that comes with Windows 95:

1. Open the Start menu by clicking the **Start** button.

2. Select the **Programs** folder. Windows 95 displays another menu that contains the items inside the Programs folder.

3. Select the **Accessories** folder. Yet another menu appears, displaying a list of the items in the Accessories folder.

4. Select the **WordPad** item.

Once you select WordPad, Windows 95 takes a few seconds to load the program and then displays it, as shown in the following figure. Note that the taskbar sprouts a button for the program. I explain why you should care about this taskbar button in "Taking Windows 95 to Task: The Taskbar" after the next section.

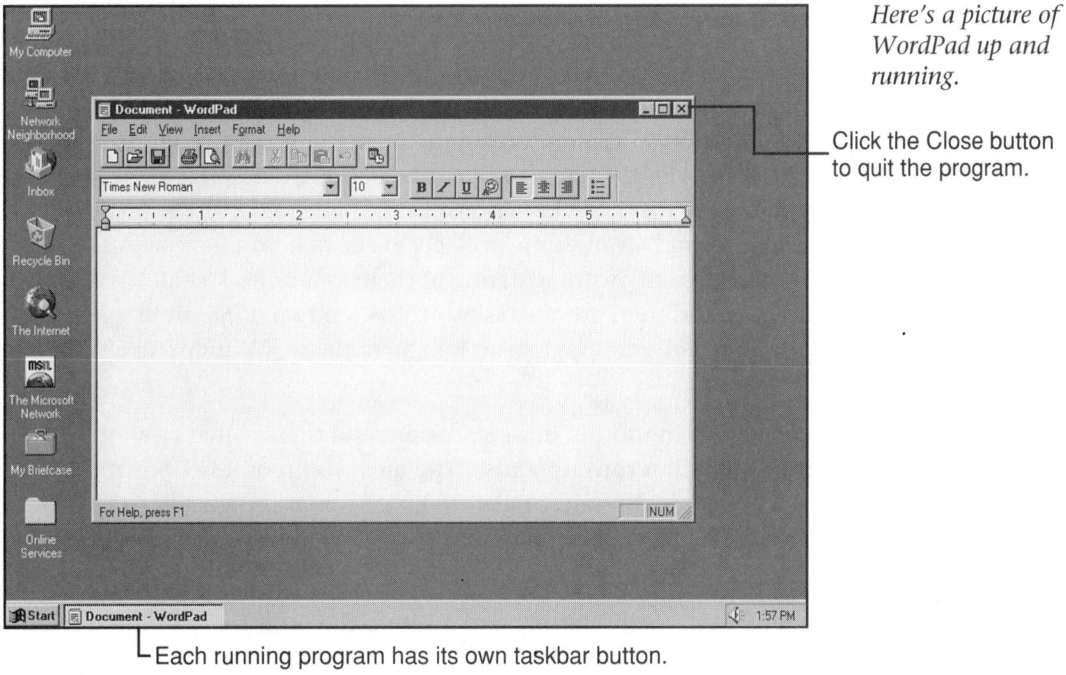

Here's a picture of WordPad up and running.

Click the Close button to quit the program.

Each running program has its own taskbar button.

Quitting a Program

When you're done with a particular program, you need to close it to clear your screen. There are actually a number of ways to shut down a running program, but the following three are the most common:

➤ With your mouse, click the **Close** button in the upper-right corner of the program's window. The Close button is the one with the **X**.

➤ From the keyboard, press **Alt+F4**.

➤ Pull down the program's **File** menu and select the **Exit** command (or, more rarely, the **Close** command). I'll tell you how to work with pull-down menus in Chapter 5.

Depending on the program you're closing and the work you were doing with it, you might be asked if you want to "save" some files. I'll tell you how to handle this in Chapter 7, in the "Save Your Work, Save Your Life" section. (If you want, you can leave WordPad open while we discuss the taskbar in the next section.)

Taking Windows 95 to Task: The Taskbar

When you started the WordPad program earlier, you saw that Windows 95 added a button for WordPad on the taskbar. What's the deal there? Well, with just one program open, there isn't much of a deal to speak of. No, the taskbar becomes useful only when you slap two or more programs onto the desktop at the same time.

At the same time? Sure. Windows 95, unlike some people you may know, can walk and chew gum at the same time. Specifically, it supports what the geeks call *multitasking*, which just means that Windows 95 is only too happy to let you run a whole passel of programs simultaneously. Why in the name of one-man bands would anyone need to run multiple programs at once? Isn't it hard enough just to use *one* program at a time? Actually, as you'll see in a second, even in the unlikely event that you have a dozen programs on the go, you really only work with one of them at a time. The idea is that you mess about in one program and then use the taskbar to switch to a different program when you need it. Here are some good reasons to take advantage of Windows 95's multitasking:

➤ You can set an operation in motion in one program and then switch to another program while the operation runs its course. The most common example of this is to start printing a document in, say, your word processor, and then switch to your spreadsheet program to crunch a few numbers.

➤ You might have a program that you use from time to time throughout the day. To avoid the tedium of continually starting and quitting the program, you can leave it open and switch to it when you need it.

➤ You might want to share information between two programs. Windows 95 lets you make a copy of, say, a chunk of text in one program, switch to a completely different program, and then insert the copy there. (This is explained in gory detail in Chapter 18.)

➤ If you're heavily into a game of FreeCell or DOOM (hey, you have to relax sometime, right?), you can quickly switch to a more corporate-looking program should the boss saunter into your office unannounced.

The Technical Truth About Multitasking

Multitasking sounds pretty slick, but don't think you can just kickstart every program you have and leave them running all day. The problem is that each open program usurps a chunk of Windows' resources. So the more programs you run, the slower each program performs, including Windows. The number of applications you can fire up at any one time depends on how much horsepower your computer has, how much memory is installed in your system, and the availability of Windows 95's *system resources*. The system resources are small chunks of memory that handle things such as the position of windows, the pattern of the desktop, and lots more. (See Chapter 21 for more info.) If you deplete the system resources, you can't open any more programs. However, even a bare-bones Windows 95-capable computer usually can get a few of the accessories going at once.

Okay, let's get down to brass tacks and check out how all this works. As you can see in the following figure, I've opened a second program—the Minesweeper game that comes with Windows 95. (To open this program on your computer, open the **Start** menu, select the **Programs** folder, the **Accessories** folder, and the **Games** folder—that's the last folder, I promise!—and then select **Minesweeper**.)

Minesweeper appears to have lopped off a good portion of the WordPad window, but in reality, Windows 95 is just displaying Minesweeper "on top" of WordPad. (You'll see later that it's easy enough to place the WordPad window back on top of the pile.) In addition, the taskbar has changed in two ways:

➤ There's now a button for Minesweeper.

➤ The WordPad taskbar button no longer appears "pressed."

The taskbar tells you two things: which programs are running and which of those programs is the *active* one. In this context, the active program is the one you're currently working in. (Technoid types say that such a program has the *focus*.) On the taskbar, the currently active program is shown with a "pressed" button.

Windows 95 with two programs running: WordPad and Mine-sweeper.

The "pressed" button represents the active program.

If that was all the taskbar did, though, it would be a waste of precious screen real estate. No, the taskbar's true value comes through when you use it to switch between your open programs. All you have to do is click the taskbar button for a program, and Windows 95 immediately brings that program to the foreground. For example, click the **WordPad** button and see what happens. As you can see in the next figure, the WordPad window now appears on top of the Minesweeper window. Nifty!

Of course, you can also use your mouse to click the window you want. However, as you'll see later (in Chapter 9, to be exact), it's possible to enlarge a program's window so that it takes up the entire desktop. If you do that, you can't see any of your other running programs, so the taskbar buttons become your best way to navigate all your programs.

Overcoming Taskbar Crunch

Here's a problem you'll run into from time to time: once you open a few programs, Windows 95 shrinks the buttons so they can all fit on the taskbar. As a result, some buttons may show only part of the program name. To see the entire name, point your mouse at the button and let it sit there for a couple of seconds. Windows 95 then displays a small banner above the button that spells out the entire program name.

WordPad is now the active program.

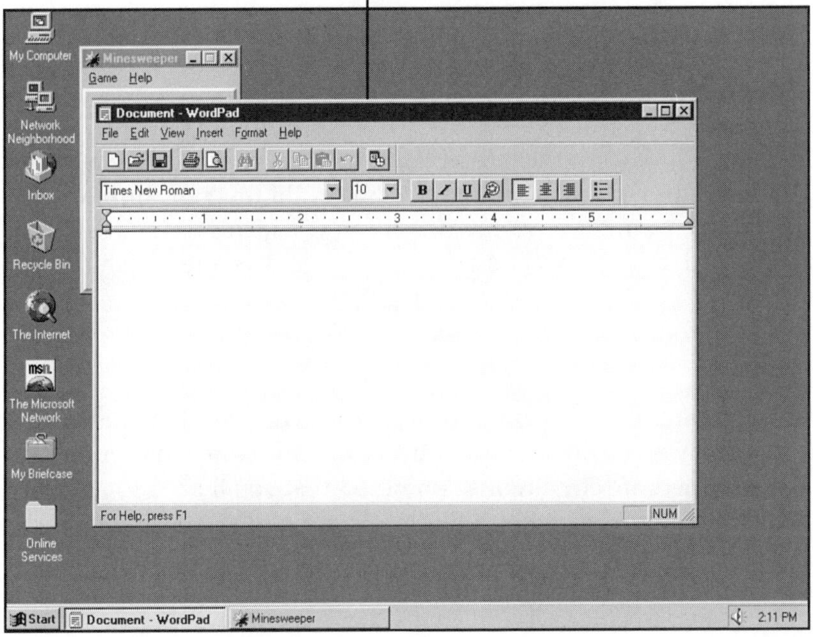

To switch to WordPad, click the WordPad button in the taskbar.

More Methods for Switching Between Programs

As you'll see throughout this book, Windows 95 never gives you just one way to perform a particular task. No, that would be too obvious (and using "Windows" and "obvious" in the same sentences borders on the oxymoronic). Instead, Windows usually serves up several different methods and then watches you sweat trying to figure out which one to use. Switching between programs is no exception: there are, in fact, three other methods you can use:

➤ If you can see any part of a program's window, you can switch to the program by clicking inside the window. This is a handy technique if your programs display in small windows (like Minesweeper's).

➤ From your keyboard, hold down the **Alt** key and tap the **Tab** key several times. Windows 95 displays the box shown in the following figure; each time you hit Tab, it cycles through the names of your open programs. When you get to the one you want, release the Alt key, and Windows 95 switches to the program. This technique is useful if you don't have a mouse or if you have only two or three programs running. (In Windows circles, the Alt+Tab key combo is known as the "cool switch.")

Hold down Alt and tap the Tab key several times to cycle through the names of your open programs.

Document - WordPad

➤ Hold down the **Alt** key and tap the **Esc** key several times. Again, Windows 95 cycles through the open programs with each press of the Esc key. In this case, however, you see the entire program window and not just its name. Use this technique if you forget what's in one or more windows and want to take a look before switching.

Help! How to Get It

This book (a savvy and prudent investment on your part) helps you learn the most-used features of Windows 95 quickly and easily. But, as you've seen, my approach is purposefully not comprehensive, so there are chunks of Windows 95 that you'll need some help with. Instead of plowing through the manual (shudder), you can use Windows' online Help system to get assistance on every aspect of the program with just a few keystrokes or mouse clicks. The rest of this chapter shows you how to use the Help system.

Getting Help: The Basics

If you run into a problem with Windows 95, or if you simply find yourself in a strange part of town, you want to get help fast before panic sets in. Thoughtfully, the Windows programmers provided you with no less than four ways to access the Help system:

➤ Press **F1** to get help that is *context-sensitive*. This means that the Help screen that appears relates to the Windows area you are in when you press F1. For example, when you're in WordPad, pressing F1 displays the Help Topics: WordPad Help window (see the following figure).

➤ Click the **?** button in a dialog box and then click something in the dialog box. This also accesses context-sensitive help: the help window that appears relates to the dialog box object you clicked. (See Chapter 6 for more info on this.)

➤ Select the **Start** button; then select the **Help** command to get help on Windows itself.

➤ In most Windows applications, you can click **Help** in the menu bar or press **Alt+H**. The Help menu that appears has one or more commands for accessing different parts of the program's Help system.

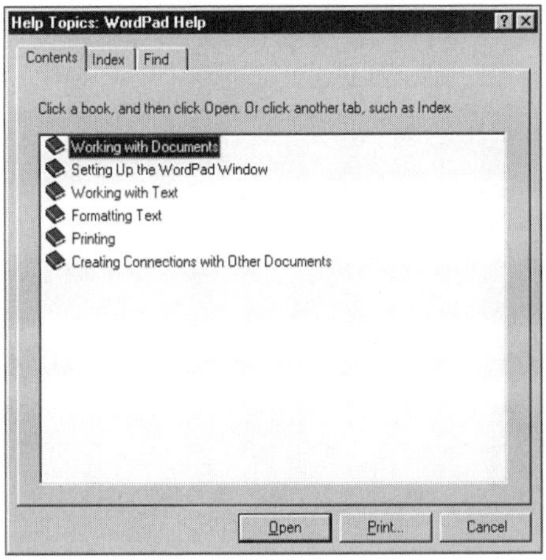

Pressing F1 in WordPad displays the Help Topics: WordPad Help window.

Displaying a Help Topic

When you invoke the Help system, the window that appears gives you a list of "books" that contain Help info. In the WordPad Help window, for example, there are books such as "Working with Documents" and "Working with Text." To open one of these books, click it and click the **Open** button (or use your keyboard's up and down arrow keys to highlight a book and then press **Enter**).

When the book opens, several topics appear under it. To display one of these topics, click it and click the **Display** button (or, again, highlight the topic using the arrow keys and then press **Enter**). For example, opening WordPad's "Working with Text" book produces a whole slew of topics, including "Copying information between documents." Selecting the latter displays the Help text shown in the following figure. In addition to reading the displayed text, you can also perform any of the following actions:

➤ If you see a word in green text with a dashed underline, you can click that word to display a definition of it. Press **Esc** when you're done reading the definition.

➤ Click **Related Topics** at the bottom of the window to see a new Help window with information related to the current topic.

➤ Click the **Back** button to see the previous Help topic.

➤ Click the **Help Topics** button to return to the topics window.

➤ Click the **Close** button to close Help.

Selecting a Help topic displays a window like this one.

To copy information into another document

1 In the document that contains the information you want to copy, select the information by highlighting it.

2 On the Edit menu, click Copy.

3 In the document where you want the information to appear, click the place where you want to put the information.

4 On the Edit menu, click Paste.

Tips

• You can also link or embed information.

• You can paste the information multiple times.

Related Topics

Searching for a Help Topic

As handy as the Help system is, it can become a bit of a maze once you start jumping from topic to topic. To make it easier to find what you want, the Help system includes an Index feature that lets you search for a Help topic in an alphabetical list of topics, or simply type a key word or phrase. Here's what you do:

1. In a Help Topics window, click **Index**.

2. Type the first few letters of the topic you want. For example, if you type **print**, Index moves to "print preview."

3. Click the topic you want and then click the **Display** button. The Help system displays the topic.

The Least You Need to Know

This chapter showed you how to use Windows 95 to get programs off the ground, as well as how to juggle them once they're in the air. (When you've got the hang of these basic techniques, you might want to pay a visit to Chapter 22 where, in the "Customizing the Taskbar and Start Menu" section, I show you how to modify the Start menu and the taskbar to suit your own style.)

Of course, starting a program is one thing, but actually getting something useful out of it is quite another. You'll take a big leap in that direction in the next chapter as you look at a few tools that enable you to take advantage of all the features and commands of any Windows 95 program.

Chapter 5

Your Click Is My Command: Menu and Toolbar Basics

In Chapter 4, you learned that you have to do some digging to discover the application nuggets and accessory trinkets that transform your computer from a doorstopper into a showstopper. However, you face a similar what-the-heck-do-I-do-now? problem once you have a program up and running.

This chapter solves that problem by showing you how to uncover the features and commands in just about any Windows 95 program. Not only that, but you'll also look at a truckload of tools and techniques that'll make it easier to wield those tools you use the most. In other words, you'll learn how to control your programs instead of letting them control you.

More Buried Treasure: Pull-Down Menus

Life, as they say, is full of surprises. One of my favorite surprises is lifting up the sofa cushions every few years and seeing what new collection awaits me. There is, of course, the usual assortment of flora and fauna: lint, crumbs, old Doritos, that kind of stuff. But you can also come across some buried treasure: coins, keys, a long-lost remote control—you name it.

The prospect of finding buried treasure is also what I like about the subject of this section: pull-down menus. These menus, which are normally hidden from view, contain all kinds of fun surprises, and they give you access to all the features of your Windows 95 programs.

Desktop Metaphor Redux

Back in Chapter 3, I introduced you to the desktop metaphor used by Windows 95. I'm returning to this metaphor now because it's perfect for describing pull-down menus.

To get your work done, it's not enough to simply shuffle papers around all day (as tempting as that may be). You usually need to do something to those papers: write on them, staple them together, take numbers from them for your calculations, make spiffy airplanes, or whatever. To accomplish these tasks, you need the proper tools: a pen, a stapler, a calculator, your boss's memos, and so on. With a few exceptions, you probably store most of these items in drawers instead of leaving them on top of your desk. (Unless, of course, you're one of those people who has to dig through layers of papers to see what kind of wood grain is on his desk.) When you need something, you just *pull* open the drawer (nudge, nudge) and select the item you want.

A pull-down menu in Windows 95 is just like a desk drawer. When you need to access a command in an application, you open the appropriate menu and select that command.

Why You Pull Down Instead of Up or Out

Why are they called "pull-down" menus and not, say, "pull-on" menus? Well, because they're hidden inside a *menu bar*: the horizontal strip on the second line of most program windows. Selecting any of the items in a menu bar displays a menu of choices. For example, the following figure shows the Windows Explorer program with its View menu pulled down. (If you want to follow along, you can start Windows Explorer by opening the **Start** menu, selecting the **Programs** folder, and then selecting **Windows Explorer**. However, I won't be showing you how to use Explorer in this chapter. That'll have to wait until Part 3, "Navigating Your Computer with Windows 95.") The effect, you'll note, is as though you pulled the menu down from the menu bar. (See, sometimes this stuff actually makes sense! Besides, a "pull-on menu" sounds like something you'd wear when the Windows weather gets a little chilly.)

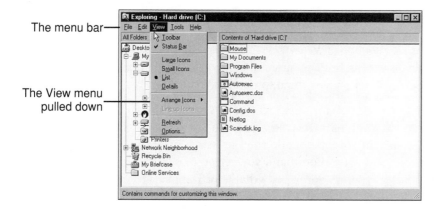

The menu bar

The View menu pulled down

Selecting Explorer's View option pulls down this menu.

How to Use Pull-Down Menus with a Mouse

If you have a mouse, using pull-down menus is a breeze. All you do is move the mouse pointer into the menu bar area and then click the name of the menu you want to pull down. For example, you simply click **View** in Explorer's menu bar to pull down the View menu.

Once your menu appears, your next chore is to select one of its commands, and you do that simply by clicking the command. Depending on the command you select, one of three things happens:

➤ **The command runs.** For example, Explorer's View menu has a Refresh command near the bottom. If you select that command, Explorer performs a quick check on your computer to see if there's anything new for it to display.

➤ **Another menu appears.** For example, if you click the View menu's Arrange Icons command, a new menu appears on the right. You then click the command you want to execute from the new menu.

➤ **A dialog box appears to ask you for more information.** For example, if you click the View menu's Options command, a dialog box named Options appears. See Chapter 6 for details on using dialog boxes. (You can press **Esc** to get rid of the dialog box.)

How to Use Pull-Down Menus with the Keyboard

Although a mouse makes it easy to use pull-down menus, there's no law against using your keyboard. In fact, the keyboard method may even be quicker because you don't have to reach all the way over to the mouse when you type on the keyboard. The secret to using pull-down menus from the keyboard is to look for the underlined letter in each menu bar option (they all have them). In Explorer, for example, look at the "F" in File and the "E" in Edit. These underlined letters are called the *hot keys*. (In geekier circles, they're also known as *accelerator* or *selection keys*.) How do they work? Simple: you just hold down the **Alt** key, press the hot key on your keyboard, and then release Alt. For example, to pull down Explorer's View menu, press **Alt+V**.

With the menu pulled down for all to see, select one of the menu commands by using the up and down arrow keys to highlight the command you want (a *highlight bar* moves up and down to mark the current command) and then pressing **Enter**. As I explained in the mouse section, depending on which command you select, one of three things happens: the command runs, another menu appears, or a dialog box appears to pester you for more info.

Bailing Out of a Menu

What do you do if you pull down a menu and then discover that you don't want to select any of its commands? You can remove the menu by clicking on any empty part of the program's window, or you can just pull down a different menu by clicking on the appropriate menu bar option.

From the keyboard, you have two choices:

➤ To get rid of the menu, press **Alt** by itself.

➤ To pull down a different menu, press **Alt** plus the letter of the new menu.

Pull-Down Menu Doodads and Doohickeys

If you've pulled down a menu or two, you may have seen a few strange things in your travels. For example, did you notice that every command in a pull-down menu has one underlined letter? Or that some commands are followed by three ominous-looking dots? Or that still other commands also list a key or key combination? These are all perfectly normal pull-down menu features (see the following figure), and you can take advantage of some of these things to make your menu chores easier. The next few sections summarize these features.

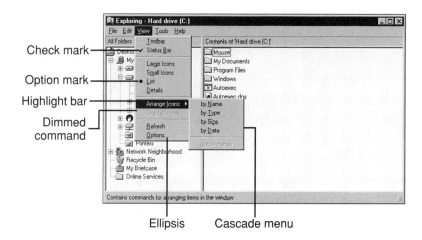

Check mark

Option mark

Highlight bar

Dimmed command

Ellipsis   Cascade menu

Some pull-down menu features.

The Highlight Bar

As you move through a menu with your keyboard, a blue bar appears across the menu. This is the *highlight bar*, and it indicates which command is current. As I've said, one way you can select a command is to press **Enter** when the command is highlighted.

Underlined Characters: More Hot Keys

Every command in a pull-down menu has one underlined character, which is called the *hot key*. Once you display a menu, you can select any command simply by pressing its underlined letter on your keyboard. (For this reason, command hot keys are also known as *selection letters*.) In Explorer's View menu, for example, you can select the Options command simply by pressing **O**. (If you're itching to try this out, go ahead and open the **View** menu and press **O**. You'll eventually see a dialog box named Options. For now, just press **Esc** to return to Explorer.)

Check This Out...

Hot Keys: Clear As Mud

"Okay, let's get this straight: each menu bar option has a hot key, and to pull down a menu I have to hold down Alt and press the hot key letter; each menu *command* also has a hot key, but to select the command, I press the letter *without* holding down the Alt key. Is it just me, or is this confusing?" It *is* confusing at first, but it's just one of those arcane Windows things you have to live with.

The Ellipsis (The Three-Dot Thing)

An ellipsis (...) after a command name warns you that a dialog box will appear when you select the command. A dialog box is a window a program uses to ask you for more information. As you saw in the previous section, selecting the View menu's Options command displays the Options dialog box. See Chapter 6 for more details about dialog boxes.

What You Can't Do: The Dimmed Commands

Sometimes, certain menu commands appear in a lighter color than the others. (For example, check out the Line up Icons command in the View menu shown earlier.) These are *dimmed commands*, and the dimming indicates that the command is not currently available. (It's the Windows equivalent of a "Gone Fishing" sign.) Generally speaking, if you see a dimmed command, it means that you must do something else with the program for the command to become available.

Arrowheads (Menus, Menus, and More Menus)

In some applications, you'll see an arrowhead (▶) to the right of a menu command. This tells you that yet another menu will appear when you select this command. Explorer has several examples of the species. To see one, pull down the **View** menu and select the **Arrange Icons** command. A new menu appears on the right with several more commands related to arranging icons. These *submenus* are called *cascade menus*.

Check Marks: Toggling Commands On and Off

Some commands operate like light switches: they toggle certain features of a program on and off. When the feature is on, a small check mark appears to the left of the command to let you know. Selecting the command turns off the feature and removes the check mark. If you select the command again, the feature turns back on and the check mark reappears. Let's work through an example so you can see what I mean.

1. Pull down Explorer's **View** menu and take a look at the Status Bar command. You should see a check mark beside it. This tells you the command is "on" which, in this case, means that Explorer is displaying its status bar. (That's the gray area at the bottom of the Explorer window.)

2. Go ahead and select **Status Bar**. This turns off the Status Bar command, and as you might expect, the status bar disappears.

3. Pull down the **View** menu again. Notice that the Status Bar command no longer has a check mark beside it.

4. Once again, select **Status Bar**. This turns the command back on, and lo and behold, the status bar reappears at the bottom of the window.

Option Marks: Selecting One Command Out of a Group

In addition to having features that you can toggle between two different states, some programs have features that can assume three or four different states. (I call them the "Three or Four Faces of Eve" features.) Microsoft designed Explorer, for example, to show you the contents of your computer, and it can display those contents in four ways: as large icons, as small icons, in a simple list, or in a list that gives the details of each item. (If you're not sure what all this means, don't give it a second thought. You'll get the full scoop in Chapter 10.)

To switch between these views, you choose from four commands on the View menu: Large Icons, Small Icons, List, and Details. Since these states are mutually exclusive (you can select only one at a time), you need some way of knowing which of the four commands is currently active. That's the job of the *option mark*: a small dot that appears to the left of the active command.

As an example, pull down the **View** menu and look for the option mark; you should see it beside the List command. Try selecting the **Large Icons** command and see what happens. Feel free to try out the other two commands as well. Notice that each time you pull down the View menu, the option mark appears beside the last command you selected.

Shortcut Keys: The Fast Way to Work

Some menu commands also show a key or key combination on the right-hand side of the menu. These are *shortcut keys* and they allow you to bypass the menus altogether and activate a command quickly from your keyboard. For example, if you pull down Explorer's **Edit** menu (see the following figure), you'll see shortcut keys listed beside the Cut command (Ctrl+X) and the Copy command (Ctrl+C), among others.

Shortcut Key Confusion

Confusingly, the shortcut keys work only when you don't have a menu displayed. If you press a key combination when a menu is pulled down, Windows 95 admonishes you with a beep and waits for you to do something sensible.

Explorer's Edit menu has several commands with shortcut keys.

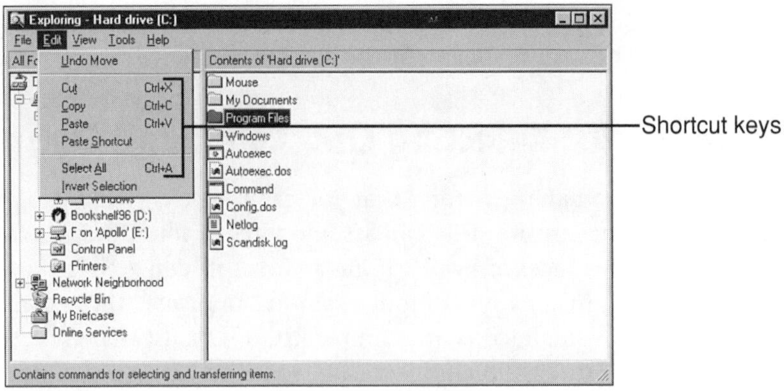

Shortcut keys

Once you've worked with your favorite Windows 95 applications for a while, you'll likely find that you often ignore the menus and just use the program's shortcut keys. It's simply a faster way to work. Some smart applications (such as Word for Windows) even let you create your own shortcut keys.

Using the Control Menu

Besides the pull-down menus attached to the menu bar, each Windows 95 window also has a Control menu. You use the Control menu to manipulate certain features of the window, such as its size and position, or to close the window (see Chapter 9 for details). Before I show you how to display a Control menu, you need to know the difference between a program window and a document window.

A *program window* is the window that contains the entire program you're running. It includes the program's menu bar, its status bar (if it has one), and the area where you do your work in the program.

A *document window*, on the other hand, is a window within the program window, which usually contains a document you've created with the program. (Here, the term "document" is used in a generic sense to include anything you create with a program. So a document can be a spreadsheet, a database, a drawing, or a word processing document.) Why bother with document windows at all? Well, some applications enable you to display multiple documents at the same time, so you need separate windows for each document. You'll find, however, that most of the accessories that ship with Windows 95 don't let you open multiple documents, so they don't use document windows.

The following figure shows the Word for Windows program window with a document window inside it.

Click here to display the document window's Control menu.

Click here to display the program window's Control menu.

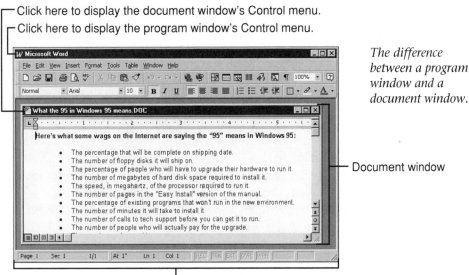

The difference between a program window and a document window.

Document window

Program window

Okay, now that all that rigmarole is out of the way, you can figure out how to display a Control menu:

➤ To display the Control menu for a program window, click the icon in the upper-left corner of the program window. (You can also press **Alt+Spacebar**.) The following figure shows the Control menu for the Word for Windows program window.

➤ To display the Control menu for a document window, click the icon in the upper-left corner of the document window (see the previous figure). Keyboarders can also press **Alt+–(hyphen)**.

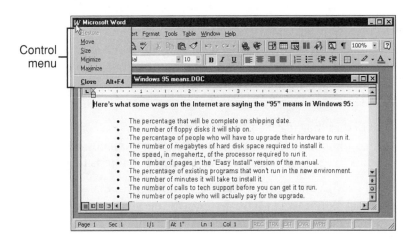

Control menu

The Control menu for Word for Windows' program window.

Quick Access to Common Commands Part I: Shortcut Menus

Windows 95 boasts a new feature that gives mouse users a real bonus: shortcut menus. These menus display a brief list of commands related to a specific feature. All you do is place the mouse pointer over the feature and then right-click. When the menu appears, just click (the left button this time) on the command you want.

For example, right-clicking the Recycle Bin displays the shortcut menu shown in the following figure. From this menu, you can select Open to open the Recycle Bin, Empty Recycle Bin to clean out the Recycle Bin's contents, or Properties to set some Recycle Bin options. (To get more details about what each of these commands does, set sail for Chapter 11 and read the "Tossing Files in the Recycle Bin" section.) To get rid of the shortcut menu without selecting a command, click an empty part of the desktop or press **Esc**.

The shortcut menu that appears when you right-click the Recycle Bin.

Quick Access to Common Commands Part II: Toolbars

In the bad old days of computers (way back in the '80s!), the only way to run a command in most programs was to press a key or key combination. Users complained, though, because not only was it hard to remember the proper keystrokes, but the hand contortions were crippling people for life.

In response to these complaints, the world's programming geniuses created pull-down menus and dialog boxes. These were a big improvement, but then people whined about having to wade through dozens of menus and windows to get to the command they needed. (You just can't please some people.)

So now you have *bars*. Whether they're called "power" bars or "tool" bars or "sushi" bars, they're all designed to give you push-button access to common commands and features. No unsightly key combinations to remember; no menu and dialog box forests to get lost in.

Windows 95 has jumped in with both feet by offering a toolbar with many of its accessories. To check one out, open Windows Explorer, pull down the **View** menu, and activate the **Toolbar** command. The toolbar appears just below the menu bar, as shown in the following figure.

When you point at a toolbar button...

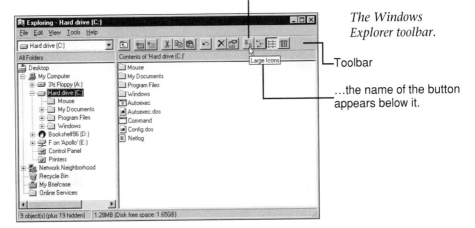

*The Windows
Explorer toolbar.*

Toolbar

...the name of the button
appears below it.

Most toolbar "tools" are buttons that represent commands you'd normally access using the pull-down menus. All you have to do is click a button, and Explorer runs the command, no questions asked. For example, clicking the Large Icons button is the same as pulling down the View menu and selecting the Large Icons command.

Okay, so which one is the Large Icons button? Ah, there's the rub. Most of those tiny pictures are pretty obscure, so icon-interpretation is quickly becoming one of the most coveted skills of the '90s. Fortunately, the Windows 95 programmers decided to have mercy on us and included an easy method for identifying toolbar buttons. Just point the mouse at the button you're furrowing your brow over and wait a second or two. Eventually, you'll see a little yellow banner below the button that tells you the button's name (see the previous figure).

The Least You Need to Know

This chapter showed you how to make Windows 95 programs toe the line. You first looked at pull-down menus and Control menus, which give you access to all of a program's features and commands. Then you looked at shortcut menus and toolbars, Microsoft's contribution to making your life in the land of Windows 95 a bit cushier.

As you saw, however, just selecting a command isn't enough to set things in motion. Instead, lots of commands leave Windows wanting more feedback from you, so it displays a dialog box. You'll see dialog boxes of every shape, size, and description as you toil in Windows 95, and you'll need to know how to handle anything that's thrown your way. Therefore, my goal in the next chapter will be to work with you as you plumb the mysteries of these dialog box things.

Chapter 6

Talk to Me: Dealing with Dialog Boxes

In This Chapter

➤ What is a dialog box?

➤ Getting around in dialog boxes

➤ Learning about dialog box buttons, boxes, and lists

➤ Working with Windows 95's wizards

➤ Your field guide to dialog box flora and fauna

Communication is in. Everywhere you go people are "establishing a dialogue," "networking," or dealing with "interpersonal dynamics." Experts from all fields appear on sleazy daytime talk shows to remind us to "listen to each other" or risk a dysfunctional fate. One tiny, famous doctor tells us that "ze key to good zex is to communicate vis your partner."

Windows 95, being the hip, modern program that it is, is also getting into the act. As you work with Windows applications and accessories, endless little windows appear on your screen to prompt you for more information. These are *dialog boxes*, and they're Windows' way of saying "Talk to me!" This chapter looks at these chatty little beasts and offers some helpful tips for surviving their relentless onslaught.

Where Do They Come From?

Dialog boxes may sometimes seem to appear out of nowhere, but they generally show up after you select certain commands from an application's pull-down menu. Whether or not a dialog box appears depends on whether or not the application needs more info from you. For example, suppose you pull down a menu and select a command called Print. You'll probably see a dialog box something like the one in this figure.

A dialog box you might see in response to a "Print" command.

The program is telling you it needs more information. In this case, it wants to know which printer to use, which pages to print, how many copies you want, and so on.

Some Dialog Box Basics

Before you can delve any deeper into dialog boxes, you need to get a specimen on-screen. I'll be using dialog boxes from WordPad as examples throughout this chapter, so you may as well crank up WordPad now. (Open the **Start** menu, select the **Programs** folder, select **Accessories**, and then select **WordPad**.) To display the Print dialog box shown earlier, pull down the **File** menu and select the **Print** command.

Brace Yourself

You can always tell when a command will generate a dialog box by looking for three dots (...) after the command name. These three dots (an ellipsis) tell you that some kind of dialog box will appear if you select the command. This gives you a chance to psych yourself up for the ordeal to come.

The first thing you should notice about a dialog box is that it has several features in common with other windows that you've seen. For example, most dialog boxes have a title (Print in the previous example) and a Close button (the X in the upper right corner). What's different, though, is what's inside. The various objects you see are *controls* because you use them to control the way the dialog box works. Each control has a name that identifies it (such as Print to file or Number of copies).

Dialog Box Controls

You'll notice that every time I refer to a dialog box control, the name appears in a special font. This is because Windows 95 uses some really long-winded control names, such as Verify backup data by automatically comparing files after backup is finished and by asking the data if it's having a nice day. It's easy to get lost in the middle of a name like that, and not know where it ends, so I'll use that special font to help you identify when I'm referring to a dialog box control.

Keep in mind that most dialog boxes like to monopolize your attention. When one is on the screen, you usually can't do anything else in the program (such as select a pull-down menu). Deal with the dialog box first, and then you can move on to other things.

Getting Around in a Dialog Box

Later in this chapter, I'll talk in nauseating detail about how the various dialog box controls operate. For now, though, you need to know how to cruise from one control to another. (This section applies only to keyboard users. Mouse maniacs do their control cruising on Easy Street because they navigate controls merely by clicking them.)

The first thing you need to figure out is which control is the *active* control. There are two things to keep your eyes peeled for:

➤ If the control displays text inside a box, the control is active either when the text appears highlighted (which means the text appears as white on a blue background instead of the usual black on a white background) or when you see an insertion point cursor blinking on and off inside the box. For example, when you first display the Print dialog box, you see the text in the Name box highlighted, indicating that the Name control is currently active.

➤ All other controls display a dotted outline around their name when they're active.

Think of these guidelines as "You are here" signs on a map, and keep them in mind as you move through the dialog boxes. There are two basic techniques you can use to move around:

➤ **Tab key** Press the **Tab** key to move forward through the controls ("forward" means that you move either left-to-right or top-to-bottom, depending on how the dialog box is laid out). Press **Shift+Tab** to move backward. (Note that Tab may not highlight every control in the dialog box. To figure out why, see the "Windows Does Multiple Choice: Option Buttons" section later in this chapter.)

➤ **Hot keys** Some control names have an underlined letter that acts as the control's *hot key*. This means you can select the control by holding down Alt and pressing the letter. In the Print dialog box shown earlier, for example, you can select the Number of copies control by pressing **Alt+C**.

To get the hang of these techniques, you really need to jump right in and get your feet wet. Feel free to use the Print dialog box for your experiments; simply moving around in the dialog box won't harm anything. As you leap around, make sure you can identify which control is active before you move on to the next one. When you finish, press **Esc** to close the dialog box without printing anything.

Negotiating the New Tabbed Dialog Boxes

One common pet peeve among Windows users over the years is that you often have to wrestle with umpteen dialog boxes to get your work done. The complaining must have worked because the designers of Windows 95 decided to do something about the dialog box deluge. Their solution was to combine all related dialog boxes into a single, multipurpose dialog box. Now that doesn't mean you're going to see dialog boxes with billions of controls jumbled together willy-nilly. Thank goodness they were a little smarter about it than that. These multipurpose dialog boxes come equipped with *tabs* that work like the tabs in a notebook. Select one tab to see a particular set of controls; select another tab to see a whole new collection of controls.

Let's take a look at an example. Pull down WordPad's **View** menu and select the **Options** command to display the Options dialog box (shown in the following figure).

The Options dialog box is an example of a tabbed dialog box.

Click these tabs to see different sets of controls.

The tabs are the rectangles that run across the top of the dialog box (Options, Text, Rich Text, and so on). When you first display the dialog box, the **Word 6** tab is selected. To choose a different tab, click it with your mouse. (If you prefer the keyboard, press **Ctrl+Tab** to cycle through the tabs from left to right or **Ctrl+Shift+Tab** to move through the tabs from right to left.) The following figure shows the controls that appear when you select the Options tab.

If you select the Options tab, a whole new set of controls appears.

Getting Help in a Dialog Box

Most dialog boxes have a **?** button in the upper-right corner (the question mark button to the left of the Close button). You can use this button to get a description of any dialog box control. To try it out, first click the **?** button. Your mouse pointer sprouts a question mark. Then click the control you're puzzling over. In a few seconds, a brief description of the control appears on-screen. (No mouse nearby? No problem. Just highlight the control and press **F1**.)

Dialog Box Gadgets and Gizmos

Now that you've dispensed with the preliminaries, look at some example dialog boxes and figure out what all those strange-looking controls are for. The next few sections give you the lowdown on each type of control.

Setting Things in Motion: Command Buttons

All dialog boxes have at least one *command button*. They're called command buttons because when you select one, you're telling the program to execute the command written on the face of the button.

WordPad's Options dialog box, for example, has two command buttons: OK and Cancel (see the following figure). These are by far the most common command buttons, and you'll see them on the majority of dialog boxes you deal with. Here's what they mean:

➤ Select **OK** when you finish with the dialog box and want to put all your selections into effect. This is the "Make it so" button.

➤ Select **Cancel** to bail out of the dialog box without putting your selections into effect. This is handy when you panic and realize that you're looking at the wrong dialog box or when you've made a mess of your selections. Think of this as the "Belay that last order" button.

Some dialog box controls.

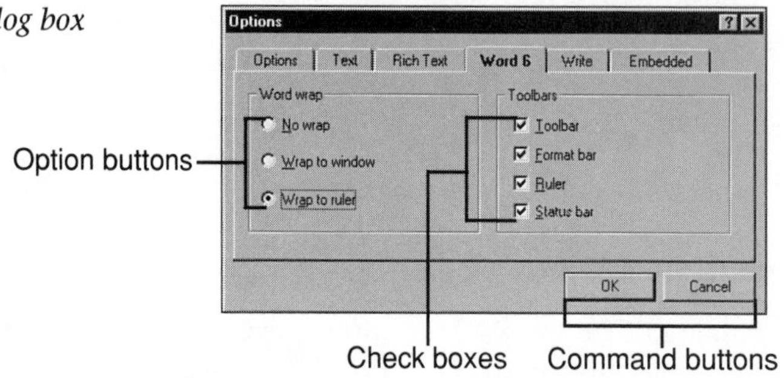

Option buttons ──

Check boxes   Command buttons

To select a command button with a mouse, just click the button. To select a command button from the keyboard, press **Tab** until the command button you want is active (a dotted outline surrounds its name), and then press **Enter**.

Here are some notes to bear in mind when working with command buttons:

➤ Many command buttons act just like the commands in pull-down menus: they might run a particular feature of the program, or they might even display *another* dialog box.

➤ Every group of command buttons has a default button that has a darker outline than the others (you need to look closely to see this). To select this button, just press **Enter** from anywhere in the dialog box. In the Options dialog box, for example, the OK button is the default.

➤ Instead of selecting the Cancel button, you can always cancel a dialog box either by pressing **Esc** or by clicking on the **Close** button (the X in the upper-right corner).

Toggling Stuff On and Off: Check Boxes

The real world is constantly presenting you with either/or choices. You're either watching *Oprah* or you're not; you either like Bac-O-Bits or you don't. Windows handles these yes-or-no, on-or-off decisions with a control called a *check box*. The check box enables you to control whether or not you want a particular program setting or option activated (checked) or deactivated (not checked). In the Options dialog box shown earlier, for example, there are four check boxes: Toolbar, Format bar, Ruler, and Status bar. The control is currently active when a check mark appears inside the box. The control is not active (deactivated) if there's no check mark.

To toggle a check box on and off with a mouse, click the box or its name. To toggle a check box on and off from the keyboard, press **Tab** until the check box you want is active (a dotted outline surrounds its name), and then press the **Spacebar**.

Windows Does Multiple Choice: Option Buttons

When I was in school, I hated multiple-choice questions. I guess I figured I could bluff my way through an essay question, but with multiple-choice, it's the law of the jungle: you're either right or wrong. I even had one perverse teacher who *subtracted* marks for wrong answers. (How do you tell your parents you got a *negative* score on a test?)

The Windows equivalent of the multiple-choice question (without all that pressure!) is the *option* button. You have two or more mutually exclusive choices, and you can pick only one.

The Word 6 tab in the Options dialog box (previously shown) contains three option buttons: No wrap, Wrap to window, and Wrap to ruler. The currently selected option has a small black dot inside its circle. You'll also notice that most option buttons appear in herds. That is, they always appear together in a box called a *group*. (This example shows the Word wrap group box.) In each group, you can select only one option button.

How do you select an option button? If you have a mouse, simply click the option you want (you can either click the button itself or the name). A black dot appears inside the circle when you select an option.

To select an option from the keyboard, you need to press **Tab** until one of the option buttons in the group is active (a dotted outline surrounds the active button). Then use the arrow keys to move through the group to the option you want. (In most cases, you'll use the up and down arrow keys to make your choice.)

Typing Text in Text Boxes

A *text box* is a control in which you type text information such as a description or a file name. A text box is active either when the text appears highlighted, or when a blinking vertical bar appears inside the box. This blinking vertical bar is the *insertion point cursor* or just *cursor*, for short.

Let's look at some text box examples. (If the Options dialog box still appears, select **Cancel** to get rid of it.) Pull down WordPad's **Format** menu, and select the **Paragraph** command to display the Paragraph dialog box shown here. There are three text boxes in this dialog box: Left, Right, and First line.

You use text boxes to type in text info.

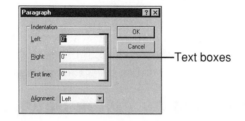

—Text boxes

To use a text box with a mouse, click anywhere inside the box and then type in your text. To use a text box from your keyboard, press **Tab** until you highlight the text inside the box; then begin typing. If you make a mistake, you can use the left and right arrows to position the cursor appropriately and use the following techniques to make corrections:

➤ Press **Backspace** to delete the character to the left of the cursor.

➤ Press **Delete** to delete the character to the right of the cursor.

➤ If the entire text box is a mess, press **Alt+Backspace** to restore the original text and then start over.

Watch Out for Highlighted Text Box Text!

When the text in a text box appears highlighted, the next letter or number you press replaces the contents of the text box! If you don't want to replace all of the text, first press the left or right arrow key to remove the highlight, position the cursor appropriately, and then start typing.

Selecting from Mucho Choices List Boxes

As you saw earlier, a check box essentially gives you two choices: having a particular feature on or off. Then I showed you option buttons, which usually give you a choice of three or four items. However, what if you need to select from a dozen items, or a hundred? As you can imagine, a dialog box with a hundred option buttons to choose from would be a navigational nightmare.

To avoid such a diabolical dialog box fate, *list boxes* are used whenever you need to select from a relatively large number of items (such as fonts, file names, or Elizabeth Taylor's ex-husbands). A list box is about what you'd expect: a box that displays a list of items. There are three list box flavors that you'll come across in your Windows travels: a *regular list box*, a *combo box*, and a *drop-down list box*.

Let's start with the garden variety *regular list box*. To see an example, pull down WordPad's **Insert** menu and select the **Object** command. (Don't forget you first need to cancel the Paragraph dialog box if it's still on-screen from the previous section.) The Insert Object dialog box appears (see the following figure). The list box is the control named **Object Type**. Notice that Windows uses a highlight bar to show the currently selected item in the list.

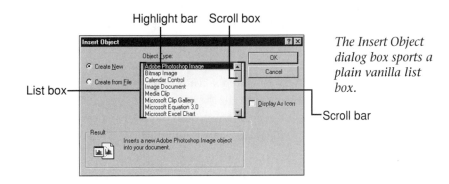

The Insert Object dialog box sports a plain vanilla list box.

To select an item from a list box with your mouse, you can use either of the following techniques:

➤ If the item is visible in the list box, click it.

➤ If the item you want isn't visible, use the *scroll bar* to display the item, and then click it. (I explain how to use a scroll bar in the next section.)

To select a list box item with your keyboard, first press **Tab** until the list is active. (Unfortunately, figuring out when a list box is active isn't as easy as it is with the other controls. You need to watch the list's highlighted item carefully as you poke the Tab key. The list is active when a hard-to-see dotted outline surrounds the highlighted item.) Then use the up and down arrow keys (or the Page Up and Page Down keys if the list is a long one) to highlight the item you want.

A *combo box* is a hybrid control that combines a list box and a text box. The idea is that you can select the item you want from the list box, or you can type what you want in the text box. An example will help make this clear. Shut down the Insert Object dialog box and then select the **Format** menu's **Font** command. WordPad displays the Font dialog box, as shown in the following figure.

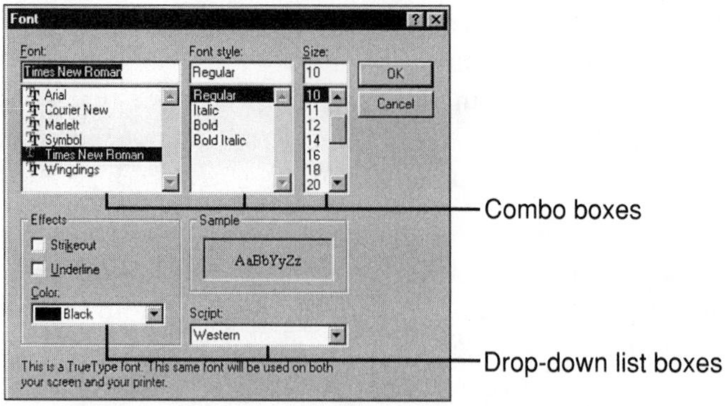

The Font dialog box has several combo boxes (and a couple of drop-down list boxes, for good measure).

Combo boxes

Drop-down list boxes

This dialog box has three combo boxes: Font, Font style, and Size. As you can see, the top section of each combo box is a text box, while the bottom section is a list box. You can choose the item you want either by scrolling through the list box (as described earlier) or by typing the name of the item in the text box.

Our final list box variety, the *drop-down list box*, normally shows only the currently selected item. (WordPad's Font dialog box has two examples of the species: the Color and Script controls.) To choose a different item, you "drop down" the list and then select the item you want just as you would in a regular list box. The next figure shows the Color list in its dropped-down state.

So just how do you go about dropping down a drop-down list box? It's easy:

➤ With your mouse, click the downward-pointing arrow on the right side of the box.

➤ From the keyboard, press **Tab** until the drop-down box is active and then press **Alt+down arrow**.

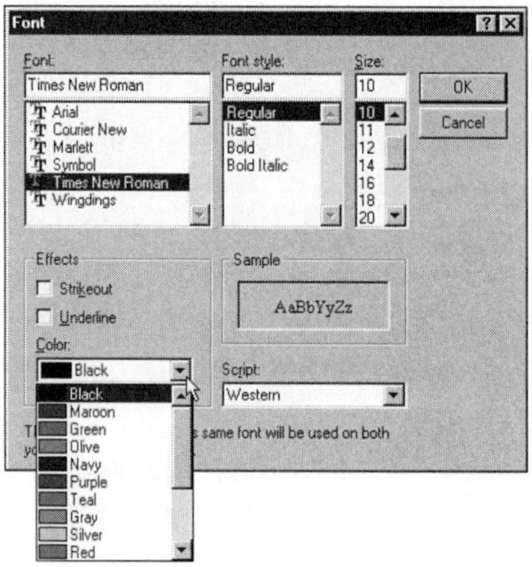

A dropped-down drop-down list box. (Try to say that three times fast.)

Check This Out...

Easier List Box Navigation

Here's a tip that can save you oodles of time when you muck about with both regular list boxes and drop-down list boxes. Once the list box is active, press the first letter of the item you want. Windows 95 leaps down the list and highlights the first item in the list that begins with the letter you pressed. For example, if you drop down the Color list and press G, the highlight immediately moves to the Green item. If you press G again, the highlight moves to the Gray item.

A Brief Scroll Bar Primer

You'll learn more about scroll bars in the next chapter, but I'll give you a brief introduction here so you can successfully negotiate list boxes with your mouse.

Some lists contain too many items to fit inside the box. When that happens, a *scroll bar* appears on the right-hand side of the box to make it easier to navigate the list. The box inside the scroll bar (called, appropriately enough, the *scroll box*) tells you where you are in the list. For example, if the scroll box is halfway between the top and the bottom of the scroll bar, you're approximately halfway down the list.

To navigate a list with the scroll bar, use the following mouse techniques:

To scroll through the list one item at a time, click either the arrow at the top of the scroll bar (to move up) or the arrow at the bottom of the scroll bar (to move down).

To jump quickly through the list, click inside the scroll bar between the scroll box and the top (to move up) or between the scroll box and the bottom (to move down).

To move to a specific part of the list, drag the scroll box up or down.

Putting the Spin on Numbers: Spinners

Spinners are controls that let you cycle up or down through a series of numbers. To see a spinner, pull down WordPad's **File** menu and select the **Print** command. In the Print dialog box shown earlier, the Number of copies control is a spinner.

Each spinner has two parts:

➤ The box on the left is a text box you can use to type in the number you want (which is the boring way to do it).

Spinner Ranges
Most spinners have a maximum and minimum value, and you can select any number within that range.

➤ The right side of the spinner contains an upward-pointing arrow and a downward-pointing arrow. You click the upward-pointing arrow to increase the number that appears in the text box. To decrease the number, click the downward-pointing arrow. For some real fun, press and hold down the mouse button on one of the arrows and watch the numbers fly!

Values Without Numbers: Sliders

To help us enter values that have no intrinsic meaning (at least to non-nerds and other mere mortals), Windows 95 uses a control called a *slider*. WordPad's dialog boxes don't use any sliders, so you'll have to look elsewhere for an example.

To get to a slider example, select the **Start** button, select the Start menu's **Settings** folder, and then select **Control Panel**. In the Control Panel window, double-click the **Keyboard** icon, or use your arrow keys to highlight **Keyboard** and then press **Enter**. The following figure shows the Keyboard Properties dialog box that appears.

The Keyboard Properties dialog box uses sliders to let you enter "values" without numbers.

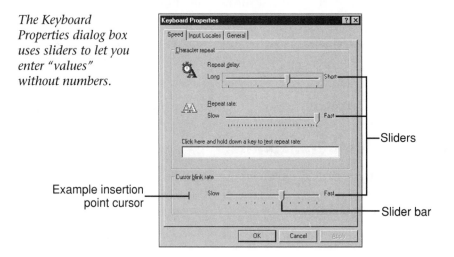

This dialog box has three sliders: Repeat delay, Repeat rate, and Cursor blink rate. Take a look at the Cursor blink rate slider. (If you're wondering what the other sliders are for, you can turn to Chapter 22 and read the "Customizing the Keyboard" section to find out.) The Cursor blink rate slider is a ruler-like line with opposite values of Slow and Fast on either end. The idea is that you enter a "value" by moving the pointer (called the *slider bar*) either left (to get, in this case, a slower blink rate) or right (to get a faster blink rate). The insertion point cursor on the left gives you a visual indication of exactly what the new value does to the blink rate.

Mouse users operate sliders using the following techniques:

➤ To move the slider bar several notches in either direction, click the slider between the slider bar and the edge of the slider.

➤ To move the slider bar to any particular position, drag it with your mouse.

You keyboarders have to press **Tab** until the slider is active (that is, surrounded by a dotted outline). Then use the left and right arrow keys to move the slider bar.

Walking with Windows 95's Way Cool Wizards

Lots of Windows tasks are multistep rituals that allow no deviation from the norm. You have to perform the steps the right way in the right order, or Windows gets all huffy and refuses to play with you anymore. To spare you from its mood swings and, even better, from having to memorize the correct rituals, Windows 95 delegates certain tasks to the care of various *wizards*. These wizards take you by the hand and lead you through the appropriate steps for a task by asking you questions and providing places for you to enter your answers.

It's quite simple, really. Each wizard displays a series of dialog boxes, and you use these dialog boxes to provide the information necessary to complete your chore. The dialog boxes use the standard controls that you looked at in this chapter, including these command buttons that let you move between the various wizard dialog boxes:

Next >	Select this button to move to the next dialog box.
< Back	Select this button to return to the previous dialog box.
Cancel	Select this button to bail out of the wizard altogether.
Finish	Select this button to complete the task. (This button normally appears only on the last wizard dialog box.)

The following figure shows an example of a wizard dialog box. (You'll use the Add Printer Wizard in Chapter 8, in the "Telling Windows 95 About Your Printer" section.)

The Add Printer Wizard takes you through the otherwise-tedious task of installing a printer in Windows 95.

The Least You Need to Know

This chapter showed you the ins and outs of using dialog boxes to communicate with Windows 95. Your Windows 95 education has now progressed far enough that you can actually crank up some programs and start working with them. In fact, that's just what you'll do in the next chapter. I'll take you through basic program chores such as opening and closing files, navigating documents, editing, and the all-important saving your work.

Chapter 7

Day-to-Day Document Drudgery

In This Chapter

➤ Opening and saving a document

➤ Launching a document from the Start menu

➤ Navigating a document

➤ Editing a document

➤ A compendium of commonplace, nose-to-the-grindstone Windows 95 tasks and chores

It may sound strange to say, but Windows 95 is the reigning sex symbol of personal computing. Think about it: all those lush screens, the siren call of the seductive icons, the cheesecake graphics. This is one good-looking program.

But even sex symbols sometimes have to take out the garbage and feed the cat. In Windows 95, this means opening and closing documents, cutting and pasting text, and saving your work. These day-to-day chores are Windows 95 without its makeup on, and that's the subject of this chapter.

To get the most out of this chapter, you probably should follow along using an actual Windows 95 application. I'll be using WordPad, the word processor that comes with

Windows 95, for my examples, but it doesn't matter a whole lot which one you use. Just make sure that the application has both File and Edit pull-down menus. If you'd like to use WordPad, you can fire it up by selecting the **Start** button, opening the **Programs** folder, opening the **Accessories** folder, and then selecting **WordPad**. (For information on actually using WordPad, though, you should head for Chapter 13.)

First Things First: What the Heck Is a Document?

I've already talked about documents a couple of times, but I enjoy beating a dead horse as much as the next guy (metaphorically speaking, of course; no actual horses were harmed in the making of this book). To reiterate, Windows 95 uses the term *document* in its broadest sense. This means a document is anything you create using an application or one of the accessories. Here are some examples:

➤ A letter, memo, or even a novel created with WordPad.

➤ A logo or cartoon produced with Paint.

➤ A budget or mortgage analysis spreadsheet put together in a spreadsheet program.

➤ An inventory or sales database maintained by a database program.

➤ Anything created with any program, anywhere, anytime.

I think that just about covers everything!

Just to keep us all on our toes, Windows 95 also uses the term *file* to refer to a document. File is a broader term in that it refers to all the little chunks of information scattered about on your computer's hard disk, which includes not only your documents, but also the items that Windows 95 uses to start programs. You'll get the full scoop on files in Chapter 11. For our purposes in this chapter, though, I (impetuous bohemian that I am) will use the terms *document* and *file* interchangeably.

Save Your Work, Save Your Life

Most people learn the importance of saving documents the hard way. For me, it was a power failure that wiped out an entire morning's writing. Believe me, that kind of thing can make you old before your time. Why is saving necessary? Well, when you work with a new document (or with an existing document), you're actually making all your changes in the volatile confines of your computer's memory. When you shut off your computer (or if—groan!—a power failure forces it off), everything in memory is wiped out. If you haven't saved your document to your hard disk (which maintains its contents even when your computer is turned off), you lose all the changes you've made. Total bummer.

Now that I've scared the wits out of you, let's see exactly how you go about saving a document. The amount of effort required on your part depends on whether you're working with a new document or an existing document.

Either way, to save the document you're working on, pull down the application's **File** menu and select the **Save** command. If you've saved the document before, the program will take a second or two to make a copy of the document on your hard drive, and then you can continue working. Easy as shooting fish in a barrel.

A Save Time-Saver
In most Windows 95 programs, you can select the Save command by simply pressing **Ctrl+S**.

 In WordPad and many other Windows programs, you can click this toolbar button to save a document.

If you're saving a new document for the first time, though, you'll see the Save As dialog box, which is shown in the following figure. This dialog box wants to know two things:

➤ Where you want the document saved on your hard disk.

➤ What name you want to give to the file.

Current folder or disk drive

Contents of the current folder or disk drive

Use the Save As dialog box to save your new documents.

Picking Out a Storage Location for the Document

The first thing you need to do is select a storage location for the document. From Windows 95's perspective, the storage location for a document has two components:

A disk drive This is most likely your hard drive, but you're free to choose one of your floppy disks. (If you intend to select a floppy disk drive, you can avoid an error message by taking a second now to insert a floppy disk in the drive.)

A *folder* on the disk drive A folder is a storage compartment on a hard drive or (more rarely) a floppy disk. They're called folders because you're supposed to think of your hard drive as a filing cabinet. As you may know, in most filing cabinets, the contents are organized into separate folders; it's the same with your hard drive: all of its files and documents are also organized into folders. As you'll see, saving your documents in a particular folder makes it easy to find them later on.

(If all this folder foofaraw isn't clear in your mind right now, don't be too concerned. We'll be taking a closer look at folders in Chapter 10.)

From Directories to Folders

If you've graduated to Windows 95 from Windows 3.1, you should know that the *directories* you used in the old program are the same as the *folders* you'll be using from now on.

In the Save As dialog box, the Save in drop-down list displays the name of the current folder or disk drive. (If you're using WordPad, the current folder is usually Desktop, but it might also be Windows.) The large box below it shows the contents of the current folder or disk drive. In general, your task is to use the Save in list to select the disk drive and folder you want to use. Let's go through a specific example for WordPad.

To make it easier to find your documents, you should store them all in a separate folder. I have a folder on my hard disk called My Documents that I use to store the documents I create. (You'll also have this folder if you've installed either Office 95 or Office 97, the suite of applications from Microsoft.) If you don't have this folder, you have to create it yourself. I'll show you how to do this in detail in Chapter 12 (see the section called "Adding On: Creating Folders"), but the following steps show you a quick way to do it from the Save As dialog box:

1. Assuming Desktop appears in the Save in list, double-click **My Computer**.

2. Double-click drive C.

3. Click the **Create New Folder** button. Windows 95 adds a new folder (see the next figure).

4. Type **My Documents** and press **Enter**. This is the folder you'll use to store your documents.

5. Double-click the **My Documents** folder.

Clicking this button…

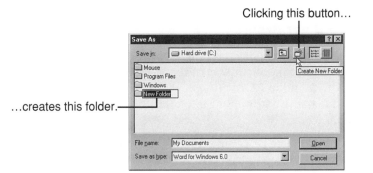

Use the Create New Folder button to slap up a new folder on your hard drive.

…creates this folder.

Happily, you won't have to go through this rigmarole every time you save a new file. Most programs "remember" the most recent folder you worked with and will select it for you automatically the next time you're in the Save As dialog box. (Unfortunately, this only applies to the current session with the program. If you exit the program and then restart it, you have to reselect the folder.)

Okay, with the folder you want now open in the Save As dialog box, you can move on to the second stage: specifying a name for the document.

Entering a Snappy Name for Your Document

Now we come to one of the all-time great features of Windows 95: the capability to use long, descriptive file names. If you're new to computers, you should thank your lucky stars that you never had to wrestle with the procrustean restrictions that were placed on file names by previous versions of Windows and DOS. In the old days, you couldn't create names any longer than eight lousy characters. (Plus, you could tack on a dot and a three-character extension. Big deal.) As you can imagine, this led to the absurdity of names like 1STQBDGT.XLS and LTR2MOM.DOC. Ugly with a capital "Ug."

With Windows 95, however, those days are gone forever. Now you can bask in the luxury of file names that can be a whopping 255 characters long! Ah, the freedom! You can include spaces, too, so it's now possible to create names that are—gasp!—comprehensible to an ordinary human being. Here are some examples:

Fiscal 1997 — First Quarter Budget Spreadsheet

Letter to Mom (the one where I plead with her to send more money)

A Document with a Really Long-Winded and Rambling Name, Just for the Heck of It!

Other than the 255-character limit, the only other restriction you face is that you can't use any of the following characters:

\ | ? : * " < >

What Do Older Programs Think of Long File Names?

The rub with long file names is that only programs written specifically for Windows 95 can take advantage of them. DOS programs and those meant to work with Windows 3.1 will scoff at your attempts to break through the old "8.3" file name barrier (8 characters for the file name and a 3-character extension).

So what happens if you create a document with a verbose name using a Windows 95 program, and then try to open that document in an older program? Well, the document will probably open just fine, but you'll notice that the file name has been knocked down to size. You see, Windows 95 actually keeps track of *two* names for each document: the long name and a shorter DOS-compatible name. The latter is just the first six characters of the long name (sans spaces), followed by a tilde (~), followed by a number. For example, a file named Fiscal 1997 — First Quarter Budget Spreadsheet would also use the DOS alias FISCAL~1.

Once you decide on a descriptive name for the document, move to the **File name** text box (see the Save As dialog boxes shown earlier) and type in the name. (Some programs include a default name in the File name text box. WordPad, for example, uses Document. Make sure you delete this name before entering your own.)

Hey, you're almost done. For your last task, just select the **Save** button, and your document, at long last, is safely stored on your hard disk.

A Fresh Beginning Starting a New Document

When you start most Windows 95 applications, you usually see a new, blank document, ready and eager to receive your input. You have two choices at this point:

➤ You can work with the new document.

➤ You can open an existing document.

Since we're just starting out, I'm going to assume you want to work with the new document. (I'll cover opening an existing document in the next section.) Besides working with this new document, you can open a fresh document anytime you want. All you do is pull down the application's **File** menu and select the **New** command or press **Ctrl+N**.

You can also click this button in WordPad's toolbar to run the New command. (Lots of other Windows programs include this button on their toolbars as well.)

Reunited Opening an Existing Document

Instead of opening a new document, you'll often want to work with an existing document that you saved previously. This means you have to *open* the document you want by pulling down the application's **File** menu and selecting the **Open** command. The Open dialog box appears (see the next figure).

Faster Opening
Pressing **Ctrl+O** in most Window 95 programs also runs the Open command.

In WordPad and many other Windows 95 programs, you can click this button in the toolbar to display the Open dialog box.

Selecting the File Open command displays the Open dialog box.

As you can see, the Open dialog box bears a remarkable resemblance to the Save As dialog box you were slaving away in earlier. In this case, you use the Look in drop-down list to select the disk drive and folder that contain the document you want to open. Then you highlight the document you want to open and select the **Open** button.

Opening a Document from the Start Menu

One of Windows 95's other handy features is its capability to open a document directly from the Start menu. You may have noticed that the Start menu includes a Documents folder. This folder maintains a list of the last few documents you opened, as shown in the following figure. To open one of these documents (and, of course, launch the program you used to create the document), select the **Start** button, open the **Documents** folder, and select the document you want.

The Start menu's Documents folder keeps track of the last few documents you opened.

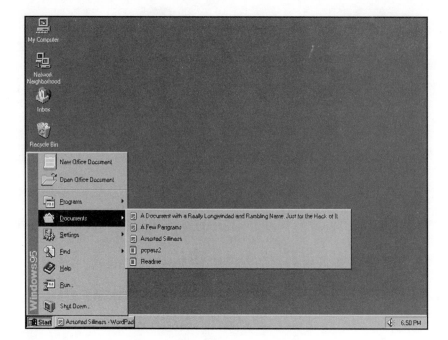

The Strange but Useful Save As Command

Your application's File menu probably also includes a Save As command. This command is a lot like Save, except it enables you to save the document to a new name or a new location, which is useful if you need to create a new document that's very similar (but not identical) to an existing document. Instead of creating the new document from scratch, just open the existing document, make the changes, and then use the Save As command to save your changes as the new document. The old document remains as it was. When you select the Save As command, you see the same Save As dialog box that I showed you earlier.

Closing a Document

Some weakling Windows 95 programs (such as WordPad) allow you to open only one document at a time. In such programs, you can close the document you're currently working on by starting a new document, by opening another document, or by quitting the application altogether.

However, most full-featured Windows 95 programs let you open as many documents as you want. Things can get crowded pretty fast, though, so you'll probably want to close any documents you don't need at the moment. To do this, activate the document you want to close, pull down the **File** menu, and select the **Close** command. If you made changes to the document, a dialog box appears asking if you want to save those changes. (Working with multiple documents in an application is an essential Windows 95 survival skill. Read Chapter 9 to learn the basics.)

Using Scroll Bars to Navigate a Document

Depending on the program you're using, an opened document might appear in its own window, or it might appear as part of the program's window. In either case, you'll often find that the entire document won't fit inside the window's boundaries. When this happens, you need some way to move to the parts of the document you can't see.

From the keyboard, you can use either the basic navigation keys (the arrow keys, Page Up, and Page Down) or the special key combinations (which vary from application to application).

Mouse users, as usual, have all the fun. To navigate through a document, they get to learn a new skill: using *scroll bars*. Scroll bars are a lot like elevators. As you can see here, they sort of look like elevator shafts, and (like your favorite Otis device) they serve a dual purpose: they can tell you where you are and they can take you someplace else.

Up scroll arrow

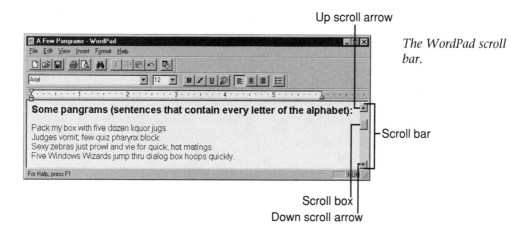

The WordPad scroll bar.

Scroll bar

Scroll box
Down scroll arrow

Check This Out...

Keyboard Navigation Tips

I've found a few key combinations that seem to work in many applications. For example, the Home key often takes you to the beginning of the current line, and the End key often takes you to the end of the line. Also, try Ctrl+Home to get to the beginning of the document and Ctrl+End to get to the end.

Where Am I? The Scroll Bar Knows

Thanks to my innately lousy sense of direction (I've been known to get lost getting out of bed in the morning), I'm constantly looking at maps and street signs to make sure I'm where I'm supposed to be. This directional defect also carries over, unfortunately, into computers. Give me a file that has more than a couple of screens of information, and I'm toast. Fortunately, I have scroll bars to bail me out. The idea is simple: the position of the scroll box tells me my relative position in the document. For example, if the vertical scroll box is about halfway down, I know I'm somewhere near the middle of the document. So the scroll box is sort of like the floor indicator on an elevator.

Can I Get There from Here? Navigating with Scroll Bars

The real scroll bar fun begins when you use them to move around in your documents. There are three basic techniques:

➤ To scroll up or down through the document one line at a time, click the scroll bar's up or down scroll arrows.

➤ To leap through the document one screen at a time, click inside the scroll bar between the scroll box and the scroll arrows. For example, to move down one screenful, click inside the scroll bar between the scroll box and the down scroll arrow.

➤ To move to a specific part of the document, drag the scroll box up or down.

Note, as well, that many of the windows you work in will also sport a second scroll that runs horizontally along the bottom of the window. Horizontal scroll bars work the same as their vertical cousins, except they let you move left and right in wide documents.

The Latest Mice Have Wheels!

In early 1997, Microsoft introduced a radical new mouse design that incorporates a little wheel between the two buttons. If you're lucky enough to have one of these rotary rodents, you can scroll up and down through a document merely by turning the wheel!

A Few Basic Document Editing Chores

You now know how to open a document, how to save it, and how to get around in it. What's missing? Oh yeah, you have to do some work eventually! Of course, most of what you do in a document depends entirely on the application you're using, but let's look at a few basic skills that you can use in almost any program.

Highlighting Text

Most documents contain some sort of text that you can format (for example, add bold or underline to) or cut and paste. Before you can do any of these things, though, you need to *highlight* the text you want to work with.

To highlight text with a mouse, simply drag the mouse over the characters you want. That is, you first position the mouse pointer ever so slightly to the left of the first character you want to highlight. Then you press and hold down the left mouse button and move the mouse to the right. As you do, the characters you pass over become highlighted (see the following figure). While you drag, you can also move the mouse down to highlight entire lines. When you release the mouse button, your text remains highlighted.

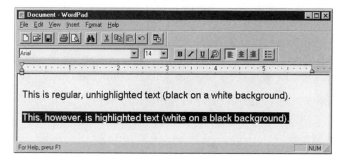

The difference between highlighted and unhighlighted text.

To highlight with the keyboard, position the cursor to the left of the first character, hold down the **Shift** key, and then press the right arrow key until the entire selection is highlighted. Use the down arrow key (or even Page Down if you have a lot of ground to cover) if you need to highlight multiple lines.

If you botch the highlight (that mouse dragging thing does take some practice) or if you decide not to work with the highlighted text, you can remove the highlight by clicking elsewhere in the document. (Keyboardists, first release the Shift key and then press one of the arrow keys.)

Accidentally Deleting Highlighted Text Is Really Easy

If you highlight some text and then press a letter on your keyboard, you'll be dismayed to see your entire selection disappear and be replaced by the character whose key you pressed! (This also happens if you press a number or even the Enter key.) This is, unfortunately, normal behavior that can cause trouble for even experienced document jockeys. To get your text back, immediately pull down the application's Edit menu and select the Undo command (for more info, see "To Err Is Human, to Undo Divine," later in this chapter).

Copying a Selection

One of the secrets of computer productivity is a simple maxim: Don't reinvent the wheel. In other words, if you have something that works (it can be a picture, a section of text, whatever) and you need something similar, don't start from scratch. Instead, make a copy of the original, and then make any necessary changes to the copy.

Happily, most Windows 95 applications make it easy to copy. In fact, once you've highlighted what you want to copy, you simply pull down the application's **Edit** menu and select the **Copy** command. You then position the cursor where you want to place the copy (it could even be in another document or another application) and select the **Edit** menu's **Paste** command. A perfect copy of your selection appears instantly.

 This is the Copy toolbar button used in billions of Windows programs.

 This is the Paste toolbar button used in many Windows programs.

Moving a Selection

If you need to move something from one part of a document to another (or from one document or application to another), you *could* do it by making a copy, pasting it, and then going back to delete the original. However, if you do this, your colleagues will certainly make fun of you because there's an easier way. Once you select what you want to move, pull down the **Edit** menu and select the **Cut** command. Your selection disappears from the screen, but don't panic; Windows 95 saves it for you. Position the cursor where you want to place the selection, open the **Edit** menu, and choose **Paste**. Your stuff miraculously reappears in the new location.

This is the Cut toolbar button used in umpteen Windows programs.

Deleting a Selection

Even the best typists make occasional typos, so knowing how to delete is a crucial editing skill. Put away the White-Out, though, because deleting a character or two is easier (and less messy) if you use either of the following techniques:

➤ Position the cursor to the right of the offending character and press the **Backspace** key.

➤ Position the cursor to the left of the character and press the **Delete** key.

If you have a large chunk of material you want to expunge from the document, you need to highlight it and press the **Delete** key. (Many applications also have Edit menu commands you can use to perform deletions; look for a command such as Delete or Clear.)

Techno Talk

Cutting versus Deleting

Okay, let's see if I have this straight. If you cut something, Windows 95 removes it from the document; if you delete something, Windows 95 also removes it from the document. So what's the diff?

Good question. When you cut a selection, Windows 95 actually saves it in a special section of your computer's memory called the Clipboard. That's why it's easy to go to a different part of the document and issue a Paste command to move the text to the new location. Paste says to Windows, in effect, "Yo! Take whatever stuff is on that Clipboard thingy and plop it right here."

When you delete a selection, however, the text is gone for good (although, as you'll see in the next section, it's often possible to retrieve accidentally deleted text).

To Err Is Human, to Undo Divine

At some point in your computing career, usually when you least expect it, you'll have the "uh-oh" experience. This occurs anytime you do something that you didn't want to, such as consigning a vital piece of an irreplaceable document to deletion purgatory. Just so you're prepared, here are the symptoms: your life inevitably flashes before your eyes (and you remember where you lost that roller skate key in Grade 3), you start hallucinating (mostly distorted images of your boss saying "You're fired!"), and your stomach does backflips that would be the envy of any gymnast.

Fortunately, many Windows 95 applications now come with an Undo feature to get you out of these jams. The Undo command restores everything to the way it was before you made your blunder. (I've had some relationships where an Undo command would have come in *very* handy!)

To use the Undo feature, pull down the application's **Edit** menu and select the **Undo** command. (Depending on the action you're trying to reverse, the command may actually say something like "Undo Paste.")

 This is the Undo toolbar button in many Windows programs.

Oodles of Editing Shortcuts

Almost all Windows 95 programs support the following keyboard shortcuts:

Copy	Ctrl+C
Cut	Ctrl+X
Paste	Ctrl+V
Undo	Ctrl+Z

In most applications, the Undo command works only on the most recent change you made. If you do anything at all after you make the mistake (such as type some text), you won't be able to reverse your mistake. For this reason, always select the Undo command immediately after your blunder. Having said all that, however, there are several applications (such as Microsoft Word for Windows and Excel) that offer a "multiple level" Undo. Check your application's documentation to find out if it's available and learn how to use it.

The Least You Need to Know

Now that was a chapter! You learned all kinds of practical stuff from opening and saving documents to basic cut-and-paste techniques. Whew! The only routine chore we didn't cover was printing, and we'll tackle that in the next chapter.

Chapter 8

Windows 95 Printing Particulars

In This Chapter

➤ Installing a printer in Windows 95

➤ Basic printing steps

➤ Controlling your print jobs

➤ A peck of pickled printing points

I've suffered with various computers over the years, but one thing has remained constant: when I'm finished working, I need some physical, tangible proof that I really did *do* something, and that this stuff isn't just all smoke and mirrors. In other words, I've gotta see some hard copy. Fortunately, Windows 95 makes printing a relatively painless procedure. You set up your printer once, and all your Windows applications fall in line and use that same setup. In this chapter, I'll cover how to install your printer, I'll show you the basic printing procedure, and I'll give you a few pointers on how to control your print jobs.

Telling Windows 95 About Your Printer

In the nasty old DOS world, every program dealt with the printer in its own special way. This sounds innocent enough, but it really means you have to perform some kind of printer setup for every program you use. Can you say "annoying"? Windows changes all that because its if-you-want-something-done-right-then-do-it-yourself approach to printing means that Windows itself handles all the printing chores. When you print from any Windows application, all the program does is pass everything over to Windows and say, "Okay, you think you're so smart, *you* print the darn thing!"

This has two major advantages. First, it means that, as you'll see in a sec, the steps required to print something in Windows 95 are more or less the same for all programs. Second, it means that the only software that needs to know about your printer is Windows 95. Your Windows applications couldn't care less; they're just along for the ride. So the upshot is that you only have to install your printer once—for Windows 95—and not for every program on your computer. Can you say "convenient"?

Printer installation is normally taken care of during the Windows 95 setup procedure. If you skipped that step or if you got a new printer for Christmas, you need to install your printer in Windows 95. This involves telling Windows 95 what kind of printer you have so it can copy the appropriate *printer driver* to your hard disk. (A printer driver isn't a chauffeur for your printer. Instead, it's a small program that translates the documents you print into some kind of gibberish the printer can understand.) The next few sections take you through all the steps you need to follow.

Getting Started

To get the printer installation show on the road, select the **Start** button to open the Start menu, select **Settings**, and then select **Printers**. Windows 95 opens the Printers folder and displays it in the window shown in the following figure. (If you haven't installed a printer yet, your Printers folder will contain only the Add Printer icon.)

The Printers folder shows the currently installed printers.

Double-click the **Add Printer** icon, or use the arrow keys to highlight it and then press **Enter**. Windows 95 calls up the Add Printer Wizard for duty.

The first dialog box just has a boring introductory message, so go ahead and select **Next >**. The Add Printer Wizard displays the dialog box shown in the following figure. (If, instead, the wizard displays a dialog box asking you whether you want to install a "Local printer" or a "Network printer," select the **Local printer** option and select **Next >**. I'll talk about setting up a network printer in Chapter 26, in the "Installing a Network Printer" section.)

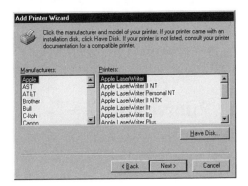

Use this wizard dialog box to select the printer you have.

Picking Out Your Printer

This dialog box lists the dozens of printers that Windows 95 is on friendly terms with. In the **Manufacturers** list, select the manufacturer of your printer, and in the **Printers** list, select your printer model.

What Do You Do If Your Printer Isn't on the Wizard's List of Printers?

You have three choices:

➤ If your printer came with a disk, select the **Have Disk** command button (it's below the Printers list) and follow the wizard's instructions.

➤ Check your printer manual to see if the printer works like (or *emulates*, as the manuals often say) another printer. If it does, see if you can find the emulated printer in the list. For example, many dot-matrix printer models emulate printers from Epson and IBM. Similarly, many laser printer models emulate the Hewlett-Packard LaserJet printer.

➤ If your printer is a dot-matrix, select **Generic** for the manufacturer and **Generic/Text Only** for the printer. For a laser printer, select **HP** for the manufacturer and try the **HP LaserJet** printer.

When you're done, select **Next >**. If the printer driver file is already on your hard disk, the wizard gives you the two choices described next. Make your choice and select **Next >** once again.

Keep existing driver (recommended)   This option is activated by default, which is fine because it's the one you'll choose 99% of the time.

Replace existing driver   If you're having trouble printing, one of the solutions you can try is reinstalling your printer in Windows 95 (as explained in Chapter 21 in the "Persnickety Printing Perplexities" section). In this case, you'll need to select the **Replace existing driver** option. If you're not having trouble printing, however, don't select this option because it may affect how your existing programs print.

Pointing Out Your Printer Port

The next Add Printer Wizard dialog box (shown in the following figure) asks you to specify which *port* to use with the printer (see the sidebar below for a short port report). Highlight the port to which your printer is attached and select **Next >**.

This wizard dialog box wants to know where your printer is attached.

The Printer Port Puzzle

A *port* is the connection where you plug in the cable for a mouse, printer, or some other computer-related toy. If you're not sure which port is the correct one, check the printer cable connection at the back of your computer. Some thoughtful computer companies actually label their ports, so look for something like LPT1 (which is the port used by the vast majority of printers) or COM2. If there are no labels, your computer manual should tell you (provided, that is, you can make heads or tails out of all that geek-speak). If you're still not sure, just choose LPT1 and cross your fingers.

Naming Your Printer and a Few Other Chores

The next Add Printer Wizard dialog box, shown in the following figure, prompts you to enter a name for the printer (you can either leave the suggested name as is, or you can enter a creative 32-characters-or-less name of your own), and it asks if you want the printer to be the *default* for Windows programs. (The default printer is the one that Windows programs use automatically when you run the Print command.) If this is the printer you use most of the time, select **Yes** and then select **Next >**.

Next, the Add Printer Wizard wonders whether or not you want to print a test page. It can't hurt, so get your printer fired up, make sure the **Yes** option is activated, and then select **Finish**.

Use the Printer name text box to enter a clever name for your printer.

Finishing Up (At Last)

Okay, you're almost out of the installation woods. Unless the Windows 95 CD-ROM is still in your CD-ROM drive, Windows 95 will beep and ask you to insert one of your Windows 95 disks. Insert the appropriate disk (or the CD-ROM, if you have one) and select **OK**. Windows 95 copies the files it needs and then cranks out the test page.

Another dialog box appears asking you if the test page printed correctly. If it did (it may take a minute or so for the page to appear), select **Yes** to return to the Printers folder and see the icon for your new printer. If it didn't, select **No** to invoke the Help system's Print Troubleshooter. (I'll take you through Windows 95's Help Troubleshooters in Chapter 21's "Some Safe Mode Diagnostics" section.)

That's all she wrote; your printer is now ready for action.

Printing: The Basic Steps

The printing process provides a good example of the consistent Windows 95 interface I babbled on about back in Chapter 1. Although there are some small differences between applications, the basic steps are the same.

Before printing, make sure your printer is powered up, has plenty of paper, and is online. (*Online* means that your printer is ready, willing, and able to handle the blizzard of characters your program will be throwing at it. Most printers have some kind of Online button that you can press, just to make sure.) When your printer is ready for duty, return to your application, pull down the **File** menu, and select the **Print** command (or press **Ctrl+P**, which is the standard keyboard shortcut for displaying the Print dialog box in Windows programs). You'll see a Print dialog box similar to the one shown here for the WordPad word processor.

 In most Windows programs (including WordPad), you can click this toolbar button to bypass the Print dialog box and print the document directly.

WordPad's Print dialog box is a typical example of the species.

The options in the Print dialog box vary slightly from application to application. However, you'll almost always see three things:

➤ A drop-down list for selecting the printer to use. In WordPad's Print dialog box, for example, use the Name drop-down list to select the printer.

➤ A text box or spinner to enter the number of copies you want. In the WordPad Print dialog box, use the Number of copies spinner.

➤ Some controls for selecting how much of the file to print. You'll normally have the option of printing the entire document or a specific range of pages. (WordPad's Print dialog box also includes a Selection option button that you can activate to print only the currently highlighted text.)

When you've chosen your options, select the **OK** button to start printing (some Print dialog boxes have a Print button, instead). Keep your eyes peeled on the information area of the taskbar (the area to the left of the time). After a few seconds (depending on the size of the document), a printer icon appears, as shown in the following figure. This tells you Windows 95 is hard at work farming out the document to your printer.

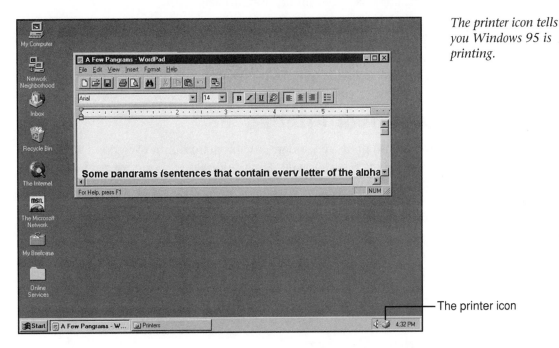

The printer icon tells you Windows 95 is printing.

The printer icon

Changing the Default Printer

As you saw earlier in the printer installation section, you can designate a printer as the default for all Windows programs. If you install a single printer driver, that printer will, of course, be the default. If you install multiple printers (drivers), however, you may need to change which of them is the Windows default.

To do this, open the Printers folder (as described earlier) and try either of the following:

➤ Highlight the printer you want to be the default, pull down the **File** menu, and activate the **Set As Default** command.

➤ Right-click the would-be default printer and then activate the **Set As Default** command from the shortcut menu.

93

Selecting a Different Printer in an Application

When you print in a Windows application, the program always assumes you want to use the default printer as previously described. If you want to print to a different printer, the Print dialog box should have a drop-down list that lets you choose which printer to use. (In WordPad's Print dialog box, for example, use the Name list.)

In some older programs, however, you'll need to either select the **File** menu's **Print Setup** command or select the **Printer Setup** button in the Print dialog box. In either case, a Print Setup dialog box appears, listing the installed printers. Select the one you want to use, and then select **OK**.

Taking Control of Your Printing

When you tell a program to print a document, the program notifies Windows 95 that a print job is pending. To get you back to your application faster, Windows performs a nifty bit of trickery. It borrows the file, makes a copy of it, and then hands control back to the application. While you continue working, Windows 95 prints the copy of the file in the background (that's why you see the printer icon in the taskbar whenever you print).

Therefore, once you send a job to the printer, you normally don't have to bother with it again. Windows 95 just goes about its business behind the scenes—and it's usually best to leave it that way. However, there may be times when you want to cancel a print job or change the order in which the documents will print, and you need to stick your finger in the printing pie to do that.

Opening the Printing Printer

If a print job you want to mess with is in progress, double-click the taskbar's printer icon. (Alternatively, you can open the **Printers** folder and double-click the printer you're using, or highlight the printer using the arrow keys and then press **Enter**.) As shown in the next figure, Windows 95 lists the print jobs in the order they were sent to the printer and displays the following info:

Document Name   The name of the document (duh).

Status   The current status of the print job. (*Spooling* means that Windows 95 is making the copy of the document that it will send to the printer.)

Owner   The username of the person who sent the document to the printer. The username matters only if you set up Windows 95 for multiple users or on a network. (I'll tell you how to set up Windows 95 for multiple users in Chapter 26.)

Progress   The size of the document and how much of it has been printed.

Started At   The time and date the document was sent to the printer.

The printer window enables you to pause a print job in progress.

A Pause for the Cause: Pausing Printing

If you need to add paper to your printer or change the toner cartridge, you can tell Windows 95 to hold its printing horses. Open the printer window as described in the previous section, pull down the **Printer** menu, and then activate the **Pause Printing** command. This prevents Windows 95 from sending any more data to the printer. When you're ready to roll again, pull down the **Printer** menu and deactivate the **Pause Printing** command.

If you just want to pause a particular document, click it (or use the up and down arrow keys to highlight it) and activate the **Document** menu's **Pause Printing** command. To resume printing, highlight the document and deactivate the **Document** menu's **Pause Printing** command.

Changing the Order of the Print Jobs

If you send more than one document to the printer in a short span of time, Windows 95 starts printing the first document and tells the others to get in line—it's literally called the print queue—and wait their turn. If you'd like to change the order that these waiting documents will print, all you have to do is use your mouse to drag any document up or down in the list. (Note, though, that you can't supplant the document that's printing—you either have to let it run its course or else cancel it, as explained in the next section.)

Bailing Out of Print Jobs

If you accidentally print the wrong document, or if you simply change your mind about printing it, deleting a print job from the queue is no problem. To do so, open the printer window, highlight the appropriate file, open the **Document** menu, and select the **Cancel Printing** command.

If the whole printing process is a complete fiasco, you can cancel every print job by selecting the **Printer** menu's **Purge Print Jobs** command.

The Least You Need to Know

This chapter gave you the lowdown on printing in Windows 95 and showed you how Windows' consistent interface makes printing a breeze. Speaking of breezes, is there a window open around here? In Windows 95, there is almost always a window open somewhere, so the next chapter tells you how to gain the upper hand on Windows' ubiquitous windows.

Chapter 9

The "Windows" in Windows 95

In ancient times, long before glass was in common use (and long before summertime air conditioning became *de rigueur*), people built their homes with holes in the walls to let in air and light. (Flintstones fans will know exactly what I mean.) Because these holes allowed the people to see out and allowed air in, they were called "wind eyes." Over time, people began covering these holes with glass and cheesy chintz curtains and the phrase "wind eyes" turned into the modern word "windows."

I tell you this seemingly pointless story by way of introduction to the subject of this chapter: the windows in Windows 95. In a sense, the old meaning of the word "window" fits quite nicely here. In Windows 95, you can "see through" a window to look at what's on your computer. But these windows also "let in" your input in the form of keystrokes and mouse clicks. It might help to keep all this in mind as you work with Windows 95's windows. Just remember that each window on the screen is a view of something on your computer and that you can "reach through" the window to make changes to what you see.

The Parts Department: Anatomy of a Window

Before you pull out your digital machete and start cutting your way through the thicket of Windows 95's windows, take a moment to get your bearings. In particular, there's a bit of unavoidable window lingo you need to get down, so you'll start with a quick lesson on window anatomy.

For openers, let's get a window specimen on-screen so you can do some poking around. You've used WordPad a few times already, so let's try something different this time: the Paint accessory. To prod Paint into action, select the **Start** button, open the **Programs** folder, open the **Accessories** folder, and select **Paint**. You'll soon see the Paint window on your desktop, as shown in the following figure. (Your look at Paint in this chapter will be superficial at best. To get the scoop on all the real Paint procedures, strike out for Chapter 14.)

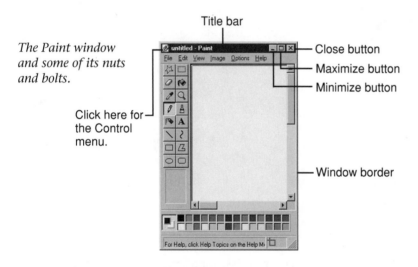

The Paint window and some of its nuts and bolts.

Here's a quick rundown of the various window features in Paint (and just about every other Windows 95 program you're likely to trip over in your travels):

Title bar   This is the blue strip across the top of the window. The title bar usually shows two things: the name of the current document ("untitled" in the Paint window shown in the previous figure) and the name of the program, separated by a dash. As you'll see later (in the section "Windows on the Move"), you can use the title bar to move a window with your mouse.

Minimize button   Of the trio of buttons in the top-right corner, the one on the left is the Minimize button. This button clears the window from the desktop without closing the program (as explained later on in the section "The Minimalist Approach: Reducing a Window to the Taskbar").

Maximize button   This is the center button of the three buttons in the top-right corner. This button enlarges the window so it takes up the entire desktop. (I talk more about this in the section "Taking It to the Max: Maximizing a Window.")

Close button   Of the three buttons in the top-right corner, the button on the right is the Close button. As I explained back in Chapter 4, this button shuts down the program.

Border   Most windows are surrounded by a thin border that you can use to change the size of a window with your mouse. I explain this technique in full in the "Sizing Up Your Windows" section.

Control menu   The Control menu sports several commands that enable keyboard users to perform routine window maintenance. For a program window, press **Alt+Spacebar** to display the Control menu; for a document window, press **Alt+-**.

New Window Buttons in Windows 95

Veterans of the Windows 3.1 wars will note that Windows 95 has made some changes to the window buttons. Specifically, the Minimize and Maximize buttons look different, and the Close button is new. Personally, I'm not sure I like having the Close button right beside the Maximize button because, mouse-maladroit that I am, I often end up closing windows I wanted to maximize. Ah well, that's life in the big Windows 95 city, I guess.

So Many Windows, So Little Space

Isn't there an old saying that talks about a person's greatest strength also being his greatest weakness? It's possible I just made it up, but in any case, it certainly applies to Windows 95. Why? Well, one of Windows 95's greatest strengths is that it enables you to work on multiple projects at the same time. This means you can have Paint running in one window, your word processor in another, a game of FreeCell in a third, and so on. And as if that isn't enough, Windows 95 also enables you to open multiple windows in a single application! So in your word processor, for example, you can have a window open for your letter to Mom, one for your shopping list, and one for your memo to the execs on the coast.

The problem with having all these open windows is that things can get real confusing, real fast. If you don't believe me, take a look at the screen in the following figure.

*Multitasking multi-
tudinousness:
opening just a few
programs can quickly
turn your screen into
a true dog's break-
fast.*

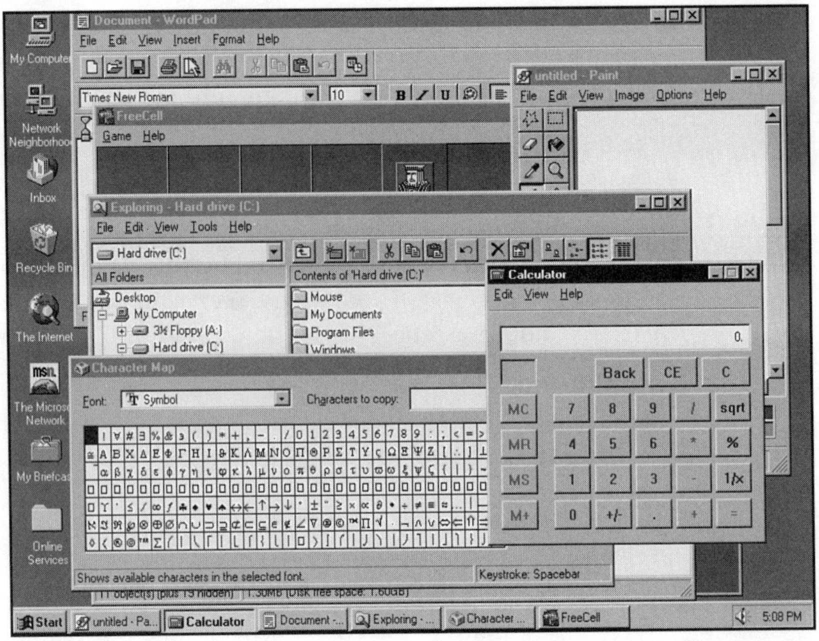

What a mess! Not only is such a screen visually unappealing, but some normally simple tasks become downright difficult. For example, just finding the mouse pointer becomes a real Where's Waldo? exercise. (Yes, there *is* a mouse pointer shown in the figure. Can you find it?) And there are only a half dozen programs running in this picture. If your computer has enough memory, you can conceivably crack open a dozen programs or more. (Although *why* you'd want to do that I can't imagine.) What you need here are some simple techniques for managing windows before they get out of hand. Fortunately, Windows 95 offers a number of methods for regaining control of your screen. Throughout the rest of this chapter, I'll bring you up to speed on the easiest and fastest of these methods.

Your Home Base: The Active Window

Anytime you find yourself with a bunch of windows on your screen, you can simplify your life immeasurably if you keep the following idea in mind: *You can work in only one window at a time.* In other words, no matter how many windows you may have open, the window you're currently slaving away in (called the *active window*, by the way) gives you its complete and undivided attention. You can, therefore, safely ignore everything else going on around it (or at least try to).

100

Which Window Is Active?

With this in mind, the first stop on our window management tour will be to learn how to make a window active. How will you know when you succeed in making a window active? There are a few clues to watch for, and they're all illustrated in the next figure.

➤ The most obvious clue is the window's title bar. If the window is active, its title bar displays the title in white letters on a blue background. If it's an inactive window, the title appears in light gray letters on a dark gray background.

➤ The active program's taskbar button appears "pressed."

➤ You'll see an insertion point cursor or some other marker to tell you where you are in the program's document.

The title bar of an inactive window shows light gray text on a dark gray background.

The title bar of an active window shows white text on a blue background.

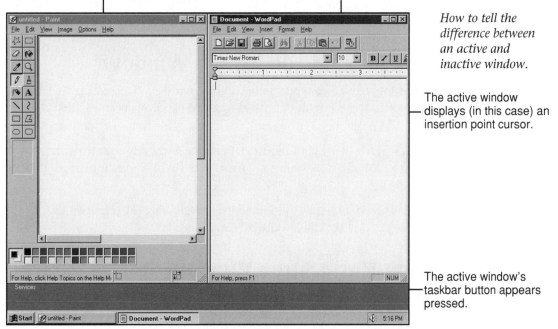

How to tell the difference between an active and inactive window.

The active window displays (in this case) an insertion point cursor.

The active window's taskbar button appears pressed.

I explained how to switch between open windows in Chapter 4, so you might want to head back there if you need to review the basic techniques.

Activating a window is important, but it's only the first step toward gaining full control over how your windows appear on the screen. The rest of this chapter shows you a number of basic Windows 95 window-control techniques.

The Minimalist Approach: Reducing a Window to the Taskbar

You'll often find that you have some windows you know you won't need for a while. You can close them, move them out of the way, or make them smaller, but all that takes time, and our goal is always to make things as easy as possible. Fortunately, there's an alternative: you can remove a window from the desktop *without* closing it. This bit of window sorcery is called *minimizing* the window.

 If you use a mouse, you can minimize a window in no time at all by clicking the window's **Minimize** button.

Minimizing a window takes a bit more effort if you use the keyboard, however. In this case, you need to pull down the window's Control menu (by pressing **Alt+Spacebar**) and select the **Minimize** command.

In either case, the window disappears from the desktop, but its taskbar button remains in view. You can open the window again at any time by clicking on its taskbar button.

Taking It to the Max: Maximizing a Window

To get the largest possible work area, you can *maximize* a window. This means that the window expands so it fills the entire desktop area (the taskbar, however, remains conveniently visible).

 To maximize a window with your mouse, all you have to do is click the window's **Maximize** button. (If you'd like a bigger target, you can also maximize a window by double-clicking its title bar.)

To maximize a window keyboard-style, pull down the window's Control menu (by pressing **Alt+Spacebar**) and select the **Maximize** command.

Back to Normal: Restoring a Window

When you maximize or minimize a window, Windows 95 is smart enough to remember the window's previous size and position. This makes it possible for you to easily restore the window to its former state.

With a mouse, you restore a window using one of these methods:

If you minimized the window, you can restore it by clicking its taskbar button.

 If you maximized the window, Windows 95 changes the Maximize button to the Restore button. Simply click the **Restore** button to return the window to its previous state.

From the keyboard, you need to do the following:

> **For a minimized window,** use either the **Alt+Tab** or the **Alt+Esc** key combination to select the window.

> **For a maximized window,** pull down its Control menu and select the **Restore** command.

Windows on the Move

One of the problems with having several windows open at once is that they have a nasty habit of overlapping each other. And what's covered up in a window is usually the information you want to see. (Chalk up another one for Murphy's Law, I guess.) Instead of cursing Windows 95's ancestry, you can try moving your windows around so they don't overlap (or so they overlap less).

If you use a mouse, you can move a window quite easily. First, activate the window you want to move. Then point the mouse at the window's title bar and drag the window to its new location. (Recall that you drag something by pointing at it, holding down the left mouse button, and then moving the mouse.) As you drag, the window itself doesn't move. Instead, Windows 95 displays a dotted outline of the window border that moves with the mouse pointer. When the border appears to be in the position you want, release the mouse button. Windows 95 redisplays the entire window in the new position.

If you use a keyboard, follow these steps to move a window:

1. Activate the window you want to move.

2. Pull down the window's Control menu by pressing **Alt+Spacebar**.

3. Select the **Move** command. A dotted gray outline appears around the window border. (Can't select the Move command? This will happen if the window is maximized. The Move command is only available in non-maximized windows.)

4. Use the arrow keys to move the window outline.

5. When the outline is in the location you want, press **Enter**, and Windows 95 redisplays the window in the new location. If you decide you don't want to move the window after all, you can press the **Esc** key at any time.

Sizing Up Your Windows

Another way to reduce window clutter is to change the size of the open windows. For example, you can reduce the size of less important windows and increase the size of windows in which you do the most work.

The secret to sizing is the window border. The idea is that you drag a section of the border (the top, bottom, left, or right side) with your mouse to create the new dimensions. Here are the explicit mouse steps:

Check This Out...

Two Sides at Once If you want to size two borders at the same time, position the mouse pointer on the corner of a window border. When you drag the mouse, Windows 95 sizes the two sides that create the corner.

1. Activate the window you want to size.

2. Point the mouse at the window border you want to adjust. For example, if you want to expand the window to the right, point the mouse at the right border. When the pointer is positioned correctly, it changes into a two-headed arrow.

3. Drag the border to the position you want. As you drag the mouse, Windows 95 shows a dotted outline of the new border position.

4. Release the mouse button, and Windows 95 resizes the window.

5. Repeat steps 2–4 for any other borders you want to size.

Diehard keyboardists need to follow these steps to resize a window:

1. Activate the window you want to size.

2. Pull down the window's Control menu by pressing **Alt+Spacebar**.

3. Select the **Size** command. A gray outline appears around the window border. (Again, you won't be able to select the Size command if the window is maximized.)

4. To select a border to size, press the corresponding arrow key. For example, to size the right border, press the right arrow key. The mouse pointer changes to a two-headed arrow.

5. Use the arrow keys to size the window outline.

6. When the outline is the size you want, press **Enter**. Windows 95 redisplays the window in the new size. If you decide you don't want the window resized, press **Esc** before you hit the Enter key.

Letting Windows Do the Work: Cascading and Tiling

All this moving and sizing stuff is fine for people with time to kill, but the rest of us just want to get the job done and move on. To that end, Windows 95 has cascade and tile features that will automatically arrange your windows for you.

To cascade your windows, right-click an empty section of the taskbar and select the **Cascade** command from the shortcut menu. This tells Windows 95 to arrange your open windows in a cool waterfall pattern, as shown in the following figure. This is good for those times when you want things nice and neat, but you don't need to see what's in the other windows.

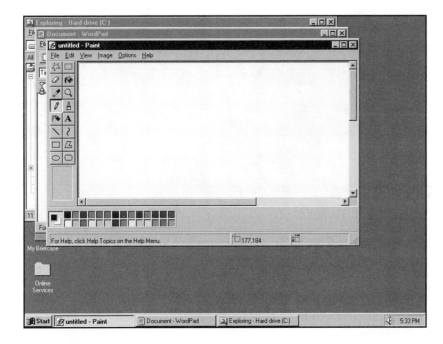

What the Cascade command does.

Tiling divides up your screen and gives equal real estate to each window. To try it out, right-click an empty part of the taskbar and select either **Tile Horizontally** (to arrange the windows in strips across the screen, as shown in the following figure) or **Tile Vertically** (to arrange the windows in vertical strips). Either pattern enables you to work in one window and still keep an eye on what's happening in the other windows (you never know what those pesky devils might be up to!).

If you'd prefer to clear off your desktop completely, you can minimize all of your running programs in one fell swoop by right-clicking an empty part of the taskbar and selecting **Minimize All Windows** from the shortcut menu.

The Tile Horizontally command gives each of your open windows an equal amount of screen space.

Arranging Windows from the Keyboard

Arranging open windows is a breeze if you have a mouse, but what if you're stuck with just a keyboard? Well, it's possible, but the method you use is a bit obscure (and *way* more work). First, press **Ctrl+Esc** to display the Start menu, and then press **Esc** by itself to get rid of the Start menu (see, I told you this was weird). Now press **Tab** and then press **Shift+F10** and, lo and behold, the taskbar's shortcut menu shows up! Now use either the up or down arrow key to highlight the appropriate command for cascading or tiling, and then press **Enter**. Ooh, my aching fingers!

Some Notes About Document Windows

So far in this chapter, we've concerned ourselves only with program windows. But lots of Windows 95 applications let you open multiple document windows, and this can also cause window clutter and navigation headaches. For example, the following figure shows how messy Microsoft Word can become with multiple documents on the go.

Opening multiple documents in a single application can quickly get out of hand.

The good news is that most of the techniques you learned earlier for program windows apply equally well to document windows. In particular, you can move them, size them, minimize them, and maximize them. (Note that keyboard users access a document window's Control menu by pressing **Alt+—**.)

Virtually any Windows 95 application that lets you open multiple windows will have a Window menu. If you pull down the Window menu, you'll see a list of the open document windows at the bottom. To activate a window, simply select it from this menu. (You can also just click the window if you can see it.) The Window menu will also probably have a few commands for arranging the document windows. Look for commands named Arrange, Cascade, or Tile, and try them out. .

The Least You Need to Know

This chapter gave you the lowdown on the windows that give Windows 95 its name. The emphasis was on gaining control over how your windows appear on your screen so you can reduce clutter and get more work done.

That ends our look at the various workaday Windows techniques. You now have all the know-how you need to successfully negotiate any Windows program, big or small. From here, most of our time together will be spent examining specific features of Windows 95.

Part 3
Navigating Your Computer with Windows 95

Just because Windows 95 has us all singing rousing choruses of "Ding, Dong, DOS is Dead," doesn't mean we can get by without having to deal with some DOS-like maintenance chores. We still have to copy files, create folders, and format floppy disks. Fortunately, as you'll see here in Part 3, Windows 95 makes most of these routine tasks a walk in the park.

Chapter 10

A Tour of Your Computer

In This Chapter

➤ Files, folders, and disks explained (in English!)

➤ Getting to know the My Computer window

➤ Navigating your computer

➤ Checking out Windows Explorer

➤ A marvelous metaphor designed to knock some sense into all this file and folder fiddle-faddle

Most people who are new to Windows 95—and especially those who are new to computers in general—would rather have a root canal than deal with files and floppy disks and such. Let's face it; that kind of stuff can be just plain intimidating: all those strange, cryptic names and the confusing terminology. Shudder.

The good news, though, is that, thanks to Windows 95 and its My Computer and Explorer tools, these kinds of things don't have to be intimidating at all. Windows 95 tames the file and floppy disk beasts and makes otherwise-unpalatable chores (such as copying files) about as painless as they can get (or, at least, a step up from a root canal). This chapter introduces you to both My Computer and Windows Explorer, gives you some plain English explanations of files, folders, and disks, and then shows you around.

What Is the My Computer Window?

For the most part, Windows 95 does a pretty good job of shielding you from the harsh realities of the computer world. You have the Start menu to start your programs, you have pull-down menus, shortcut menus, and toolbars to access commands, and you have dialog boxes to talk to Windows 95. All very civilized, if you ask me.

With the My Computer window, Windows 95's civil behavior extends to normally uncivil things such as files and floppy disks. Dealing with such unpleasantries in DOS meant you had to jump through all kinds of techno-hoops just to find out what was on your hard drive, and then you had to peck out various bizarre and cryptic commands to get anything done. My Computer, on the other hand, maps out everything on your computer and presents it to you in an easy-to-digest visual format. Instead of entering unfathomable commands, you do things by simply selecting the appropriate pull-down menu commands or toolbar buttons. Easy as pie (really!).

My Computer versus File Manager

If you upgraded to Windows 95 from Windows 3.1, you may be wondering how My Computer compares with File Manager. Well, they're similar in that they both give you a visual map of what's inside your machine. There are, however, two main differences:

➤ My Computer, by default, opens up a new window every time you open a different folder or disk drive. File Manager, as you may recall, used the same window to display whichever disk drive or folder you were working in.

➤ My Computer shows you the contents of only the current drive or folder. There is no "directory tree" like you had in File Manager.

If you liked File Manager, you probably won't get along with My Computer very well. Instead, you'll probably prefer Windows Explorer, which I'll discuss later in this chapter.

Before you dive headfirst into My Computer's waters, take a step back and see if you can make some sense of a few misunderstood fundamentals. Specifically, in the next few sections, I'll give you some nontechnical explanations of files, folders, and disks.

Getting a Grip on Files, Folders, and Disks

Remember the silly desktop metaphor I tried to pass off on you back in Chapter 3? Well, things are about to get even sillier as I (in true daredevil, throw-caution-to-the-wind, fashion) attempt to extend that metaphor to include your entire computer! Bear with me, here, because this exercise in metaphor-stretching should (I hope) give you a pretty good idea of what files and folders are all about, and it should make it easier for you to figure out My Computer (and the Explorer) later on.

Your Computer: Just a Fancy Filing Cabinet

Okay, here goes (insert dramatic drumroll here): instead of thinking about just a desktop, let's expand our metaphoric view to include an entire office (or, if you home users prefer, a den). Any office worth its salt includes, of course, a filing cabinet, which is handy because that's just what I want you to think of your computer as. In particular, I want you to imagine a filing cabinet where each drawer represents a disk drive on your computer. The next picture shows what a typical computer might look like if it came back in the next life as a filing cabinet. As you can see, there are drawers for the 3^1/$_2$-inch floppy disk (drive A), the hard disk (drive C), and the CD-ROM drive (drive D).

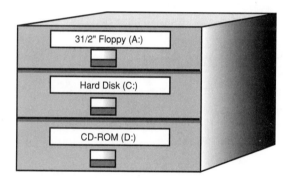

Metaphor madness: if a computer is a filing cabinet, each disk drive is a drawer.

A Peek Inside the Filing Cabinet: Folders

So far so good. Now, what do you find if you open up a drawer in a typical filing cabinet? Folders, of course, lots of folders. Depending on whose filing cabinet you're dealing with (and how organized she is), you'll find folders for different customers, different projects, different employees, different strokes, different folks, well, you get the idea. The key is, though, that each folder contains only related information. If the first folder is for a customer named H. R. Poopenscoop Dog Walking Service, everything in that folder has something to do with that company.

Disk drives, too, can have lots of folders. In this case, you can think of a folder as just a chunk of disk real estate set aside for storage. As with filing cabinet folders, computer folders usually contain only related items. In the next picture, the Hard Disk drawer has been opened to reveal four different folders: Mouse, My Documents, Program Files, and Windows.

Whether you open a filing cabinet drawer or a computer disk drive, you see lots of folders.

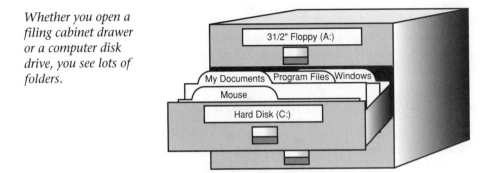

What Happened to Directories?

Windows 3.1 users and the old DOS diehards in the crowd may be wondering what in blue blazes happened to directories. They're still around, but Windows 95 now calls them *folders*.

A Peek Inside the Folders: Files

What kinds of "related items" am I talking about folders containing? Well, let's head back to our old friend the filing cabinet. Most filing cabinet folders contain memos, invoices, letters, lists, contracts, artwork, and whatever else relates to the subject of the folder. The computer equivalents of these items are *files*. A typical folder on a disk drive contains all kinds of files, which fall into three categories:

➤ Files that run your programs. They're—surprise, surprise—*program files*.

➤ Files used by your programs once they're up and running. These are *data files*.

➤ Files you create using these programs. These are the *documents* discussed *ad nauseam* in the previous chapters.

But filing cabinet folders can contain other folders, as well. In my income tax folder, for example, I have a separate folder for each of my tax returns from the past few years. (It's a *very* depressing folder.) This folders-within-folders idea also extends to disk drive folders (you knew it would). For example, your hard disk includes a Windows folder that contains most of your Windows 95 files. But there are also several subfolders within the Windows folder. One of them, to give you a for instance, is called Start menu; it includes the items you see when you open the Start menu.

So there you have it: disks, folders, and files explained in one easy-to-digest, no muss, no fuss metaphor. As you work with My Computer (and Explorer later on), try to keep these concepts in mind. They should help you out if (or perhaps I should say *when*) things become a bit overwhelming.

Checking Out the My Computer Window

 Fine words butter no parsnips, as they say, (no, they really do)—so let's get the My Computer show on the road. Go ahead and double-click the **My Computer** icon in the upper-left corner of the desktop. Windows 95 displays the My Computer window, as shown in the following figure (your window probably looks a bit different from mine).

Techno Talk

Displaying My Computer from the Keyboard

The My Computer desktop icon appears accessible only to mouse martins, so the rodent-deprived in the audience may think they're out of luck. Not so. There *is* a way to display My Computer with a keyboard, but it's not even close to being obvious. What you do is press **Ctrl+Esc** to display the Start menu, press **Esc** to close the Start menu, and then press **Tab** twice and marvel at the fact that the My Computer icon now appears highlighted! Press **Enter** and you're there. (Bonus tip: Once you highlight the My Computer icon, you can use the up and down arrow keys to highlight other desktop icons. Pressing **Enter** while any icon is highlighted will launch that icon.)

The My Computer window.

What you see here, essentially, are the drawers to your computer's filing cabinet! All your disk drives are shown as icons, and My Computer even throws in another couple of icons for good measure. (In the Windows 95 world, an *icon* is a picture that represents something else, such as a disk drive, a folder, or a file.) The following table shows some of the icons you're likely to see and what each of them represents.

The My Computer Icons

This Icon	Represents This
	A 5 ¼-inch floppy disk drive.
	A 3 ½-inch floppy disk drive.
	A hard disk drive.
	A CD-ROM drive.
	The Control Panel. (You use the Control Panel to adjust the settings for your computer in lots of future chapters, but especially in Part 5.)
	The Printers folder.
	A garden-variety folder.

Disk Driving: Selecting a Disk Drive

From here, checking out the contents of a particular disk drive is really easy:

➤ With your mouse, double-click the drive icon.

➤ From the keyboard, use the arrow keys to highlight the drive icon, and then press **Enter**.

The following figure shows the window that appears when I select my hard disk (drive C). As you can see, I have four folders on my hard disk—Mouse, My Documents, Program Files, and Windows—as well as a few files.

The contents of my hard disk drive (drive C).

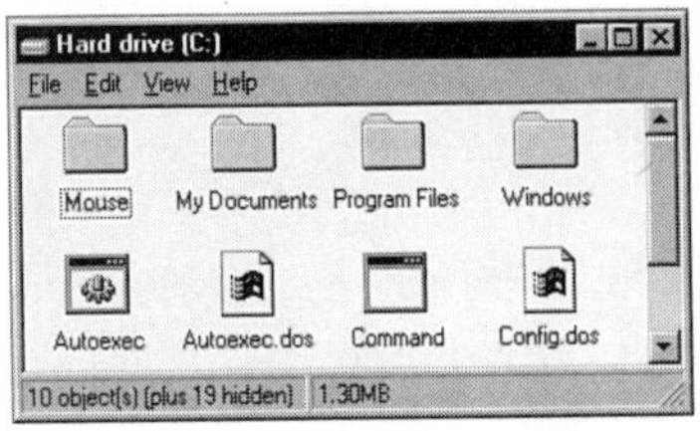

Folder Surfing: Looking in Folders

To see the contents of a folder, double-click it, or use the arrow keys to highlight it and then press **Enter**. For example, try opening your Windows folder. A new window appears, similar to the one shown here.

The contents of my Windows folder.

As you can see, the Windows folder contains even more folders (these are examples of the subfolders mentioned earlier), as well as all kinds of other interesting-looking icons. These are all *files*, and the icons indicate what type of files they represent.

Before you can work with a file (for instance, to rename it or to delete it), you need to select it. Easy money: just click the file's icon with your mouse, or use your keyboard's arrow keys to highlight the icon.

A Nifty Navigation Tip

First, some lingo: The folder/subfolder connection is often regarded as a sort of parent/child relationship because a subfolder is, in a sense, the "offspring" of the main folder. (I know, I know: the geeks who make up this stuff *really* need to get out more.) Anyway, if you open a subfolder and then decide not to stay, closing the window returns you to the parent folder. No big deal there. However, if you prefer to keep the subfolder window open, you can do that *and* return to the parent folder by pressing **Backspace**. (You can also just click the parent folder's taskbar button.)

Some Options for the My Computer Windows

To make My Computer a bit easier to manage, there are several options you can try out. The next few sections tell you all about them.

Changing the File Display

By default, My Computer shows you just the name and icon for each folder or file. You can adjust this display to show more items or to show more detail about each item. Here are your choices:

➤ To show more folders or files in the current window, pull down the **View** menu and select either **Small Icons** (which displays the contents left to right and down the window) or **List** (which displays the contents in a vertical list).

➤ To see details such as the size of the file, the file type, and the date and time it was last modified, select the **View** menu's **Details** command.

Sorting the Window Contents

My Computer normally shows your files in alphabetical order by name, which makes it easy to find the file you want. However, the View menu's Arrange Icons command displays a cascade menu that enables you to choose how you want the icons arranged. In most cases, you have four commands at your disposal: **by Name** (the default sort order), **by Type** (to sort the files in alphabetical order by file type, which corresponds, roughly, to the three kinds of files discussed earlier: program files, data files, and documents), **by Size**, and **by Date**.

Mouse users can also sort the contents of a My Computer window using the Details view. If you look at the screen in Details view (see the next figure), you see that the headings for each column are actually buttons. Clicking one of these buttons sorts the contents according to the data in the column. (To reverse the sort order, click the column button again.) For example, you can click the Modified column's button to have Windows 95 sort the contents in descending order by date.

Click on these buttons to sort the folder's contents.

In Details view, you can sort a folder's contents by clicking the buttons at the top of each column.

Taming My Computer's Windows

One of the things I don't like about My Computer is that its windows multiply like rabbits. Every time you select a new drive or folder, a new window sprouts up. If you do a lot of work with your files and folders, the desktop can get overpopulated in a hurry. To prevent this, you can tell My Computer to cool its jets and not display a new window with each new drive or folder. To give this a try, simply hold down the **Ctrl** key whenever you open a folder. Instead of displaying the folder in a new window, Windows will just use the current window.

If you prefer this behavior, it's possible to make Window 95 do it all the time (so you don't have to remember to hold Ctrl every time you open a folder). To do this, pull down the **View** menu and select the **Options** command. In the Options dialog box, make sure the **Folders** tab is selected, and then activate the following long-winded option button: **Browse folders by using a single window that changes as you open each folder**. Select **OK** to return to My Computer, and then try some folder hopping. My Computer recycles the same window each time you move to a different drive or folder.

Another Approach: Windows Explorer

If you're more of a "big picture" kind of person, you may prefer to use Windows Explorer for all your folder and file fun and games. To understand why, let's get Explorer up to bat. Select the **Start** button to display the Start menu, open the **Programs** folder, and select **Windows Explorer**. You'll see a window like the one shown in the following figure.

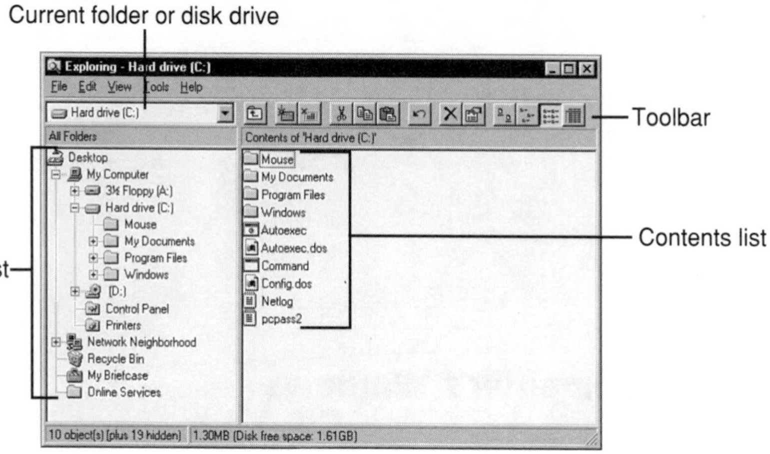

Current folder or disk drive

Windows Explorer lets you see disk drives and folders in one fell swoop.

All Folders list

Toolbar

Contents list

To get the same view as the one shown in the previous figure, you may need to enlarge the window by clicking the Maximize button (see Chapter 9). Also, if you don't see the toolbar, pull down the **View** menu and activate the **Toolbar** command.

The bulk of the Explorer screen is taken up by two list boxes: the All Folders list on the left and the Contents list on the right.

Navigating the All Folders List

As you can see, the All Folders list shows the Desktop at the top of the list and has several other items branching off below it. So Explorer takes a tree-like view of your system. (Well, okay, it's only semi-tree-like, but what the heck, it's close enough for my money.)

Tree-like? You mean yet another metaphor? Groan!

Wait, work with me on this. Let's try a couple of experiments so you can see what I mean.

First, click the Desktop item at the top of the All Folder list. (From the keyboard, press **Tab** until a highlight appears inside the All Folders list, and then press the up arrow key until Desktop appears highlighted.) When you highlight any item in the All folders list, the item's contents appear in, appropriately enough, the Contents list. In the next figure, notice that the contents of the Desktop item are precisely the same doodads that appear on your Windows 95 desktop! Far out.

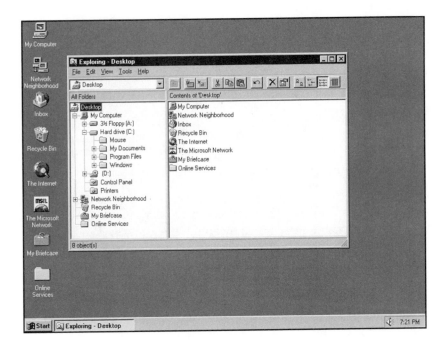

With Desktop highlighted, notice that the items in the Contents list exactly match the items on the desktop itself.

Okay, time for experiment number two. See the minus sign (–) to the left of My Computer in the All Folders list? Go ahead and click that. (From the keyboard, highlight **My Computer** in the All Folders list and press the minus key on your numeric keypad.) You just simplified the All Folders list so that it looks like the one shown in the following figure.

The simplified All Folders list.

Notice in this figure that I highlighted the My Computer item. You can see in the Contents list that the contents are exactly the same as they were in the My Computer window I showed you earlier. In other words, Explorer is just a different way of looking at the same thing.

To see how this difference can come in handy, click the plus sign (+) beside the My Computer item. (Or highlight **My Computer** and press the plus key on your numeric keypad.) This returns you to your original Explorer view. Notice, though, that when Explorer opens My Computer, its contents appear in the All Folders list and they branch off from the My Computer item. This is the fundamental way you work with the All Folders list. To summarize:

> **To expand a branch,** click the plus sign (+) to the left of the folder's name. (If the plus sign is too small a target, you can also double-click the folder's name.) From the keyboard, use the arrow keys to highlight the item, and then press your numeric keypad's plus (+) key.

> **To collapse a branch,** click the minus sign (–) beside the folder's name. (You can also double-click the folder's name.) Keyboarders can use the arrow keys to highlight the item, and then press the numeric keypad's minus (–) key.

The advantage to this approach is that instead of opening all kinds of My Computer windows to get down to a folder or subfolder, you can just open up the appropriate "branch" in the All Folders list and then highlight it. The subfolders and files contained in that folder then appear in the Contents list.

One last thing to note: most of the options I told you about earlier for My Computer also apply to Explorer. In particular, you can display large icons, small icons, or file details in the Contents list, and you can sort the Contents list in various ways.

Explorer: File Manager on Steroids

Fans of Windows 3.1's File Manager will probably feel right at home in Explorer. The layout is more or less the same, with directories (oops, I mean *folders*) on the left and subfolders and files on the right. As you'll see in the next couple of chapters, though, Explorer is more powerful, more flexible, and easier to use than File Manager.

Which One Should I Use: My Computer or Windows Explorer?

Now that you've eyeballed both My Computer and Windows Explorer, which one should you use? That depends on what you need to do and how you prefer to do it. You'll probably have to work with each tool for a time to see which one feels right for you. Here's a quick summary that may help you decide:

Use My Computer if:

➤ You don't mind juggling multiple windows. (Although bear in mind that, as described earlier, you can turn off this feature if you prefer the single window approach.)

➤ You need to place a couple of folder or disk drive windows side by side for easy file copying or moving. (As you'll learn in Chapter 11, you can use your mouse to copy or move files from one My Computer window to another.)

➤ You're only interested in the small picture (what's inside a particular folder or disk drive).

Use Explorer if:

➤ You prefer to keep your desktop uncluttered with windows.

➤ Your computer is attached to a network and you need to access the other computers on the network.

➤ You need to access other desktop stuff such as the Recycle Bin and the My Briefcase folder. (I'll talk about Briefcase in Chapter 17, in the "Taking Files on the Road with Briefcase" section.)

➤ You want to get the big picture (everything that's available on your system).

The Least You Need to Know

This chapter took you on a scenic tour of your computer using two not-unrelated Windows 95 tools: My Computer and Windows Explorer. I hope my computer/filing cabinet metaphor helped put some of this in perspective for you. I think it'll really help you get through the next two chapters as you turn your attention to actually working with files, folders, and floppy disks.

Chapter 11

Fooling Around with Your Files

In This Chapter

➤ Copying and moving files

➤ Renaming and deleting files

➤ Searching for files

➤ Drag-and-drop demystified

➤ A slew of file maintenance shortcuts and speedups

➤ Various other nifty file techniques that are sure to impress your family and friends (at least those who are easily impressed)

In Chapter 10, I tried to sell you on the idea that your computer was like a filing cabinet full of folders. I told you to think of the files that inhabit your hard disk as being akin to the letters, contracts, and other papers you might find in a typical filing cabinet folder. In this chapter, you learn some basic secretarial duties, such as moving and copying files, deleting files, and searching for files. (Throughout most of this chapter, my instructions apply to both My Computer and Windows Explorer. Where there are differences, I'll point them out as we go along.)

Making Copies of Files

In an office, photocopying memos, reports, and various parts of one's anatomy (after hours, of course) is a big part of the everyday routine. In your computer, you'll find that copying files, whether you copy them from one part of your hard disk to another or between your hard disk and a floppy disk, is one of your most common chores. This section shows you three ways to copy files: the old-fashioned way (using the Copy command), a faster way for hard-disk-to-floppy-disk copying (the Send To command), and the newfangled way (using something called "drag-and-drop").

Copying Files with the Copy Command

Before you can copy a file, you need to select it, which you can do by opening the file's folder and highlighting the file. Go ahead and select a file—any file. Now pull down the **Edit** menu and select the **Copy** command. Hmm, nothing happened. Actually, it only *seems* like nothing happened. Windows 95, sneaky devil that it is, really did make a copy of the file, but it's storing the copy in a hidden part of your computer's memory. Fortunately, the mechanics of all this isn't something that need concern the likes of you and me, so we'll move on.

The next step is to select the folder or disk drive where you want to store the copy of the file. When you've done that, pull down the **Edit** menu and select the **Paste** command. Windows 95 takes the copy it made earlier and stuffs it into the folder. As it does, a window appears to show you the progress of the copy, as you can see in the following figure. (I'm a big fan of the animation that shows papers flying from one folder to another, because it reminds me of those flying squirrels you often see in *National Geographic* specials.)

The Copying window appears to let you know how the copy operation is proceeding.

> **Copying...**
> A Few Pangrams.doc
> From 'My Documents' to 'A:\'
> [Cancel]

This Ain't File Manager's Copy Command!

When I first started using Windows 95, it threw me for a loop that I couldn't find a Copy command on the File menu of either Explorer or My Computer. I had to poke around for a bit before I realized that the Copy command is now on the *Edit* menu and that copying a file has become a copy-and-paste routine. Weird.

An Easier Way to Copy Files to a Floppy Disk

A good chunk of your copying labors will involve sending files to a floppy disk to make backup copies of important data or for transportation to another machine. (Computer nerds, proving that at least some of them have a sense of humor, refer to transporting files on foot via floppy disk as *sneaker net*.) Instead of trudging through separate Copy and Paste commands, you can toss a file onto a floppy in one easy step. All you do is highlight the file, pull down the **File** menu, and select the **Send To** command (or right-click the file and select **Send To** from the shortcut menu that appears). As you can see in the following figure, selecting **Send To** produces a cascade menu that lists, among other things, your floppy drive (or drives, if you have more than one). Select the appropriate command from this menu, and Windows 95 sends the file to the floppy without further prodding.

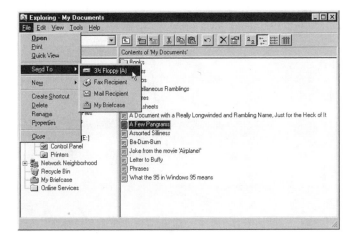

The File menu's Send To command displays a list of your computer's floppy disk drives.

Check This Out...

Don't Copy to a Floppy Without a Floppy!

Before you copy a file to a floppy disk, make sure you have a disk in the appropriate drive. If you don't, your computer makes a rude noise, and Windows 95 chastises you by displaying a dialog box with an error message. If you're not sure how to insert a floppy disk or which of your floppy disk drives to use, see Chapter 12.

Drag 'Til You Drop: Yet Another Way to Copy

Now turn your attention to the *drag-and-drop* method. It sounds like something you do when you get home after a hard day's work, but it's actually a handy mouse method for copying stuff from one locale to another. First, however, you need to arrange your windows appropriately:

➤ If you're using Explorer, make sure the Contents list shows the file you want to copy, and make sure the All Folders list shows the destination—the disk drive or folder to which you want to copy. (If you can't see the destination drive or folder, use the All Folders list's scroll bar to move up or down through the list until you see the destination you need. For a scroll bar refresher course, head back to Chapter 7 and read the "Using Scroll Bars to Navigate a Document" section.)

➤ If you're usingMy Computer, you need to arrange two windows side by side. In one, display the folder that contains the file you want to copy, and in the other, display the destination—the folder or disk drive to which you want to copy. (Need a refresher course on arranging windows? Check out Chapter 9.)

With that out of the way, point your mouse at the file you want to copy, hold down the left mouse button, and (using your other hand, of course) hold down the **Ctrl** key. Now move the mouse toward the destination folder (this is the dragging part). As you drag the mouse, the pointer shows the file name and a little square with a plus sign (+) attached to it. (The next figure shows a file in mid-drag.) The plus sign is Windows 95's way of telling you that you're copying the file.

A file in the process of being dragged

When you drag a file, the mouse pointer shows the file name. The little square with the plus sign (+) tells you that you're copying the file.

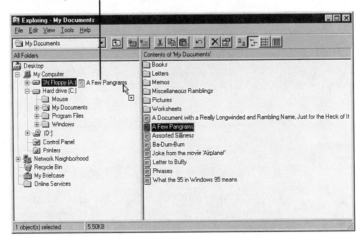

Now move the mouse over the destination folder, release the mouse button (this is the dropping part), and then release **Ctrl**. Windows 95 copies the file to the destination as pretty as you please. (This is about as much fun as files get, so enjoy the moment while it lasts.)

Moving Files from One Location to Another

When you copy a file, the original stays intact, and Windows 95 creates an exact replica in the new location. If you don't want to keep the original, however, you need to pack up the file and *move* it instead of copying it. Fortunately, moving stuff in Windows 95 doesn't require hunting down boxes and tape or hiring big, beefy guys to sweat all over your possessions. This section looks at two simpler methods you can use to move files.

Using the (Yawn) Cut and Paste Commands

As you might expect, moving a file is quite similar to copying one. You highlight the file you want to move and pull down the **Edit** menu, but this time you select the **Cut** command. Again, nothing much happens except that the file's icon becomes a ghostly shadow of its former self. Then head to the disk drive or folder that'll be the file's new home, and select the **Edit** menu's **Paste** command. Windows 95 extracts the file from its original location and adds it to the destination.

Using (Yea!) Drag-and-Drop

Moving a file is easiest when you drag-and-drop it into its new location. You use the same technique that I outlined for copying a file, with one important exception: instead of holding down the Ctrl key when you drag, you hold down the **Shift** key. (When you're dragging, notice that there isn't a little square with the plus sign; this is your clue that you're moving the file instead of copying it.) Once you've dropped the file, you can release the Shift key.

You Need to Shift to Move

If you're used to Windows 3.1, you'll have to get out of the habit of holding down the Alt key when you move a file with drag-and-drop, because Windows 95 has opted to use the Shift key, instead.

A Slight Improvement on the Basic Drag-and-Drop Technique

Drag-and-drop is a handy way to sling files around on your computer. However, I do have one nit-picky complaint: I don't like having to remember to hold down Ctrl or Shift to designate a copy or a move.

To avoid this and keep drag-and-drop as a one-handed, all-mouse affair, Windows 95 also lets you use the *right* mouse button for drag-and-drop. Here's how it works:

1. Point your mouse at the file you want to copy or move, and then hold down the right mouse button.

2. Drag the file and drop it on its destination. When you release the right mouse button, a shortcut menu appears, as shown in the following figure.

When you drag-and-drop a file with the right mouse button, this shortcut menu pops up.

> Move Here
> **Copy Here**
> Create Shortcut(s) Here
>
> Cancel

3. If you're copying the file, click the **Copy Here** command. If you're moving it, click **Move Here**, instead.

Techno Talk

Hopelessly Confusing Drag-and-Drop Drivel

Actually, there are times when you can copy or move files with drag-and-drop and avoid both holding down a key *and* using the right mouse button method. It's all a bit convoluted, but here goes nothing:

➤ If you're dragging a file to a *different* disk drive, Explorer assumes you're copying it. So, if you *are* copying the file, you don't have to hold down Ctrl. (If you're moving the file, though, you need to hold down Shift.)

➤ If you're dragging a file to another folder on the *same* disk drive, Explorer assumes you're moving it. So, if you *are* moving the file, you don't have to hold down Shift. (However, if you're copying the file, you need to hold down Ctrl.)

Confusing? Absolutely.

A File by Any Other Name: Renaming Files

If you don't like the name of one of the files you've created, you can easily rename it to something you can live with. For example, if you have a Christmas present wish list document named "Christmas Goodies 1996" that you want to reuse in 1997, you can rename the file to "Christmas Goodies 1997."

Renaming is easy; you begin by using any of the following techniques:

➤ Highlight the file and select the **File** menu's **Rename** command.

➤ Highlight the file, and then click the file again to edit the name. (Note, however, that you want to avoid double-clicking the file. Click it once to highlight it, wait a couple of beats, and then click it again.)

➤ Highlight the file and press **F2**.

Regardless of which method you choose, Windows 95 creates a text box around the file name, highlights the name, and throws in an insertion point cursor for good measure (see the next figure). Now you're free to edit the name just like you would any text in a text box. (If you need to learn more about how text boxes work, see Chapter 6's "Typing Text in Text Boxes" section.) When you're done, press **Enter** to remove the text box and confirm the new name.

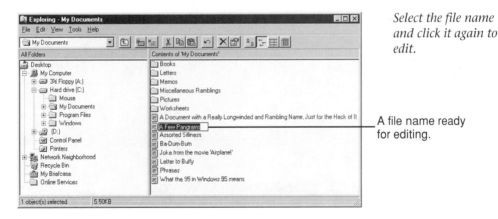

Select the file name and click it again to edit.

A file name ready for editing.

Avoiding Wrong Steps When Renaming

When renaming your files, you need to watch out for a couple of things. First of all, remember that although Windows 95 is happy to accept long file names (up to 255 characters) with spaces in them, it chokes on names that include the following characters: \ | ? : * " < >.

Also, rename only those files that you've created yourself. Any other files on your computer are probably used by your programs, and those programs can be quite picky about what names these files have. If you mess around with the wrong file, your program may refuse to run altogether.

Tossing Files in the Recycle Bin

In real estate, it's taken for granted that property values will always rise because nobody's making any more land. This is true in hard disk real estate, as well. As applications (especially Windows applications) become bigger and bigger, your hard disk becomes more and more cramped (remember how *huge* it seemed when you first got it?). This section shows you how to free up disk space by deleting files you no longer need. And, just in case you delete a vital file by accident, I'll also show you how to use the Recycle Bin to get a file back.

Deleting a File

Okay, it's time to take out the garbage. Here are the steps you follow to delete a file:

1. Highlight the file you want to delete.

2. Pull down the **File** menu and select the **Delete** command. Windows 95 displays the Confirm File Delete dialog box (shown here) to ask if you're sure you want to go through with the deletion.

Windows 95, ever paranoid, asks if you're sure you want to delete the poor file.

Confirm File Delete	✕
Are you sure you want to send 'A Few Pangrams' to the Recycle Bin?	
	Yes No

3. After giving the whole thing a second thought (and maybe even a third, just in case), select **Yes** to delete the file. (Alternatively, you can select **No** if you get cold feet at the last second.)

Retrieving Files from the Recycle Bin

One of the sad realities of computing life is that sometime, somewhere, you'll accidentally delete some crucial file that you'd give your eyeteeth to get back. Well, I'm happy to report that you can keep your teeth where they are because Windows 95's Recycle Bin is only too happy to restore the file for you. (Actually, if the deletion was the last thing you did, you don't have to bother with the Recycle Bin. Just pull down the **Edit** menu and select the **Undo Delete** command.)

The Inner Mysteries of the Recycle Bin

Holy Lazarus! How the heck can the Recycle Bin restore a deleted file?

Good question. You can get part of the answer by looking at the Recycle Bin icon on your Windows 95 desktop. It looks like a garbage can, and that's sort of what the Recycle Bin is. Think about it: if you toss a piece of paper in the garbage, there's nothing to stop you from reaching in and pulling it back out. The Recycle Bin operates the same way: it's really just a special, hidden folder (called Recycled) on your hard disk. When you delete a file, Windows 95 actually moves the file into the Recycled folder. So restoring a file is a simple matter of "reaching into" the folder and "pulling out" the file. The Recycle Bin handles all this for you (and even returns your file *sans* wrinkles and coffee grounds).

However, keep in mind that the Recycle Bin has a finite size (the default is 10 percent of your hard disk; you can adjust this by right-clicking the Recycle Bin icon and selecting Properties). When the Recycle Bin gets full, Windows 95 gets rid of the oldest deleted files in order to make room for new ones.

Your first step to retrieving a deleted file is to open up the Recycle Bin. If you're in Explorer, select **Recycle Bin** in the folder list. Otherwise, double-click the desktop's **Recycle Bin** icon. Then highlight the file you want to undelete, open the **File** menu, and select **Restore**. The Recycle Bin instantly returns the file to its original location, safe and sound. (Insert sigh of relief here.)

Making Life Easier: Selecting Multiple Files

So far, I've only shown you how to work with one file at a time. But if you have, say, a dozen files to copy, even drag-and-drop can get old in a hurry. The solution is to select *all* the files you want to work with and then do the copy (or move, or delete, or whatever).

Selecting Multiple Files, Mouse Style

With your mouse, there are three methods you can use to select multiple files:

➤ If the files you want to work with are all in a row, click the first file, hold down the **Shift** key, and then click the last file.

➤ If the files aren't displayed consecutively, you can select files randomly by holding down the **Ctrl** key and clicking each file.

➤ To select a group of files, "lasso" them with your mouse. Move the mouse pointer beside the first file (make sure it's not over the file's name or icon), and then drag the mouse down and to the right. As you're dragging, Windows 95 displays a dotted box, and every file that falls within that box becomes highlighted (see the following figure). When you have all the files you need, release the mouse button.

You can select a group of files by dragging your mouse over them.

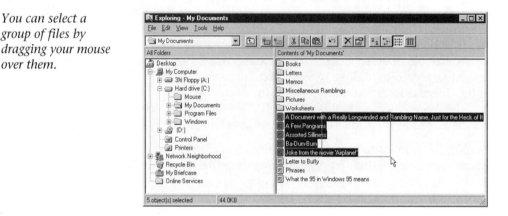

Selecting Multiple Files, Keyboard Style

For dedicated keyboardists, here's how to select multiple files:

➤ To select every file in the current folder, press **Ctrl+A**.

➤ To select nonconsecutive files (files not touching each other), use the arrow keys to highlight the first file, and then press and hold **Ctrl**. For each of the other files you want, use the arrow keys to move to the file and then press the **Spacebar**. When you're done, release **Ctrl**.

➤ To select consecutive files (several files in a row), highlight the first file, press and hold down **Shift**, and use the arrow keys to highlight the other files.

Finding File Needles in Hard Disk Haystacks

Today's behemoth hard disks can easily hold hundreds or even thousands of files. If you use your computer a lot, you know it's no sweat to add to this hard disk overpopulation by creating dozens of your own documents. So it's inevitable that you'll misplace the odd file from time to time. However, instead of wasting time scouring your folders, why not let Windows 95's Find program do the work for you?

Find is available from the Explorer and My Computer windows as well as from the Start menu. Here are the three methods you can use to fire it up:

➤ Pull down Explorer's **Tools** menu, select **Find**, and then select the **Files or Folders** command.

➤ In My Computer, highlight the disk drive in which you want to search, and then select the File menu's Find command.

➤ Select the **Start** button to display the Start menu, open the **Find** folder, and select the **Files or Folders** icon.

In each case, the Find window leaps onto the desktop (see the following figure).

Use the Find program to scour your computer for a particular file.

The first thing you need to do is use the Look in drop-down list to tell Find where you want it to snoop for the files. By default, the Look in box shows either the current Explorer directory (if you started Find from Explorer) or your hard disk (if you started Find from the Start menu). If you'd prefer to begin your search from a different starting point, you have two choices:

➤ If you want to search in a particular disk drive, drop down the **Look in** box and select a drive from the list that appears.

➤ If you want Find to rummage through a particular folder, select the **Browse** button, choose the folder you want from the Browse for Folder dialog box that appears (it works just like Explorer's All Folders list), and then select **OK**.

Once all that's out of the way, you need to use the Named text box to tell Find the name of the file you want to track down. Fortunately, you don't have to type the entire name (a blessing if the file you're looking for has a lengthy moniker). Your best bet is to enter only one word or part of a word from the file name. (The problem with entering multiple words is that Find matches any files that contain one word *or* the other.)

On the other hand, what do you do if you're not sure about the name of the file? For example, suppose you want to hunt for last year's Christmas list, but you haven't the faintest idea what you named it. Well, it's a good bet that the file contains the word "Christmas," so you can tell Find to sniff around for any file that contains *Christmas* somewhere in the text. To do that, click the **Advanced** tab and enter the word in the **Containing text** box.

Techno Talk

Fancier Finds

If you're the adventurous type, you might also want to check out some of Find's other options:

The Date Modified tab: Instead of searching through all the files on your system, you can use the controls in this tab to restrict Find to looking for only those files that were created or modified on a certain date or within a range of dates. For example, to find a file you created yesterday, activate the during the previous option and then make sure 1 appears in the accompanying spinner.

The Advanced tab: Besides the Containing text box mentioned earlier, you can also use the options in this tab to tell Find to look for only certain types of files or files of a certain size.

When that's done, select the **Find Now** button. Find forages through the drive or folder you selected and displays its results in the box at the bottom of the window. From here, you can use the commands on Find's File and Edit menus to do what you will with the file. (If you want Windows 95 to go ahead and open the file's folder, select the **File** menu's **Open Containing Folder** command.) When you're done with Find, you can shut it down by selecting the **File** menu's **Close** command.

Using the Open and Save As Dialog Boxes for More Convenient File Fun

If you're working in an application and need to perform one or two quick file mainte-nance chores (such as renaming or deleting a file), it often feels like overkill to have to crank up My Computer or Explorer, find the folder you want, and then run the necessary commands. Fortunately, Windows 95 gives you a more convenient way to handle these kinds of quickie tasks.

If the application is built specifically for Windows 95 (as are, say, WordPad and Paint) and you have a mouse, you can handle a good chunk of your file labors inside the program's Open and Save As dialog boxes. (We talked about these dialog boxes back in Chapter 7.) All you do is open either dialog box, find the file you want to work with, and then right-click it. As you can see in the next figure, the shortcut menu that appears sports all kinds of file-related commands, including Send To, Cut, Copy, Delete, and Rename.

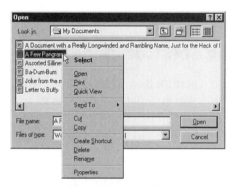

In the Open or Save As dialog boxes, right-click a file to get a handy menu of file maintenance commands.

Using Toolbars and Shortcuts for Faster File Fun

As you've seen, Explorer and My Computer make it easy to play around with the files on your computer. However, there are lots of faster ways to perform most of the techniques you've looked at. This section shows you how to use the toolbar, the right mouse button, and the keyboard to shift your file chores into overdrive.

As I explained back in Chapter 5, the toolbar gives you point-and-click access to a program's commands. You can also take advantage of the toolbar in Explorer and My Computer. The following table presents a summary of the file-related toolbar buttons and the keyboard equivalents you can use in these programs.

Toolbar Buttons and Keyboard Shortcuts for Windows Explorer and My Computer

Click this	Or press this	To do this
✂	Ctrl+X	Cut the highlighted file
📋	Ctrl+C	Copy the highlighted file

continues

Toolbar Buttons and Keyboard Shortcuts for Windows Explorer and My Computer   Continued

Click this	Or press this	To do this
📋	Ctrl+V	Paste the cut or copied file
↩	Ctrl+Z	Undo the most recent action
✕	Delete	Delete the highlighted file

A Quick Click: The Shortcut Menus

You can usually get to a common command faster by right-clicking an object to display the shortcut menu than you can by pulling down menus. Folders and disks also have shortcut menus that contain some common commands. In particular, you can use these menus to access the Find command and the Paste command.

The Least You Need to Know

This chapter took you through several techniques for working with the files on your computer. Now that you have files figured out, it's time to move on to bigger game. In Chapter 12, you'll close out Part 3 by examining lots of useful techniques for monkeying around with folders and disks.

Fiddling with Folders and Floppy Disks

This chapter closes the tour of your computer by showing you how to mess with folders and disks. You'll tackle such crowd-pleasing subjects as creating your own folders, performing routine maintenance on existing folders (moving them, renaming them, deleting them, and so on), formatting floppy disks, and creating a potentially life-saving Windows 95 "startup" disk.

Adding On: Creating Folders

Remember that computer-as-a-filing-cabinet metaphor I threw at you back in Chapter 10? At the time, I mentioned in passing that the purpose of folders—real ones or computer ones—is organization. For a filing cabinet or hard disk to make sense and for you to find things in it quickly, its folders should contain only related items.

The programs installed on your hard disk are probably already set up this way. When you install most programs, they take the liberty of creating a folder for themselves (the polite ones ask you first if it's okay), and then they install most of their files in that folder.

You should follow their lead by creating some folders of your own and organizing your documents in the same way. You can create multiple folders and use each one to store only related documents. For example, you might create a Spreadsheet folder to hold your spreadsheet files, a Memos folder to hold your office notes, a Shocked and Appalled folder to hold your letters to the editor, and so on. And, if several people have access to your computer (such as your spouse and kids), you can set up separate folders for each person.

The best way to do this is to create a new folder called, for example, My Documents (or perhaps Our Documents, depending on who's peering over your shoulder), and then add the other folders as subfolders under My Documents (or whatever). These, of course, are just suggestions. It is, after all, a free country, and you can organize your hard disk any way you darn well please.

The Standard Way to Create a Folder

Okay, enough of the theory. Let's see just how you go about creating a folder. Before you add a folder, you have to decide *where* you want it:

➤ Do you want it to branch off from your hard disk? If so, you need to first open your hard disk window if you're using My Computer, or select the hard disk in Explorer's All Folders list.

➤ Do you want it to be a subfolder of an existing folder? In that case, you need to open the folder's window (if you're using My Computer) or highlight the existing folder in the All Folders list (if you're using Explorer).

Once you select the location, pull down the **File** menu, select **New**, and select **Folder**. Windows 95 adds a new folder and displays a text box in which you can enter a name for the folder (see the following figure). Folder names follow the same rules as file names: 255 characters max, and spaces are okay but the characters \ | ? : * " < > aren't. When you're done, press **Enter**, and your new folder is official.

```
Exploring - My Documents                                    _ □ ×
File  Edit  View  Tools  Help
My Documents          ▼              X             
All Folders                   Contents of 'My Documents'
 Desktop                       Books
 └ My Computer                 Letters
    ├ 3½ Floppy (A:)           Memos
    └ Hard drive (C:)          Miscellaneous Ramblings
       ├ Mouse                 Pictures
       ├ My Documents          Worksheets
       ├ Program Files         A Document with a Really Longwinded and Rambling Name, Just for the Heck of It
       └ Windows               A Few Pangrams
    ├ (D:)                     Assorted Silliness
    ├ F on 'Apollo' (E:)       Ba-Dum-Bum
    ├ Control Panel            Joke from the movie 'Airplane!'
    └ Printers                 Letter to Buffy
 ├ Network Neighborhood        Phrases
 ├ Recycle Bin                 What the 95 in Windows 95 means
 ├ My Briefcase                Tirades, Harangues, Rodomontades, and Other Tub-Thumpings
 └ Online Services
 1 object(s) selected
```

Windows 95 displays a text box for entering the name of your new folder.

Enter a name for the new folder in the text box that appears.

A Nonstandard Way to Create a Folder

Here's a scenario you'll probably stumble over umpteen times in your computing career: you create a new document in a Windows program and select the Save command to preserve your work. When you get to the Save As dialog box, though, you realize that you need to store this particular document in a new folder.

However, if you're using a program designed for Windows 95, you don't have to trudge over to My Computer or Explorer because you can create the folder right from the Save As dialog box! I showed you how to do this back in Chapter 7 (see the section named "Picking Out a Storage Location for the Document").

Copying and Moving Folders

The techniques for copying and moving folders are, mercifully, almost exactly the same as those for copying and moving files. And, as with files, you also have the choice of using the Edit menu commands or the drag-and-drop method.

Copying and Moving with the Edit Menu Commands

To copy a folder, select it, pull down the **Edit** menu, and select the **Copy** command. Then select the folder where you want the copy to appear, pull down the **Edit** menu again, and select the **Paste** command.

Moving a folder is similar. Begin by selecting it, pulling down the **Edit** menu, and selecting the **Cut** command. Then select the folder to which you want to move the original folder, pull down the **Edit** menu, and select the **Paste** command.

141

Shortcut Methods for Folders

Most of the shortcut methods for working with files that I showed you at the end of Chapter 11 work equally well when you deal with folders.

Copying and Moving Folders Using Drag-and-Drop

Copying and moving folders is much more fun using the drag-and-drop method. As with files, you first need to make sure you can see both the original folder (the one you're copying or moving) and the destination folder.

To copy a folder, hold down the **Ctrl** key, drag the folder, and drop it on the destination folder. To move a folder, hold down the **Shift** key, drag the folder, and drop it on the destination folder.

If you don't want to bother with the Ctrl and Shift keys, use the right mouse button to drag the folder. When you drop it, a shortcut menu appears from which you can select either **Copy Here** or **Move Here**.

Renaming Folders

If you don't like the name of one of your folders, go ahead and rename it. To start, all you have to do is highlight the folder and use any of the following techniques:

Moving and Renaming Warning Avoid moving or re-naming folders created by your applications. Most programs are finicky: they expect to find their files in specific folders. Changing even a single letter of one of these folders can put an application in a huff and make it refuse to run. As with files, move or rename only folders you created.

➤ Select the **File** menu's **Rename** command.

➤ Click the folder again to edit the name. (As with files, remember that you want to avoid double-clicking. Click the folder once to highlight it, wait a couple of seconds, and then click it again.)

➤ Press **F2**.

Windows 95 displays a text box so you can edit the folder name. Type the new name and press **Enter**.

More Recycle Bin Fun: Deleting Folders

If you no longer need one of the folders you created, there's no sense letting it clutter up the Explorer or My Computer window. You may as well delete the thing and get it out of your life.

To delete a folder, highlight it and select the **File** menu's **Delete** command. Because deleting a folder is a fairly big deal, Windows 95 displays the dialog box shown in the following figure to ask if you're sure you want to go through with the deletion. If all looks well, click the **Yes** button to get rid of the folder. (You may see other dialog boxes appear asking you to confirm the deletions of program files and other "important" files inside the folder.) Otherwise, you can click **No** to bail out of the deletion. Whew—just in the nick of time!

Windows 95 displays this dialog box to ask if you're sure you want to delete the folder.

Just in case you're wondering: yes, you *can* bring back a folder from the dead. If the folder contained files, Windows 95 tossed them into the Recycle Bin. So all you have to do is head for the Recycle Bin, select the files that were in the folder, and run the **File** menu's **Restore** command. Windows 95 re-creates the appropriate folder and returns the files to their rightful (that is, original) place.

Working with Multiple Folders

If you want to copy, move, or delete two or more folders, working with them all at once is no problem. To select multiple folders, use the same techniques that I outlined for selecting multiple files back in Chapter 11. Keep in mind, however, that you have to select your folders in Explorer's Contents list; you can't select multiple folders in the All Folders list.

Types of Floppy Disks

I'm now going to spend a little time talking about floppy disks—those fun little plastic platters your kids have been using for frisbees. For starters, this section tells you about the different species of floppy disk that exist. (This is the kind of information you can use to impress your friends at parties.)

Floppy Disk Sizes

Although the technowizards in the labs have been showing off a few weird-sized disks recently, your basic floppy disks come in the two sizes you see on the next page: 5$^1/_4$-inch and 3$^1/_2$-inch.

The 5$^1/_4$-inch disks are usually black, and they come safely ensconced in a flexible plastic case. (The flexibility of the 5$^1/_4$-inch disks is where the "floppy" in "floppy disk" comes from.) The 3$^1/_2$-inch disks come in all kinds of designer colors. Their cases are quite sturdy, and they even have moving parts! They also fit nicely into a shirt pocket (if this doesn't feel like too nerdy a thing to do).

5$^1/_4$-inch and 3$^1/_2$-inch disks.

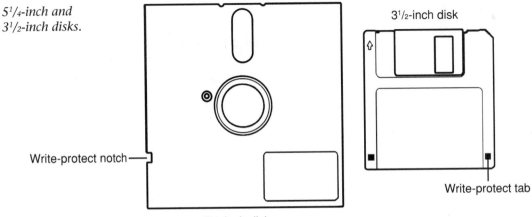

3$^1/_2$-inch disk

Write-protect notch

Write-protect tab

5$^1/_4$-inch disk

Which type of disk you use depends on the type of floppy disk drive (or drives) you have installed in your computer. If you're not sure, you can tell easily enough just by looking at the drive. If the opening is a little more than 5$^1/_4$-inches wide, it's a 5$^1/_4$-inch floppy drive. If it's about 3$^1/_2$-inches wide, it's a 3$^1/_2$-inch floppy drive. As you can see, this is not rocket science.

The Capacity of a Floppy Disk

A slightly more subtle issue is the *capacity* of a floppy disk. A disk's capacity is simply the number of bytes of information the disk is designed to hold.

What's a Byte?

A *byte* is a single character of information. So, for example, the phrase *This phrase is 28 bytes long* is, yes, 28 bytes long (you count the spaces, too). To make things really confusing, a *kilobyte* is equal to 1,024 bytes, and a *megabyte* is equal to 1,024 kilobytes. If you want to be hip, always say "K" instead of "kilobyte" and "meg" instead of "megabyte."

What's with this fetish for the number 1,024? You may be sorry you asked. You see, "kilo," as you may know, means "thousand," and it turns out that 2 to the power of 10 (2×2×2×2×2×2×2×2×2×2) is 1,024, which is close enough. Why *2* to the power of 10? Well, internally, computers can deal with only two states: on or off. A circuit has either a high current (it's on) or a low current (it's off). Amazingly, the world's computer geniuses have created everything from Pac Man to Windows 95 out of these two simple states.

Don't be fooled by their physical sizes. You may think that since the 5^1/$_4$-inch disk is bigger, that it holds more data. Actually the 3^1/$_2$-inch disk has a higher storage capacity. Both 5^1/$_4$- and 3^1/$_2$-inch disks are available in two capacities: *double-density* and *high-density*. (Actually, the term "double-density" is relatively meaningless nowadays. It comes from the old days of computers—way back in the '80s!—when there were such things as "single-density" disks. Many people now refer to double-density disks simply as "low-density.") The following table summarizes the four most common floppy disk types.

The Most Common Floppy Disk Types

Disk Type	Storage Capacity
5^1/$_4$-inch double-density	360 kilobytes (KB)
5^1/$_4$-inch high-density	1.2 megabytes (MB)
3^1/$_2$-inch double-density	720 kilobytes (KB)
3^1/$_2$-inch high-density	1.44 megabytes (MB)

Normally, the only way to tell whether a disk is high-density or double-density is to look at the disk's markings. For a high-density disk, look for the words "High-Density" (of course) or the letters "HD." For a double-density disk, look for "Double-Density" or "DD." If the disk has no markings at all, assume it's a double-density disk.

Which type should you use? Well, high-density disks are better because they can hold more info, but you should use them only if you have a high-density disk drive. The vast majority of computers shipped in the past two or three years are equipped with at least one high-density drive; so if your computer is fairly new, that's probably what you have. If you're not sure, your computer's manual ought to tell you. (You can also check out the machine's packing slip or receipt, if you still have either one.)

Disk Dos and Don'ts

Here are a few things to bear in mind when working with floppy disks.

Do:

➤ Place your 5¹/₄-inch disks inside their protective covers when not in use.

➤ Label your disks so that, six months from now, you can figure out what they contain.

➤ Buy cheaper, no-name disks for everyday use.

➤ Buy top-quality disks for important needs, such as backing up your hard disk.

➤ Try to get out more.

Don't:

➤ Touch the magnetic surface of a disk.

➤ Expose a disk to direct sunlight or excessive temperatures.

➤ Place a disk near a strong magnetic or electronic source.

➤ Fold, spindle, or mutilate a disk.

➤ Use a pen or pencil to write on a label attached to a 5¹/₄-inch disk (felt tip pens are okay).

➤ Try to remove a disk from a disk drive if the drive's light is still on.

➤ Take any wooden nickels.

Formatting a Disk

As you can imagine, you can't just stick any old piece of plastic in a disk drive and expect it to read and write information. Even official I-bought-it-at-the-local-computer-store floppy disks often need to be *initialized* first so that you can store information properly on the disk.

It's like the difference between a peg board and an ordinary piece of wood. Buying new disks (unless the box says they're *preformatted*) is like buying a bunch of flat, featureless pieces of wood. You can try all day to stick pegs in 'em, but they'll just fall off. What you need to do is *format* the wood with holes so you end up with peg board. *Then* you're in business. Floppy disks are the same way. Brand new disks are a bunch of flat, featureless pieces of plastic. You need to *format* each disk so it's capable of storing your files and documents.

Why aren't all disks preformatted? Well, you can use most disks with both Windows and non-Windows computers (such as Macintoshes), but different machines require different formats (think of peg boards with differently sized holes). So disk manufacturers simplify their lives by shipping their disks unformatted.

Fortunately, though, Windows 95 makes disk formatting a relatively painless affair. The following steps show you how to format a new disk or a used one:

1. Insert the disk you want to format in the appropriate drive.

2. Using Explorer or My Computer, select the drive. (If you're using Explorer, you need to select **My Computer** in the All Folders list and then highlight the drive in the Contents list. Strangely enough, Explorer won't let you format a floppy disk if you highlight it using the All Folders list.)

3. If the disk has never been formatted, Windows 95 displays a dialog box that lets you know and asks if you want to format it. In this case, click **Yes**.

   Otherwise, pull down the **File** menu and select the **Format** command. (You can also right-click the drive and select **Format** from the shortcut menu.) Windows 95 displays the Format dialog box, as shown here.

Use the Format dialog box to set some formatting options.

4. Fill out the following options in this dialog box:

Capacity Use this drop-down list box to select the proper capacity of the disk.

Format type For a new disk, select the **Full** option button. For a used disk, select the **Quick (erase)** option. (You can safely ignore the **Copy system files only** option.)

Label Fill in this text box (11 characters maximum) if you want to give the disk a name. This option is, well, optional.

5. When you've set up your options, click **Start** to get the formatting show on the road. When Windows 95 is done, it displays a dialog box full of incomprehensible data about the disk.

6. Click **Close** to return to the Format dialog box.

7. Click **Close** to return to Explorer or My Computer.

The Quick (Erase) Option

When you format a used disk, selecting this option is a real time-saver because it cuts the format time from a minute or so to a few seconds. Why would you want to format a used disk? Well, for one thing, it's a quick way to erase all the files and folders on a disk. For another, formatting can help protect you against computer *viruses*, those nasty programs that like to terrorize innocent machines. Most viruses transmit from computer to computer via floppy disks, so if you inherit some old disks, the best thing to do is format each one to eradicate everything on the disk, including any viruses lurking in the weeds. The only problem with the Quick (erase) option is that it doesn't check the disk for damage. If you're dealing with a really old disk or if you've had problems with the disk, use the Full option instead.

Creating a Startup Disk

The next time you start your computer, keep your eye on disk drive A. A few seconds after you throw the switch, the drive light should come on briefly. This means the drive is being set up for use, and once that's done, the light goes out again. A few seconds later, though, the light reappears. When the light comes back on, your system is looking to see if there's a floppy disk in the drive. If there is, the computer attempts to load Windows 95 from the floppy disk. If the disk contains the proper files—specifically, the Windows 95 *system files*—Windows 95 loads, but you'll see an A:\> prompt instead of the usual

Windows 95 screen. This process is called *booting from a floppy*, and a disk with the Windows 95 system files is called a *startup disk.*

What good is such a disk? Well, it's possible that, thanks to a virus or a system crash, you can lose access to your hard drive. This would be bad news because Windows 95 normally uses your hard drive to start itself up when you turn on your computer. Therefore, no hard drive means no Windows 95, which means no work (or play, for that matter). If you have a startup disk, however, you just insert it in drive A and reboot your computer. Since the startup disk tells Windows 95 to boot from the floppy disk instead of the hard disk, you regain at least some control over your machine. You (or some nearby computer wiz) can then proceed to investigate the problem. Not only that, but the start-up disk also contains some programs that you (or your troubleshooting guru) can use to diagnose the problem. For example, the startup disk includes the ScanDisk program (which I'll talk about in Chapter 16, in the section "Avoiding Hard Disk Hard Times: ScanDisk").

Is it hard to create a startup disk? Not at all. All you have to do is shuffle a couple of disks in and out of your computer, and Windows 95 takes care of all the dirty work. Here are the steps to follow:

1. Select the **Start** button, open the **Settings** folder, and select **Control Panel**. The Control Panel window appears.

2. Double-click the **Add/Remove Programs** icon (or highlight it with the arrow keys and press **Enter**). This displays the Add/Remove Programs Properties dialog box.

3. Select the **Startup Disk** tab.

4. Click the **Create Disk** button. Windows 95 displays a dialog box asking you to insert one of your Windows installation disks. (If you have the Windows 95 CD-ROM and it's still in the CD-ROM drive, you won't see this dialog box. Instead, Windows 95 eventually asks you to insert a disk in drive A. Skip to step 6.)

5. Insert the disk (or the Windows CD-ROM, if that's what you have) and select **OK**. After a few seconds, you're prompted to insert a disk in drive A, as shown in the next figure.

6. Pick out a disk that doesn't have any files on it that you need (Windows 95 will obliterate all the current info on the disk), insert it, and select **OK**. Windows 95 chugs away for a minute or two while it creates the startup disk. When it's done, it returns you to the Add/Remove Programs Properties dialog box.

7. Click **Cancel** to return to the Control Panel, and then select the **File** menu's **Close** command.

8. Remove the disk, attach some kind of label to it so you know what it is, store it in a safe place, and keep your fingers crossed that you never have to use it!

When you see the Insert Disk dialog box, insert a disk in drive A.

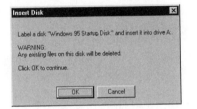

The Least You Need to Know

This chapter told you everything you need to know about dealing with folders and floppy disks in Windows 95. It's all very practical information that's sure to come in handy as you work with Windows and Windows applications.

That ends Part 3 and your tour around your system with Explorer and My Computer. In Part 4, "Okay, Enough Gawking. It's Time to Get Some Work Done!," you'll turn your attention to the accessories that come as part of the Windows 95 package. First up: the WordPad word processor.

Part 4

Okay, Enough Gawking. It's Time to Get Some Work Done!

Windows 95 is supposed to be "intuitive" and (ugh) "user-friendly," but it has taken you a full 12 chapters to figure out how to use it! Now, however, your investment starts paying off as you delve into the Windows 95 programs that you can use to, at last, get some work done.

Don't worry though: work won't be your only focus in these chapters (you know what they say about all work and no play). You'll find info on games, multimedia, drawing and painting, and other Windows 95 leisure-time activities.

Chapter 13

Word Processing with WordPad

In This Chapter

➤ Getting around in WordPad

➤ Editing text

➤ Formatting text and paragraphs

➤ Previewing documents before printing them

➤ A vast number of tips and tricks for getting the most out of WordPad

Almost everyone who uses a computer uses it to write something from time to time. It could be a letter to Mom, a memo to the honchos at HQ, or yet another attempt at the Great (insert nationality here) Novel. Most computer-based writing is handled by a *word processor*, which is a geekoid term for a program that lets you not only type in text, but also edit it and format it so it looks all nice and pretty.

WordPad is the word processor that comes free with Windows 95. Granted, WordPad may not have all the fancy-schmancy features you get in the more glamorous word processors (such as Word for Windows or WordPerfect for Windows), but it can handle simple day-to-day chores such as memos, letters, résumés, or ransom notes, without a complaint. So unless you're a professional word jockey, WordPad can do the job. This chapter gets you up to speed with this useful little writing tool.

Taking a Look Around the WordPad Window

To start WordPad, select the **Start** button, open the Start menu's **Programs** folder, open the **Accessories** folder, and select **WordPad**. (What's that? You can't find hide nor hair of WordPad in your Accessories folder? Ah, then you need to install it on your computer. To find out how, travel ahead to Chapter 23 and read the "Adding Windows 95 Components" section.) The following figure shows the WordPad window and points out a few landmarks.

The WordPad window.

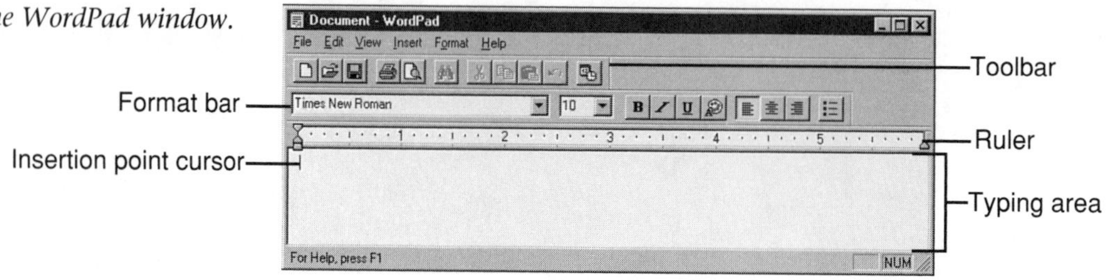

Here's a summary of the important features of the WordPad window:

Toolbar   As described back in Chapter 5, you use a toolbar for one-click access to important everyday commands such as Open, Save, Cut, Copy, and Paste.

Format bar   This is a variation on the toolbar theme. These buttons give you point-and-click service for many of WordPad's formatting commands. I'll talk about formatting later in this chapter in the "Sprucing Up Your Text" and "Getting Your Paragraphs Just So" sections.

Ruler   You use the ruler for setting tabs, indenting paragraphs, and changing margins. The left edge of the ruler (at 0 inches) represents the left margin, and the right edge (at 6 inches) represents the right margin.

Typing area   This is the vast white expanse that takes up the bulk of the WordPad window, and it's where your document text appears.

Insertion point cursor   The text you type always appears to the right of this blinking vertical line.

3.1 WordPad Can Out-Write Write Any Day!

If you've been using Write, the word processor that came with Windows 3.1, you'll *love* WordPad. Why? Well, let's just say that if WordPad and Write had an arm wrestling match, WordPad would win hands-down (no pun intended) every time. I mean, right off the bat you can look at the handy toolbar and format bar, and you just *know* WordPad is easier to use. It also includes some nice features (such as the capability to preview your documents before printing them) that Write could only dream about.

The Ol' Hunt and Peck: Entering Text in WordPad

Unlike with some of today's big-bucks word processors, you don't need a degree in rocket science to get up and running with WordPad. Once you load the program (and, if necessary, open a file you saved before), you can simply go ahead and start pounding out your deathless prose. Each character you type appears beside the insertion point cursor, and the cursor then leaps ahead to show you where your next character will appear.

If you're used to typing with a typewriter, you may be tempted to press the Enter key when you approach the end of a line. No way, José! You don't have to bother, because WordPad handles that chore for you. No guff. You see, when you hit the end of a line, WordPad automatically dispatches the cursor to the beginning of the *next* line. Even if you're smack in the middle of a word, WordPad automatically trucks the entire word to the start of the next line. (This handy feature is called *word wrap*, in nerdspeak.) The only time you need to press Enter is when you want to start a new paragraph. Hey, this ain't no Selectric!

Can I Get There from Here? Navigating a Document

For the terminally verbose, WordPad can handle tome-like documents as large as your computer's memory allows. When your writings become several pages or more in length, however, you need some way to navigate them quickly. If you use a mouse, you can move the cursor by clicking the appropriate text inside the window. To move to other parts of the document, use the scroll bars to leap giddily from page to page. (Need a scroll bar refresher course? Head back to Chapter 7 and re-read the section "Using Scroll Bars to Navigate a Document.")

From the keyboard, you can use the techniques outlined in the following table to navigate a document.

Handy WordPad Navigation Keys

Press	To Move
Left arrow or right arrow	Left or right one character
Ctrl+left arrow or Ctrl+right arrow	Left or right one word
Home or End	To the beginning or end of a line
Up arrow or down arrow	Up or down one line
Ctrl+Page Up or Ctrl+Page Down	To the top or bottom of the window
Page Up or Page Down	Up or down one screen
Ctrl+Home or Ctrl+End	To the beginning or end of the document

Some Text-Selection Tricks

When editing and formatting a WordPad document, you often need to select a group of characters or lines to work with. Because selected text appears as white letters on a dark background, this is also called *highlighting* text.

I showed you some basic methods for highlighting text back in Chapter 7 (in the "Highlighting Text" section), and these techniques will stand you in good stead for most text-selection chores. But WordPad also has a few other tricks you can stuff up your word processing sleeve:

To select a word, double-click it.

To select a line, click inside the narrow strip of white space to the left of the line (that is, between the line and the WordPad window's left border). This area is known in the word pro trade as the *selection area*.

To select a paragraph, double-click to the left of the paragraph. If you're feeling athletic, you can also select a paragraph by *triple*-clicking anywhere inside the paragraph. (I'd suggest a good half-hour finger warm up before attempting this maneuver.)

To select the entire document, hold down **Ctrl** and click anywhere inside the selection area.

Check This Out...

Formatting?
Formatting a WordPad document involves altering the look of your text to make the document more effective or more presentable. For example, you can make a word **bold** so it stands out from the crowd, *or you can change a phrase to italics to add emphasis.* Formatting your documents gives them a real professional look.

Now that you know how to select text, you're ready to add formatting. The next few sections show you how to use formatting to dress up your WordPad prose so it looks respectable.

Sprucing Up Your Text

When you get to Chapter 20, you'll find out all about *fonts*. Font is a catchall term that refers to the formatting of your document text. I'll save the details for Chapter 20, but the following figure shows a WordPad document with a few font examples.

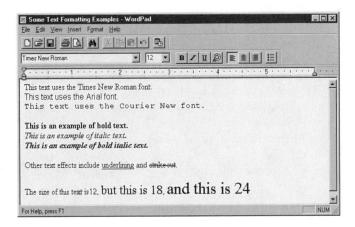

Some of the ways you can format your WordPad text.

Here are the WordPad steps you plow through to format text with a particular font:

1. Select the text you want to format using the techniques described earlier.

2. Pull down the **Format** menu and select the **Font** command (or right-click the selection and then choose **Font** from the shortcut menu). WordPad displays the Font dialog box, as shown in the following figure.

3. Use the controls in the Font dialog box to pick out the various font options you need. As you make your selections, watch the Sample box to see what havoc you'll wreak on your text.

4. When you finish playing, select **OK**. WordPad returns you to the document and reformats the selected text.

Use WordPad's Font dialog box to add all kinds of fancy formatting to your text.

Formatting New Text

Instead of typing some text and then going back to format it, you can apply some formatting options to new text. First, position the insertion point where the new text will appear. Now launch the Font dialog box, make your formatting selections, and then return to the document and start typing. WordPad displays the new text using the formatting you selected. To return to your normal text formatting, display the Font dialog box again and reset the options you adjusted earlier.

If you just want to throw a little bold or italic at a word or two, it's a bit of a hassle to fire up the Font dialog box every time. (Lazy? Moi? Nah. Merely efficient!) To make your text formatting tasks go faster, WordPad offers all kinds of shortcut methods. The following tables list the format bar buttons and shortcut key combinations you can use to fancy up some text quickly.

Format Bar Buttons for Formatting Text

Click	To Get
Times New Roman ▼	A list of fonts
10 ▼	A list of font sizes
B	**Bold**
I	*Italics*

Click	To Get
 **U**	Underline
 🎨	A list of colors to apply to your text

Shortcut Key Combos for Formatting Text

Press	To Get
Ctrl+B	**Bold**
Ctrl+I	*Italics*
Ctrl+U	Underline

Getting Your Paragraphs Just So

Although the content of your documents is important, how the documents look on the page is equally (if not more) important. Why? Because in these busy times, people will simply ignore (or trash) a document if it looks cramped and uninviting.

To avoid this fate, use WordPad's paragraph formatting options to make yourself look good on paper. To try them out, first place the cursor in the paragraph you want to format. (If you want to format multiple paragraphs, select the text for each paragraph.) Then select the **Format** menu's **Paragraph** command to display the Paragraph dialog box, as shown in the following figure. (You can also coax this dialog box onto the desktop by right-clicking the paragraph and selecting **Paragraph** from the shortcut menu.)

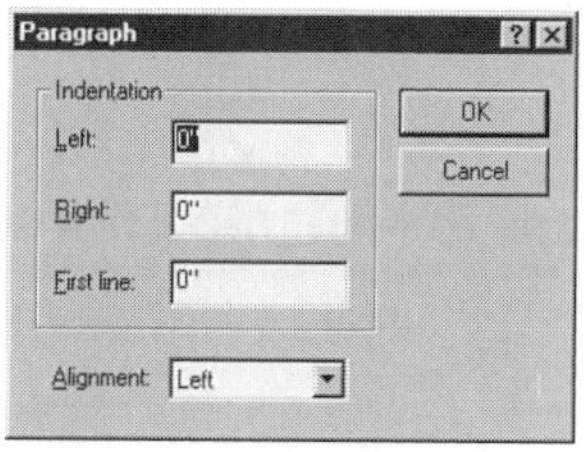

Use the Paragraph dialog box to format your paragraphs.

The Paragraph dialog box contains the following controls:

Left   Use this text box to control how far (in inches) the paragraph is indented from the left margin. For example, if you enter 1, the paragraph is indented one inch from the left margin; entering .5 indents the paragraph one-half inch.

Right   Use this text box to control how far the paragraph is indented from the right margin.

First line   Use this text box to control how far the first line (and only the first line) of the paragraph is indented from the left margin.

Alignment   Use this drop-down list to adjust the alignment of the paragraph's lines. If you select **Left**, all lines in the paragraph are aligned with the left margin; if you select **Right**, all lines in the paragraph are aligned with the right margin; if you select **Center**, all lines in the paragraph are centered between the margins. Just so you have some idea of what the heck I'm talking about, the following figure shows examples of the paragraph formatting options.

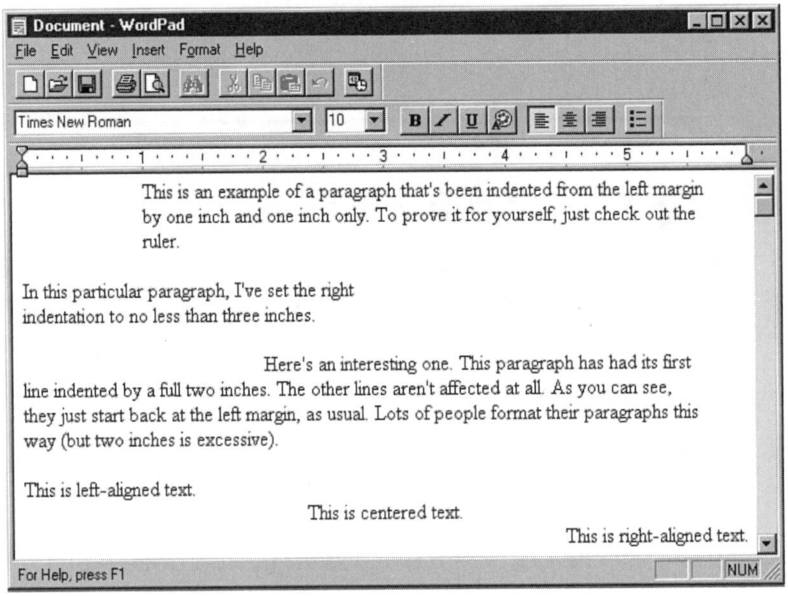

WordPad's paragraph formatting options.

As the following table shows, you can also pick out an alignment using the format bar.

Format Bar Buttons for Aligning Paragraphs

Click	To Get this alignment
	Left
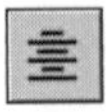	Center
	Right

Setting Tab Stops

Documents look much better if they're properly indented and if their parts line up like soldiers on parade. One easy way to do this is to use *tabs* instead of spaces whenever you need to create some room in a line. Why? Well, a single space can take up a different amount of room depending on the font, the type size, and so on. So your document can end up looking pretty ragged if you try to use spaces to indent your text. Tabs, on the other hand, are meticulously precise. When you press the Tab key, the insertion point moves ahead to the next tab stop, no more, no less. (If you don't have any tab stops set, pressing Tab moves the insertion point ahead exactly half an inch.)

However, if you don't like the tab stops currently set in WordPad, don't just boycott tabs altogether; change 'em! After all, you're the one who's running the show around here. You'll need to make your way through the following steps to set your own Tab stops.

1. Place the insertion point inside the paragraph you want to format. If you want to set the same tab stop for multiple paragraphs, select them all. (Keep in mind, too, that if you set some tab stops for the current paragraph, each new paragraph you create below it will also use the same tab stops.)

2. Pull down the **Format** menu and select the **Tabs** command. The Tabs dialog box appears, as shown in the following figure.

Enter the new tab position here.

Tabs you've already set appear here.

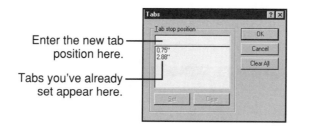

Use the Tabs dialog box to set up one or more tabs for the current line.

3. In the Tab stop position text box, enter a location for the tab stop. For example, if you want the tab stop to be one inch from the left margin, enter **1**.

4. Click the **Set** button, and WordPad adds the tab to the list.

5. If you're feeling gung-ho, repeat steps 3 and 4 to enter any other tabs you want to set.

6. When you've had just about enough, select **OK**. WordPad adds the tab stops to the document and displays them in the ruler.

Faster Tab Stops

Instead of entering tab stop positions blindly in the Tabs dialog box, WordPad gives you a way to set your tabs visually. As usual, place the cursor in the paragraph you want to work with; then move your mouse into the ruler, point at the position where you want your tab stop, and click. A tab stop appears instantly. If the tab isn't quite in the right spot, just drag it to the left or right with your mouse. To get rid of a tab, drag it off the ruler.

Finding Lost Text in Humongous Files

Finding a particular word or phrase is usually no problem in small WordPad files. But, as your competence with WordPad grows, so will your documents. When you start dealing with 10- and 20-page extravaganzas, you'll find yourself singing "Where, oh, where has my little text gone? Where, oh, where can it be?"

To help out (and to prevent your family or coworkers from thinking you've gone completely off the deep end), WordPad has a Find feature that does the searching for you. To try it out, pull down the **Edit** menu and select the **Find** command (or press **Ctrl+F**). The Find dialog box appears, as shown in the following figure.

 You can also fire up the Find command by clicking on this button in the WordPad toolbar.

Use the Find dialog box to search for a word or phrase in your document.

Find	? X
Find what:	Find Next
☐ Match whole word only	Cancel
☐ Match case	

— Type what you want to look for here.

In the Find What text box, enter the word or phrase you want to locate. You can also refine your searches by using the two check boxes provided:

Match whole word only   WordPad normally tries to find partial matches for your search text. For example, if you enter waldo, WordPad finds *Waldorf*, *Gottwaldov* (a city in the Czech Republic), and, of course, *Waldo*. If *Waldo* is all you want, activate the **Match whole word only** check box, and WordPad ignores partial matches.

Match case   Activate this check box to make WordPad's searches *case-sensitive*. For example, if you enter **Curt** as your search text and you activate this check box, WordPad ignores the word *curt* and finds only the name *Curt*.

Continuing the Search

Once you're back in the document, you may realize you have to locate another occurrence of the search text. Instead of going through the hassle of the Find dialog box, you can continue the search by selecting the **Edit** menu's **Find Next** command (or you can simply press **F3**). WordPad remembers the last word(s) you were searching for.

When you're ready to go, click the **Find Next** button. If WordPad finds the text, it highlights it in the document's typing area. If that's not the occurrence of the text you're looking for, keep clicking **Find Next** until you locate it. When you do, click the **Cancel** button to return to the document. If WordPad can't locate a match, a dialog box appears to tell you it has finished searching the document.

Finding and Replacing Text

A slightly different kettle of fish involves finding text and *replacing* it with something else. For example, you might want to change each occurrence of *Ave.* to *Avenue* or some occurrences of *affect* to *effect* (yeah, I have a hard time remembering which is which, too).

To do this, pull down the **Edit** menu and select the **Replace** command (or press **Ctrl+H**). The Replace dialog box that appears is almost identical to the Find dialog box you saw earlier. As before, enter the text you want to locate in the **Find what** text box. In the **Replace with** text box, enter the replacement text. You now have two ways to proceed:

➤ If you know you want to replace every occurrence of the search text with the replacement text, click the **Replace All** button. WordPad trudges through the entire document, finding and replacing as it goes. When it's done, it displays a dialog box to let you know. Select **OK** to return to the Replace dialog box, and then select **Close** to return to the document. (You'll need to exercise a bit of caution before using the Replace All feature willy-nilly. For example, suppose your search text is *ave* and your replacement text is *avenue*. Since *ave* may also match *avenge* or *average*, Replace All changes these words into the nonsensical *avenuenge*, and *avenuerage*.)

➤ If you want to replace only *certain* occurrences of the search text, click the **Find Next** button. Whenever WordPad finds an occurrence you want to replace, click the **Replace** button.

Some Notes About a Few Basic WordPad Chores

Back in Chapter 7, I took you through a few routine tasks that are more or less the same in most Windows applications. Thankfully, most of the techniques you learned in that chapter are also readily applicable to WordPad. However, WordPad does have a few minor quirks you should know about:

➤ To make our lives more complicated, every word processor has its own format for the documents it creates. The format WordPad uses is the same as that used by Microsoft's high-end word processor, Word for Windows 6.0. So when you run the Open command, WordPad's Open dialog box shows only those documents that conform to the Word for Windows 6.0 format. If you want to open a different type of document (such as a straight text file), you need to use the Open dialog box's Files of type drop-down box, which lists various other document types.

➤ If you select the File menu's New command, WordPad displays the New dialog box. Here, WordPad wants to know what kind of document you want to create: Word 6 (the normal WordPad type, and the type you'll use most often), Rich Text (a special text file that lets you add formatting), or Text Only (a pure text file that can't contain any formatting).

➤ WordPad has a Print Preview feature that can save you lots of time (and paper). What Print Preview does is give you a bird's-eye view of your document so you can see if your formatting looks the way you want it to. To give it a go, pull down the **File** menu and select the **Print Preview** command.

Clicking this toolbar button also displays the Print Preview window.

➤ The WordPad window can display only one document at a time. If you need to copy or move a chunk of text between two WordPad documents, just start up a second copy of WordPad and open the other document in it. Then cut or copy the text from the original WordPad window, switch to the second window, and paste it. See Chapter 9 for instructions on switching between open applications.

The Least You Need to Know

This chapter gave you a basic introduction to WordPad, Windows 95's not-overly-powerful-but-hey-whaddya-want-for-nothing word processor. We covered all the must-know word pro tasks, including entering text, navigating a document, formatting text and paragraphs, setting tab stops, and finding and replacing text. So go out and land that fat publishing contract and spend your lavish advance on something completely self-indulgent, because that successful writing career is now surely just around the corner.

Chapter 14

The Art of Windows 95: The Paint Program

In This Chapter

➤ Navigating the Paint window

➤ Drawing lines, boxes, circles, and other funky shapes

➤ Drawing freehand lines

➤ Editing your drawings

➤ More ways of reliving your youth than you can shake a stick at

If you enjoyed finger painting when you were a kid, you'll get a kick out of Paint, Windows 95's drawing program. Oh sure, you can use it for practical stuff like logos, charts, and whatnot, but to my mind, Paint's real reason for being is sheer fun. Think about it: all you do is select a "tool" to work with and then just wiggle your mouse around the screen. Magically, you get all kinds of cool shapes and patterns. Throw in a few colors and a dash of imagination (or just plain silliness), and you have a recipe for hours of entertainment (and—bonus!—your fingers stay nice and clean).

Powering Up Paint

When the creative urge hits, you can start Paint by selecting the **Start** button, opening the Start menu's **Programs** folder, opening **Accessories**, and then selecting **Paint**. (If

Paint is nowhere to be found in your Accessories folder, you need to install it on your system. The "Adding Windows 95 Components" section in Chapter 23 gives you the goods on installing Windows 95 accessories.) Eventually, the Paint window shown in the following figure appears.

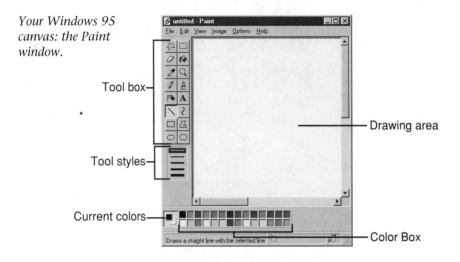

Your Windows 95 canvas: the Paint window.

Tool box

Tool styles

Current colors

Drawing area

Color Box

Paint: A New and Ever-So-Slightly Improved Paintbrush

If you're a fan of Windows 3.1's Paintbrush accessory, you'll be happy to know that Paint carries on the tradition. In fact, the two programs are almost identical, although Paint does bring a few improvements to the easel. For example, some of the tools have a few more options to try out, and the Zoom command is a bit more flexible. The one thing that Paint lacks is probably the one thing nobody will miss: keyboard support.

A Look Around the Paint Studio

As you can see, the Paint window is chock-full of artistic goodies. Let's take a close look at the various toys you can play with:

Tool Box   This section contains the various tools you use to create or edit your drawings. You get a Pencil, a Brush, an Airbrush, an Eraser, and all kinds of utensils for drawing lines and shapes. I'll show you how to wield each tool as you work (or should I say *play*) in this chapter. Don't even think about memorizing which Tool Box tool is which. If you draw a blank (sorry about that), just point your mouse at the Tool Box button in question. In a second or two a small banner appears to tell you the name of the tool.

Tool styles   Some of the tools give you a selection of styles so you can add some variety to your drawings. When you select one of these tools (such as the Brush tool or the Line tool), the available styles appear in the area below the Tool Box.

Color Box   This section shows the available colors and patterns you can use for drawing or filling shapes. Think of this as your own personal 28-color box of Crayola crayons (sans that icky flesh-colored crayon) that never need sharpening.

Current colors   These two boxes display the currently selected foreground color (the top box) and background color (the bottom box). What do I mean by *foreground* and *background* colors? Well, that's actually a tough question to answer! It really depends on which tool you use, so I'll pass the buck and just explain everything as you go along. To select a new foreground color, click one of the color rectangles in the Color Box. To select a new background color, right-click a color.

Drawing area   This is the large blank area that takes up most of the Paint window. The drawing area is your Paint canvas: it's where you do the actual drawing and painting that leads to the creation of your digital masterpieces. It is, in short, the place where all the fun happens.

Drawing with Paint

The best way to approach Paint is simply to have a good time fooling around with the various tools, styles, and colors. Go on, let loose; toss off those inhibitions, free yourself from the shackles of adult responsibilities, and allow yourself to revert to a more immature, to-heck-with-it-I'm-going-to-be-at-one-with-my-inner-child state. (You may want to close the door for this.)

Once you're suitably juvenile, you can pick a tool and start playing. However, there *is* a basic four-step method you use for each tool:

1. Select the tool you want to work with by clicking it in the Tool Box.

2. Click one of the available tool styles (if the tool has any, that is).

3. Select a foreground and background color from the Color Box.

4. Move the pointer into the drawing area and draw the shape you want. (As you can see, the specifics of the drawing process vary from tool to tool.)

The next few sections flesh out these generic steps by showing you how to wield specific tools.

Don't Forget to Save!

When you draw something just right, you should save your work right away (by pulling down the **File** menu and selecting the **Save** command, or by pressing **Ctrl+S**). Once you save the drawing, if you mess things up, you can get back to the saved version by closing the drawing and then opening it again. (To close, select the **File** menu's **New** command; in this case, make sure you select **No** when Paint asks if you want to save your changes.)

A Note About Bailing Out of Your Mistakes

Before you start, you should probably know how to get rid of the botched lines and mutinous shapes that inevitably appear when you learn to use each tool.

Using any of Paint's tools requires that you hold down one of the mouse buttons while drawing. If you make a mess during the drawing, you can start again by simply clicking the other mouse button *before* you release the button you're using.

What if you've already finished drawing the shape? No problem. Just select the **Edit** menu's **Undo** command (or press **Ctrl+Z**). In fact, Paint can handle up to three levels of Undo. So, if you need to, you can wipe out the last three shapes you created by selecting the Undo command three times. What happens if you have more stray shapes to get rid of? (My, you *are* messy, aren't you? Maybe you should just tell everyone the drawing is *supposed* to look like that.) Happily, Paint comes with a couple of erasers that can expunge any wayward lines or colors. See the section "Erasing Parts of a Drawing" later in this chapter.

If the drawing is a total disaster, you can start over by selecting the **Image** menu's **Clear Image** command (or by pressing **Ctrl+Shift+N**).

Drawing Lines

The simplest drawing element is probably the straight line, so (as you might expect) it's the easiest to use of Paint's drawing tools.

 Begin by clicking the Line tool in the Tool Box.

Now click one of the line widths displayed below the Tool Box, and then select your colors.

Move the pointer into the drawing area (as you do, the pointer will change to a crosshair; this is perfectly normal behavior) and position it where you want the line to start. Press and hold the left mouse button, drag the pointer until the line is at the angle and length you want, and then release the mouse button. (Mouse Refresher Course—Dragging 101: Remember that dragging the mouse means holding down one of the mouse buttons and moving the mouse at the same time.) If you want the line to appear in the current foreground color, use the left mouse button to drag the pointer; if you prefer the current background color, use the right mouse button.

Keeping Lines on the Straight and Narrow
To draw a perfect horizontal or vertical line, or to draw your line at exactly a 45-degree angle, hold down the **Shift** key while dragging the mouse.

Drawing Rectangles and Circles

You can use rectangles, circles, ellipses, and rounded rectangles (along with lines) to create most of the basic shapes in your drawing. The Paint tools you use to create these shapes are, not surprisingly, the Rectangle, Ellipse, and Rounded Rectangle tools.

   The Rectangle tool

The Ellipse tool

The Rounded Rectangle tool

 To use any one of these tools, click the tool in the Tool Box, and then click one of the three border styles that appear at the bottom of the Tool Box.

Next, click your foreground and background colors. (I'll explain how the colors work with these tools in a sec.)

Then move the pointer into the drawing area and position it where you want the shape to start. Drag the pointer toward what will be the opposite side of the shape until the object is the size and shape you want. Then release the mouse button.

Perfect Circles and Squares
To draw a perfect square or circle, hold down the **Shift** key while dragging the pointer.

The colors that Paint uses for the shape depend on which style you selected, which mouse button you drag with, and what mood Paint is in that day:

Border only   This style draws only the border of the shape. If you left-drag (click the left mouse button and drag the mouse), the border appears in the current foreground color; if you right-drag (click the right mouse button and drag the mouse), the border appears in the current background color.

Border and fill   This style draws a border and fills it with a color. If you left-drag, the border appears in the foreground color, and the fill appears in the background color; right-dragging applies the background color to the border and the foreground color to the fill.

No border   This style leaves off the shape's border and draws only the fill. If you left-drag, the fill appears in the current background color; if you right-drag, the fill appears in the current foreground color.

Got all that? No? Well, not to worry; there's plenty of time before tomorrow's pop quiz.

Drawing Curves

For your nonlinear moods, Paint has a Curve tool you can use to draw wavy lines. It's actually a bit tricky to use, so you may need to play around with it a bit. Here are the steps to follow:

1. Click the **Curve** tool, click the style (you get the same choices you saw earlier for the Line tool), and select the color you want to use.

2. Position the pointer where you want the curve to start.

3. Drag the mouse until the line is the length you want and then release the button. (As with the Line tool, drag with the left button to use the foreground color or drag with the right button to use the background color.)

4. Drag the mouse again to curve the line. For example, if you drew a horizontal line in step 3, you can drag the mouse down to curve the line downward. Similarly, you can drag the mouse up to curve the line upward. When you have the curve you want, release the button.

5. If you want to add a second curve to the line, drag the mouse again and release the button when you're done.

Drawing Polygons

Polygon may sound like a parrot that's flown the coop (here, I'll save you the trouble: "Groan!"), but it's really just a highfalutin' mathematical term for a collection of straight lines that forms an enclosed object. (A triangle is a common example of a polygon.) Follow these steps to create a Paint polygon:

1. Click the **Polygon** tool, click the style (you get the same choices that you saw earlier for the Rectangle and Ellipse tools), and select the color you want to use.

2. Move the pointer into the drawing area and position it where you want the polygon to start. The pointer changes to a cross.

3. Drag the pointer (using the left button for the foreground color or the right button for the background color) until the first side is the length and angle you want.

4. Release the mouse button.

5. Position the pointer where you want the next side to end.

6. Click a mouse button, and Paint draws a line from the end of the previous line to the pointer.

7. Repeat steps 5 and 6 to define the other sides of the polygon. To finish the shape, connect the last side with the beginning of the first side.

Drawing Freehand Lines

As you've seen, Paint makes it easy—some would say *too* easy—to draw lines, circles, and polygons. To become a true Paint artiste, or just to have some real fun, try using the Pencil tool or the Brush tool to draw freehand lines.

 Begin by clicking the **Pencil** tool or the **Brush** tool.

If you choose the Brush tool, you can also choose from one of the dozen different styles that appear at the bottom of the Tool Box.

Next, you can select a foreground and background color for each tool.

Move the pointer into the drawing area and position it where you want to start drawing. (If you use the Pencil, the pointer changes to a pencil; if you use the Brush, the pointer changes to the style you select.) Then just drag the pointer, and a line follows your every twitch. (As usual, you left-drag to display the line in the foreground color and right-drag to display the line in the background color.) When you're done, release the mouse button.

Filling Shapes with Color

What do you do if you create, say, a rectangle using the "border only" style, and then later decide you'd like the rectangle filled with a particular color? Or suppose you create an enclosed area with the Pencil or Brush and would like to fill it in with a color.

The solution to these Paint problems is the Fill With Color tool. As its name implies, the Fill With Color tool fills in any enclosed shape with whatever color you select. It's really easy to use, too: just click the **Fill With Color** tool in the Tool Box, and then click anywhere inside the shape. If you left-click, Paint fills the shape with the current foreground color; if you right-click, Paint uses the current background color.

Check This Out...

Sometimes Fill With Color Does Too Good a Job

Before foisting the Fill With Color tool on a shape, make sure to enclose the shape completely. If you don't enclose the shape—even if there's just the tiniest gap—Fill With Color's color leaks out and fills in any enclosed area that surrounds the original shape, which usually means the entire drawing area! Argh! This will happen more times than you think, so it's important to know what to do. After counting to ten or chanting your mantra or doing whatever it is you do to calm yourself, immediately select the **Edit** menu's **Undo** command (or press **Ctrl+Z**). Then return to the shape and close the pesky gap that caused the leak. (For best results, you may need to magnify the shape. See the "A Zoom with a View" section later in this chapter.)

Using the Airbrush Tool

The Airbrush tool (as its icon shows) is actually more like a can of spray paint. This is useful for satisfying those graffiti urges without breaking the law.

Click one of the three Airbrush styles (these define the size of the "spray") and then click your colors.

Move the mouse pointer into the drawing area (the pointer changes to a spray can), and hold down a mouse button to start spraying. You know the drill by now: hold down the left button for the foreground color or the right button for the background color. Simply drag the pointer around the drawing area, and you're an instant graffiti artist.

Adding Text to a Drawing

Paint is mostly for your right brain, but if your left brain wants to get in on the act, you can use the Text tool to add text to a drawing. Here's what you do:

1. Click the **Text** tool, click either the opaque or transparent style (the following figure shows an example of each style), and then click your colors.

2. Position the pointer where you want the text to start, and drag the mouse to create a box large enough to hold the text. When you release the mouse button, an insertion point cursor appears inside the box.

3. If this is the first time you've used the Text tool, a Fonts toolbar appears (see the following figure). If you don't see the Fonts toolbar, right-click the **Text** box and select **Text Tool** from the shortcut menu.

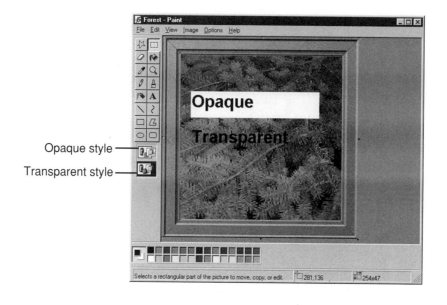

You can add text to your drawing using either an opaque or transparent style.

Opaque style

Transparent style

Use the Fonts toolbar to format your text.

4. Use the drop-down lists and buttons on the Fonts toolbar to establish a format for your text. (To find out more about fonts, pay a visit to Chapter 20.)

5. Type your text. When you're done, click the **Text** tool again.

Cutting, Copying, and Pasting Drawings

You can apply the cut and paste techniques that I described in Chapter 7 to Paint drawings; however, there are some extra steps involved. The next couple of sections explain everything you need to know.

Selecting Parts of a Drawing

If you need to cut or copy a piece of a drawing (to paste either elsewhere in the drawing or, perhaps, in a different program altogether), you first need to select the image you want. Paint gives you two tools to do the job: the Select tool and the Free-Form Select tool.

The Select tool

 The Free-Form Select tool

173

Use the Select tool to select a rectangular area of the drawing. Click the tool and move the pointer to the upper-left corner of the area you want to select. Drag the mouse until the box encloses the area you want to work with, and then release the mouse button.

Use the Free-Form Select tool to select any area that's not rectangular shaped. After clicking the tool, move the pointer into the drawing area and drag the mouse around the area you want to select. Release the button when you've completely outlined the area.

Pasting Cut or Copied Images

Once you cut or copy your selected image (by using the Edit menu's Cut or Copy commands), you need to paste the image.

With text, as you may recall, you first position the cursor where you want the new text to appear. However, Paint doesn't have a cursor. So when you select the **Edit** menu's **Paste** command, the image appears in the upper-left corner of the drawing. To position it, move the mouse pointer inside the image, and then drag the image to the location you want.

Pasting into Another Drawing

Paint, like WordPad, doesn't let you work with more than one document at a time, so if you need to paste some or all of one drawing into another Paint drawing, just start up a second copy of Paint and open the other drawing in it. You can cut or copy the image from the original Paint window, switch to the second window, and paste it. See Chapter 9 for instructions on switching between open applications.

Erasing Parts of a Drawing

Because it takes a little time to get used to the Paint tools, you'll probably have a number of stray lines and shapes that you don't want in the finished drawing. Fortunately, you can use Paint's Eraser tool to remove any rogue elements. Actually, Eraser is two tools in one: a normal eraser and a color eraser.

 As a normal eraser, the Eraser tool does pretty much what you'd expect: it wipes out everything in its path. (This is not a tool to wield carelessly!)

Select the eraser width from the styles that appear at the bottom of the Tool Box. If you have a lot to erase, pick a wider shape; if you want fine control, pick a thinner shape.

Move the pointer into the drawing area and position it near where you want to start erasing. (The pointer changes into a box.) Drag the pointer to start erasing, and everything in the path of the box is erased. (Technically, everything in the path of the box is replaced by the current background color.) When you're done, release the mouse button.

What's the Eraser tool's other personality—the color eraser—all about? Well, suppose you want to preserve the outlines of a drawing but wipe out the color that fills it, or suppose you want to replace one color with another. These sound like tricky operations, but the color eraser can do the job without breaking a sweat.

You use the color eraser just as you do the eraser, except that you right-drag the eraser box. When you drag the tool over your drawing, it replaces anything it finds in the current foreground color with the current background color.

A Zoom with a View

For fine detail work, Paint lets you "zoom" in on a section of a drawing. This magnifies the drawing so you can get a closer look at a particular section. At the maximum magnification (a whopping 800%), you can even see the tiny individual elements (the *pixels*) that make up a Paint picture.

Pixel Perfect

The elements that comprise a picture are called pixels ("pixel" is a combination of the term "picture element"). A typical Paint image has pixels arranged in 640 columns and 480 rows, which totals more than 300,000 pixels!

To try this out, click the **Magnifier** tool and then click a magnification from the choices that appear at the bottom of the Tool Box. When you move the mouse into the drawing area, the pointer changes into a box. Move the box over the area you want to magnify, and then click. Paint zooms in, as shown in the following figure. The little Thumbnail window shows the normal view of the magnified area so you can keep things in perspective. (If you'd prefer not to see the Thumbnail window, open the **View** menu, select the **Zoom** command, and deselect the **Show Thumbnail** command in the cascade menu.)

The Zoom tool in action.

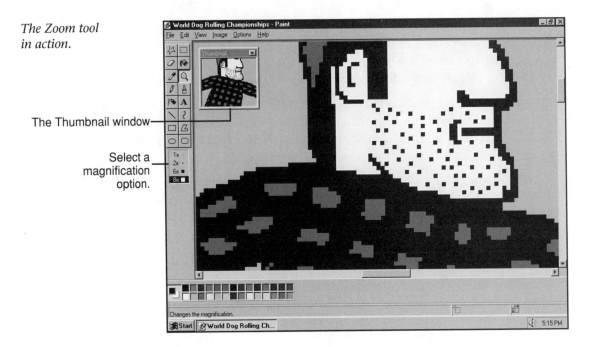

The Thumbnail window⏤

Select a magnification option.

You can work on the drawing normally in this view because almost all the other tools are available (the Text tool is the only exception). When you finish, click the **Zoom** tool and then click the **1x** style to return to the normal view.

There are actually a few other methods you can use to zoom in and out:

➤ Pull down the **View** menu, select the **Zoom** command, and then select **Large Size** from the cascade menu. (Or you can bypass the menus altogether by simply pressing **Ctrl+Page Down**.) This command magnifies the drawing by 400%.

➤ Select the **View** menu's **Zoom** command, and then select **Custom** from the cascade menu. In the Custom Zoom dialog box that appears, select one of the zoom percentages, and then select **OK**.

➤ Pull down the **View** menu, select the **Zoom** command, and then select **Normal Size** from the cascade menu. (Or you can press **Ctrl+Page Up**.) This command returns you to the regular view.

Getting a Bigger Picture

Instead of seeing less of your drawing, you may prefer to see more of it. This section lets you in on a few Paint techniques for seeing the big (or, at least, bigger) picture.

To expand the picture so it takes up the entire screen, pull down the **View** menu and select the **View Bitmap** command (or press **Ctrl+F**). To return to Paint, click the mouse or press any key.

Alternatively, you can give yourself more elbow room by hiding certain elements of the Paint window:

➤ To hide the Tool Box, deselect the **View** menu's **Tool Box** command (or press **Ctrl+T**).

➤ To hide the Color Box, deselect the **View** menu's **Color Box** command (or press **Ctrl+A**).

➤ To hide the status bar, deselect the **View** menu's **Status Bar** command.

If you'd prefer to keep the Tool Box and Color Box on-screen, you can still create more room by dragging them out of their normal locations. (Be sure to use the margins surrounding the tools or color squares to drag each box.) As you can see in the following figure, this turns the boxes into "floating" windows that sit on top of your drawing.

To see more of your drawing, move the Tool Box and Color Box anywhere you like.

Use the margins surrounding the tools or color squares to drag each box.

The Least You Need to Know

This chapter showed you how to have all sorts of fun with Paint, Windows 95's drawing program. Most of the tools take a bit of getting used to, but even your experiments will probably be a lot of fun! Unfortunately, I didn't have the space to get into some of Paint's wilder features. The Image menu, in particular, is a rich source of wow-your-friends special effects. Feel free to try out the Flip/Rotate, Stretch/Skew, and Invert Colors commands on your own.

Chapter 15

Working with a Net: Using Microsoft Backup

In This Chapter

➤ Starting Microsoft Backup

➤ Going through the backup steps

➤ Understanding backup sets

➤ Restoring backed-up files

➤ Real-world backup tips and strategies designed to help you sleep better at night

These days, there's no shortage of books and magazine articles that list all the possible ways your hard disk can crash. Computer veterans seem to delight in telling war stories about hard disks going down for the count, rogue programs running amok, lightning storm meltdowns, and—more and more often—vicious, disk-trashing viruses that give no quarter to your valuable data.

All these stories lead us to one inescapable conclusion: our precious files are at risk and they need our protection. Fortunately, protecting data doesn't mean investing in an arsenal of semi-automatic weapons and heavy artillery. No, all you need to do is to make backup copies of your data at regular intervals. Now here's the good news: Windows 95 comes equipped with its own backup artillery (oops, I mean accessory) called Microsoft Backup. This chapter takes you through the Backup basics.

Up an' at 'Em: Starting Backup

As you'll see later on, the Backup program makes backing up your data a relatively painless procedure. You just select the files you want to back up, and the program dutifully copies them to floppy disks. Then, if any disaster occurs, you can use Backup to restore your data safe and sound from the disks. For now, though, uncrate Backup so you can get a good look at it.

To start Backup, first open the Start menu by selecting the **Start** button. Then open the **Programs** folder, the **Accessories** folder, and the **System Tools** folder. Take a second or two to catch your breath, and then select **Backup.** (Is panic setting in because Backup is nowhere in sight in your System Tools folder? Don't worry: you just need to install it from your Windows 95 disks. Leap ahead to Chapter 23 and read the "Adding Windows 95 Components" section to find out how to install it.)

When Backup comes up, you see the Welcome to Microsoft Backup dialog box, shown in the following figure. This otherwise-useless dialog box just gives you a not-very-complete overview of the whole backup process. Unless you want to read this drivel every time you crank up Backup, activate the **Don't show this again** check box and select **OK**.

The Welcome dialog box gives you a backup summary that's a few geese shy of a gaggle.

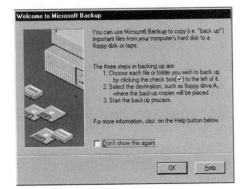

Backup rummages around in your system for a couple of seconds, and then it displays a dialog box (shown in the following figure) telling you it has created a "full backup set" named Full Backup Set (how imaginative). You gotta love it: you just started the program a few moments ago, and already it's throwing some jargon in your face. Here's the quickie explanation: a *backup set* is a collection of files selected for backup (it also includes a couple of other things as well, as you'll soon see). A *full backup set* is a backup set that includes every file on your hard drive. So why don't they just say "everything on your hard drive"? Ah, technogeeks: you can't live with 'em, and you can't (unfortunately) live without 'em.

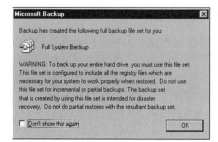

Some not-even-close-to-comprehensible mumbo-jumbo about backup sets.

With that out of the way, activate the **Don't show this again** check box, and select **OK** so you won't be pestered by this dialog box again. If you don't have a tape drive installed on your system, another dialog box appears to let you know that. Select **OK** to move on.

At last, you end up at the Backup window shown in the following figure. As you can see, it looks a lot like the Explorer window, with a folders list on the left and a contents list on the right.

The Microsoft Backup window.

Backing Up Is Hard to Do—Here's How to Make It Easier

Before getting down to business, you need to ask yourself which files you want to include in the backup. Your first inclination might be to use the infamous Full Backup Set that the Backup program mentioned earlier, just to be safe. The problem with this approach is that even a small hard disk contains enough data to fill a couple of dozen floppy disks. Believe me, shuffling that many disks in and out of your machine every time you do a backup will get old *really* fast. "Sorry, I'd like to do a backup, but I have to delouse my Rottweiler."

181

Instead, you need to take a "real-world" approach to backups:

➤ The problem with a full backup is that it includes all your program files (the ones that run your applications). Presumably, however, you have these files on disk somewhere, so why include them in a backup? If worse comes to worst, you can always reinstall your programs (and even Windows 95 itself, if necessary).

➤ If you leave out your program files, however, you should seriously consider making backup copies of your program disks (unless they come on CD-ROM). You only have to do it once, and you probably only have to do it for your most important programs.

The Full Scoop on Copying Disks

If you need to make a copy of a floppy disk, Windows 95 is up to the task. Here are the steps you need to follow:

1. Insert the disk you want to copy (this is the *source* disk). If your system has a second drive of the same type, insert the disk you want to use for the copy (this is the *destination* disk) in the other drive.

2. Highlight the source disk drive and select **File**, **Copy Disk**. Windows 95 displays the Copy Disk dialog box.

3. The Copy from box lists the floppy drives on your system. Highlight the drive that contains the source disk.

4. The Copy to box also lists the floppy drives on your system. Highlight the drive that you want to use for the destination disk. Make sure that this drive uses disks of the same type as the source disk. If your system has two drives of different type, you can use the same drive for the copy procedure. (For example, suppose drive A is $3^1/_2$-inch and drive B is $5^1/_4$-inch, and you want to copy a $3^1/_2$-inch disk. Then you can select the $3^1/_2$-inch drive in both **Copy from** and **Copy to**.)

5. Select **Start**. Windows 95 reads the data from the source disk. If you use the same drive for the copy, Windows 95 prompts you to insert the destination disk.

6. Insert the destination disk and then select **OK**. Windows 95 copies the data to the destination disk.

7. When the copy is complete, select **Close**.

➤ All the energy you put into backing up should go toward protecting your documents because, unlike your programs, these are usually irreplaceable. To make life easier, you should create separate folders to hold only your documents (as described back in Chapter 12). Then you only have to back up those folders.

➤ Take advantage of Backup's two different backup types: full and incremental. *Full* backs up all the files you select; *incremental*, on the other hand, backs up only those files that have changed since the last full backup, which can really cut down on the number of files involved. Your overall backup strategy might look something like this:

1. Perform a full backup of all your documents once a month or so.

2. If you do most of your work in one or two programs, do a full backup of these programs' documents every week or two.

3. Do an incremental backup of modified files every couple of days (although you might think about backing up your really important documents every day).

➤ If, after all this, you still have a few dozen megabytes or more to back up, forget floppies altogether and invest in a tape drive. They're a little pricey, but they can hold hundreds of megabytes of data, and they do it all while you're doing lunch.

Backup's Five-Step Procedure

The first dialog box you saw told you that backing up requires three steps, but that's not quite true. "Oh, great, now Windows is lying to me. And after all we've been through together!" It's sad, but true, because it can actually take as many as five steps when you start out:

1. Select the files you want to back up.

2. Select the type of backup (full or incremental).

3. Select the drive you want to use for the backup.

4. Save your backup set.

5. Start the backup.

The next few sections take you through the details for each step.

Step 1: Selecting the Files to Back Up

I mentioned earlier that the Backup window resembles the Explorer window. There's one important difference, however: in the Backup window, all the disk drives, folders, and files have a check box next to them, as you can see in the following figure.

Click here to select an entire drive.

To make backup selection easier, Backup displays check boxes beside your drives, folders, and files.

Click here to select an entire folder.

	Name	Size	Type	Modified
☐	ShellNew		Folder	12/18/96 12:10 PM
☐	Netdet	7885	Configuratio...	8/24/96 12:11 PM
☑	Dionysus.pwl	688	PWL File	12/18/96 12:20 PM
☐	Smartdrv	44867	Application	8/24/96 11:11 AM
☐	Himem.sys	33191	System file	8/24/96 12:11 PM
☐	Regedit	105984	Application	8/24/96 12:11 PM
☐	Accstat	24576	Application	8/24/96 12:11 PM
☐	Calc	59392	Application	8/24/96 12:11 PM
☐	Notepad	34304	Application	8/24/96 12:11 PM
☐	Packager	65024	Application	8/24/96 12:11 PM
☐	Pbrush	4608	Application	8/24/96 12:11 PM
☐	Write	5120	Application	8/24/96 12:11 PM
☐	Rsrcmtr	15360	Application	8/24/96 12:11 PM
☐	Dialer	63240	Application	8/24/96 12:11 PM

File set: Untitled   Files selected: 684   38,096 Kilobytes selected

Click here to select a file.

The general idea is that you activate the check box for each drive, folder, and file you want to include in the backup. (You activate the check boxes either by clicking them, or by highlighting the disk, folder, or file and pressing the **Spacebar**.) Here are the specifics:

➤ To back up all the files on a disk drive, activate the disk drive's check box.

➤ To back up all the files inside a folder, activate the folder's check box. (For example, see the My Documents folder in the figure.) Now you see why it's so convenient to include all your documents in a single folder.

➤ To back up a file, activate the file's check box.

Why the Grayed Check Boxes?

If you take a close look at the previous figure shown, you'll notice that the check boxes for Hard disk (C:) and the Windows folder have a gray background. The gray tells you that only some of the disk's or folder's contents have been selected for backup.

Step 2: Selecting the Type of Backup

As I said earlier, Backup can perform two kinds of backups:

Full   Backs up all the files you selected in step 1.

Incremental   Of all the files you selected in step 1, this backs up only those files that have changed since the last full backup.

To select the backup type you want to use, pull down the **Settings** menu and select the **Options** command. In the Settings - Options dialog box that appears, select the **Backup** tab (see the following figure). Choose either the **Full** or **Incremental** option button, and then select **OK**.

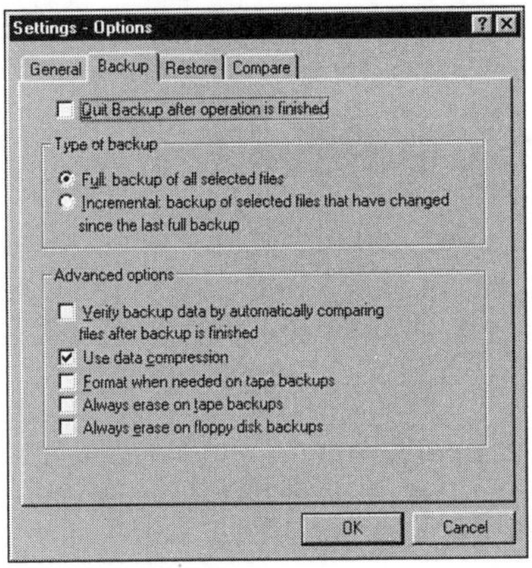

Use the Backup tab to choose either a Full or an Incremental backup.

Step 3: Selecting the Backup Destination

Once you select all the documents you want to back up, select the **Next Step** > button. Backup redisplays the window as shown in the following figure. You use this window to highlight the drive or folder where you want to place the backup copies of your documents. You'll usually select a floppy disk drive or a tape drive (if you have one). Note, as well, that the < Previous Step button is active in this window. You can use it to go back and make adjustments to your file selections at any time.

Use this window to specify where you want your documents backed up.

![Untitled - Microsoft Backup window showing Backup, Restore, Compare tabs. "Where to back up:" with Previous Step and Start Backup buttons. Select a destination for the backup: Desktop, My Computer with 3½ Floppy [A:], Hard drive [C:], [D:], F on 'Apollo' [E:], Network Neighborhood, Microsoft Backup did not detect a tape dri. Selected device or location: A:\. File set: Untitled, Files selected: 684, 38,096 Kilobytes selected.]

Step 4: Saving Your Backup Set

Together, the files you selected in step 1, the backup type you selected in step 2, and the destination you selected in step 3 make up your *backup set*. Because this is a combination you'll likely use quite often, it's a good idea to preserve your selections by saving your backup set.

To do that, pull down the **File** menu and select the **Save** command (or press **Ctrl+S**). In the **File name** text box, enter a descriptive name for the backup set (such as Documents only - incremental), and then select **Save**.

Check This Out...

Reusing a Backup Set

Once you save a backup set, reusing it in the future is easy. Just select the **File** menu's **Open File Set** command, select the backup set in the Open dialog box that appears, and then select **Open**.

Step 5: Doing the Backup Thing

Well, at long last, you're just about ready to roll. Here are the steps to follow to back up your data:

1. Place a floppy disk in the drive you selected.

2. Select the **Start Backup** button. Backup displays the Backup Set Label dialog box, as shown in the following figure.

3. Your files aren't backed up individually. Instead, they're combined into a single file, and that file is backed up. Use the Backup Set Label dialog box to enter a name for this file, and then select **OK**.

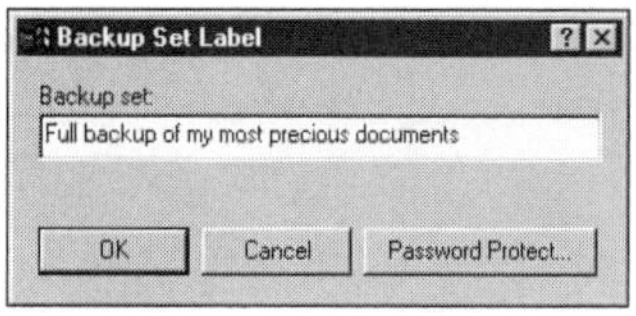

Use this dialog box to enter a name for the backup file.

4. If the disk is full, Backup asks if you want to erase the data. If that's not what you want, remove the disk and insert another one. Select **Yes** when you're ready to go. The Backup dialog box appears to keep you posted on the progress of the backup (see the next figure).

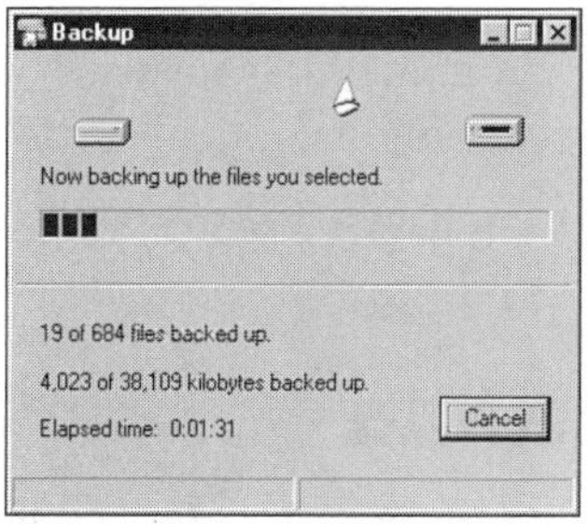

This dialog box shows you how much of the backup has been completed.

5. Depending on the number and size of the files you selected, Backup occasionally prompts you to enter more disks. When it does, insert the new disk and select **OK**. When you're done with a disk, you should label it for future reference (for example, Backup Disk #1).

6. Backup displays a dialog box to let you know when it's finished. Select **OK** to return to the Backup dialog box, and then select **OK** again to return to the Backup window.

Backup DOs and DON'Ts

Here are a few more hints and suggestions to make backing up easier and safer:

Do:

➤ Decide on a backup strategy and stick to it. Otherwise, you'll fall victim to one of computerdom's strictest laws: hard disks only crash when they contain priceless, irreplaceable data that isn't backed up.

➤ Use backup sets to configure the program quickly.

➤ Run the ScanDisk program before a major backup to look for any problems. (For the lowdown on using ScanDisk, read the "Avoiding Hard Disk Hard Times: ScanDisk" section in Chapter 16.)

➤ Have your pet spayed or neutered.

Don't:

➤ Use $5^1/_4$-inch disks if you don't have to. With high-density $3^1/_2$-inch disks, you not only get a little more data on each disk, you also get the added safety of a sturdy case.

➤ Keep all your backup disks in one place. If a thief happens upon them, you'll be out of luck. Some folks go as far as keeping a copy in an offsite location such as a safety deposit box.

➤ Use low-priced, no-name disks for your backups. Stick with high-quality disks, and you'll sleep better at night.

➤ Be lazy or put it off. Back up your files now!

Restoring Your Data

If some unforeseen disaster occurs, you need to restore your data from the backups. Here are the steps to follow:

1. Start Microsoft Backup, as described earlier in this chapter.

2. In the Backup window, select the **Restore** tab.

3. Insert the first floppy disk from the backup set.

4. Use the **Restore from** list to select the floppy drive. The name of the backup set should appear in the box on the right side of the window (see the following figure).

5. If there are multiple backup sets, select the one you want to use.

6. Select the **Next Step >** button. The window changes to show the folders and files in the selected backup set.

7. Use the check boxes to choose which folders or files you want to restore.

8. Select the **Start Restore** button. Backup restores the files.

9. Backup displays a dialog box to let you know when it's finished. Select **OK** to return to the Restore dialog box, and then select **OK** again to return to the Backup window.

Use the Restore screen to select the backup file that contains the files you want to restore.

The Least You Need to Know

This chapter showed you how to use Microsoft Backup to achieve the peace of mind that comes when you know your precious data is safe and sound. As a reminder, here's a recap of the basic five-step backup procedure:

1. Select the files you want to back up.

2. Select the type of backup (full or incremental).

3. Select the drive you want to use for the backup.

4. Save your backup set.

5. Start the backup.

To put your worried mind even more at ease, the next chapter presents a few more of Windows 95's system tools, a couple of which can scope out and repair problems on your hard disk.

Chapter 16

Routine Maintenance: The System Tools

In This Chapter

➤ Using ScanDisk to scope out hard disk woes

➤ Using Disk Defragmenter to tidy up a messy hard disk

➤ Using DriveSpace to double the size of your hard disk

➤ The lowdown on three tools that put the "routine" in routine hard disk maintenance

As you work with your computer, you usually focus on just the external appendages that you can readily eyeball: the mouse and keyboard, the monitor, maybe a floppy disk or two. But the old phrase "It's what's inside that counts" has no more apt a subject than that big beige box squatting impassively on your desk. An internal tour of your machine would reveal some crucial digital anatomy, including the processor that runs the whole show (that's the *386*, *486*, or *Pentium* everyone's always talking about), the memory chips that give your programs room to roam, and the cooling fan that keeps everything from melting into a silicon puddle.

But, for my money, the most critical component inside my computer's case is by far the hard disk. Processors process, memory chips remember, and cooling fans cool, and you can replace or upgrade each one without a moment's thought. But the hard disk is where you store your program and document files. Without a hard disk, you have no way to run Windows 95 and all its applications, and your computer becomes simply a two-thousand-dollar paperweight.

This chapter focuses on three tools that help you get the most out of your precious hard disk. ScanDisk watches your hard disk for signs of trouble, Disk Defragmenter keeps your files and folders shipshape, and DriveSpace performs the impressive feat of effectively doubling the size of your hard disk!

A Caveat or Two Before You Begin

Before starting your maintenance chores, there are a couple of things you should know that will help you avoid problems. You can think of these caveats as electronic versions of the physician's "Above all, do no harm" credo.

First, you may know that DOS 6.2 came with its own version of ScanDisk. However, you should avoid it like the plague. Why? Because the DOS ScanDisk can't figure out some of the Windows 95-specific stuff on your hard disk, and it may report errors where none exist (or, even worse, try to fix them!). You should also steer clear of similar utilities from other companies—such as the Norton Disk Doctor—that were designed in the pre-Windows 95 era.

Second, even some disk utilities that were designed for Windows 95 may cause difficulties. The problem here, you see, is that Microsoft created a revised version of Windows 95 (called Windows 95B) and made it available to computer manufacturers toward the end of 1996. (This revised version isn't available through regular software retail channels.) Windows 95B uses a completely different method of working with your hard disk, so disk maintenance programs designed for the original Windows 95 (Windows 95A) will choke on this new system.

How do you know which version of Windows you have? There's an easy way to find out: Right-click the **My Computer** icon and then click **Properties**. The dialog box that shows up (see the next figure) tells you which version of Windows 95 you have. Just look for the letter after the 4.00.950: if you see an **A** (or nothing), then you have the original Windows 95; if you see a **B**, then you have Windows 95B.

If you have Windows 95B and you're going to go out and buy disk utilities (such as the Norton Utilities), make sure you get the latest version, which should work fine with Windows 95B. If in doubt, either ask the salesperson or see if the package tells you that it works with something called FAT-32 (this is the technogeek name for the new hard disk system in Windows 95B).

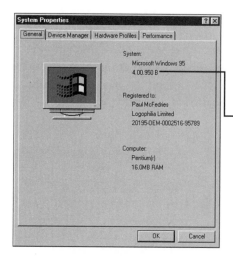

Use this dialog box to figure out your Windows 95 version.

This letter tells you which flavor of Windows 95 you have.

Avoiding Hard Disk Hard Times: ScanDisk

Computers are temperamental, finicky beasts that often seem all too eager to act strangely or to give up the ghost altogether. Most computer components can be easily (albeit expensively) replaced if they head south. But if your hard disk goes haywire, you may lose irreplaceable data (you might lose a few hairs, too, and gain a shiny, new ulcer).

Of course, as a responsible practitioner of the arcane art of computing, you *do* perform regular backups of your documents, right? I thought so. However, replacing a hard disk, reinstalling and reconfiguring your programs, and then restoring your data from the backups is a real pain in the you-know-what. To put it off for as long as possible, you can use Windows 95's ScanDisk accessory to give your hard disk regular checkups.

When you have a physical exam, your family doctor pokes you and prods you and generally gives you the once-over. In the same way, ScanDisk performs a battery of tests on your hard disk to make sure it's up to snuff and that there are no chinks in its electronic armor. If it finds any minor problems, ScanDisk lets you know and offers to fix them for you on the spot. If it finds a more serious problem, the program warns you that hard disk failure is, if not imminent, at least a possibility in the near future.

Check This Out...

Installing the Tools As you work through this chapter, if you find that one or more of these programs aren't installed on your system, you'll need to load them from your original Windows 95 disks (or the Windows 95 CD-ROM). Flip to Chapter 23 and read the section "Adding Windows 95 Components" to find out how to do this.

Getting ScanDisk Started

As you'll see, the great thing about ScanDisk is that it's so easy to use. For now, though, let's just get it started. Begin by selecting the **Start** button to display the Start menu. Then open the **Programs** folder, open the **Accessories** folder, and open the **System Tools** folder. Now select **ScanDisk**, and you see a ScanDisk window similar to the one shown in the following figure.

Use the ScanDisk window to select a disk and get the show on the road.

Selecting a Disk to Scan

ScanDisk's Select the drive(s) you want to check for errors list is where you choose the drive or drives you want to check. The program automatically selects the hard disk where Windows 95 is installed, but you can select another hard disk (if you have one) or even one of your floppy disks.

To select another disk, just highlight it in the list. (If you're going to select a floppy disk, first make sure there's a disk in the drive.)

Selecting the Type of Test

ScanDisk is no mere one-trick pony. It is, in fact, fully capable of performing not one, but *two* types of tests: Standard or Thorough. Which of the two you choose depends on how much time you have to kill, how patient you are, and how paranoid you are about your hard disk having a nervous breakdown.

The Standard test runs various checks to ensure the integrity of your hard disk's files and folders. It shouldn't take more than a few seconds to perform this test. The Thorough test delves deeper and checks not only your hard disk's files and folders, but also the surface of the hard disk itself. Depending on the size of your hard disk, this test can take 15 minutes or more.

Which one should you choose? Well, if you've never run ScanDisk before, you should probably run a Thorough test just for the extra peace of mind it'll bring. After that, you can set up a ScanDisk schedule (assuming, of course, you're a schedule setter-upper type of person). For example, you can run a Standard test every day and run a Thorough test once a week.

Scanning a Disk with ScanDisk

Okay, you're almost ready for action. Your last remaining chore is to decide if you want ScanDisk to automatically fix any errors it finds. This is handy if, for example, you want to perform the lengthy Thorough test and you'd like to head off to a three-martini lunch while it's running. To have ScanDisk fix any errors, activate the **Automatically fix errors** check box.

To commence the ScanDisk checkup, select the **Start** button. ScanDisk begins nosing around in your hard disk's private parts and displays its progress at the bottom of the window. If ScanDisk finds a problem (and you didn't tell it to fix errors automatically), a dialog box appears that gives you several options. In the example shown in the following figure, ScanDisk has found some "lost file fragments" (aw, how sad) and wants to know what to do with them.

In this case, it's best to just chuck these fragments. So select the **Discard lost file fragment(s) and recover disk space** option and select **OK**. If you're really not sure what to do, you could try selecting the **More Info** button to display a dialog box with a few more facts. (Select OK when you're done with this dialog box.) If that still doesn't help, just select **OK** and let ScanDisk figure things out for itself.

Use ScanDisk if Windows 95 Crashes and Burns Windows 95 was designed to be more robust and to crash less often than its previous incarnations. However, if Windows 95 does go wonky on you, reboot your computer and run a Standard ScanDisk test when you get back to Windows 95. This should weed out any lingering bad effects from the crash.

ScanDisk displays a dialog box like this one when it finds an error.

When ScanDisk's labors are complete, it displays the Results dialog box to let you know what happened. This dialog box is jam-packed with stats and numbers that are sure to warm the cockles of nerdy hearts everywhere. Nod your head knowingly and select **Close** to return to the ScanDisk window.

Putting Your Hard Disk Affairs in Order with Disk Defragmenter

You can use Windows 95's Disk Defragmenter program to *defragment* the files on your hard disk. Defragmenting sounds pretty serious, but it's just Windows 95's way of tidying up a messy hard disk. It puts your files in order and does a few other neat-freak chores. (Don't worry though: Disk Defragmenter doesn't change the contents of the files, and they'll still appear in the same places when you look at them in Explorer or My Computer.)

A Plain English Explanation of Defragmenting

Why bother with this arcane defragmenting business? Well, imagine, if you will, a particularly disorganized household where, say, the cutlery and dishes are scattered throughout the house. The knives are in the basement, the spoons are in the den, the plates are out on the porch, and so on. Imagine how long it would take you to set the table for dinner if you had to run around to all these different locations to get what you needed. Obviously, storing these items in one place (the kitchen, silly) would reduce table-setting times to a fraction of what they were before.

Defragmenting does the same thing for your files. You see, Windows 95 is, to be blunt about it, a real pig. When it stores files on your hard drive, it often just throws them anywhere it can find space. This is a simple way to work (Windows 95 can be a bit dim at times, so it likes to keep its life as simple as possible), but it often means that pieces of your files are scattered willy-nilly around your hard disk. And the more pieces there are, the longer it's going to take to load the file the next time you want to use it. After a while, this can get so bad that your hard drive slows to a crawl.

Clusters, FATs, and Other Useless Terminology

Windows 95 stores hard disk files in fixed-sized chunks called *clusters*. The size of each cluster depends on the disk, but 4,096 bytes and 8,192 bytes are typical sizes. Because most files are larger than 4,096 (or even 8,192) bytes, each file is divided into many different clusters.

Windows 95 keeps track of all the clusters on a disk by means of the *file allocation table* (or FAT for short). When Windows 95 needs to store a file, it looks at the FAT to determine where the empty clusters are, and then just starts storing clusters wherever it can find room. So it ends up putting part of the file here, another chunk there, and so on. The result is a *fragmented* file. Disk Defragmenter's job is to rearrange everything so that each file's clusters are reunited. Remember how earlier I told you that Windows 95B uses something called FAT-32? This is a new and improved FAT that uses smaller cluster sizes. This makes file storage more efficient, but it doesn't do anything about file fragmentation, unfortunately.

Doing the Defragmenting Thing

Before you use Disk Defragmenter, you need to do a little preparation:

➤ As described in Chapter 11, you should delete any files from your hard disk that you don't need. Defragmenting junk files only slows down the whole process.

➤ Check for hard disk errors by running Windows 95's ScanDisk program as described earlier in this chapter. You should probably run a Thorough test just to be safe.

When you've done these preliminary chores and are ready to use Disk Defragmenter, follow these steps:

1. Display the Start menu, open the **Programs** folder, open the **Accessories** folder, open the **System Tools** folder, and select **Disk Defragmenter**. The Select Drive dialog box appears so you can select the drive you want to defragment.

2. Use the **Which drive do you want to defragment?** drop-down list to choose a drive, and then select **OK**. Disk Defragmenter analyzes the fragmentation of your files, and if it's not too bad, it displays the dialog box shown in the following figure.

Disk Defragmenter	? X
Drive C is 2 % fragmented.	
You don't need to defragment this drive now. If you want to defragment it anyway, click Start.	
Start Select Drive Advanced... Exit	

Disk Defragmenter lets you know if your hard disk isn't too messy.

3. If you want to go ahead with the defragment, select **Start**. Disk Defragmenter starts tidying up your hard disk and displays a dialog box that lets you view its progress.

4. If you'd like to see a visual representation of the Disk Defragmenter's labors, select the **Show Details** button. The window that appears looks something like the one shown in the following figure. To find out what all those squares mean, select the **Legend** button to display the Defrag Legend dialog box.

Select the Show Details button to watch Disk Defragmenter do its thing.

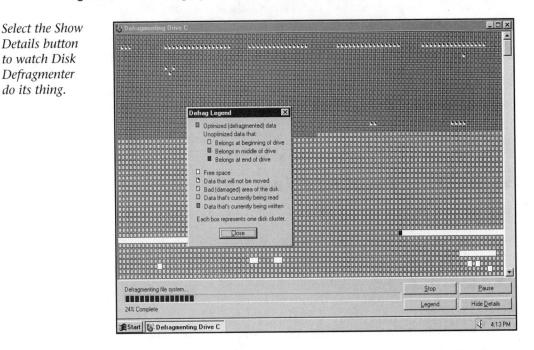

5. When Disk Defragmenter finally finishes its chores (it may take 10–15 minutes depending on the size of your disk, how cluttered it is, and how fast your computer is), your computer beeps, and a dialog box appears to tell you the defragmentation is complete and ask if you want to exit Disk Defragmenter. If you do, select **Yes**. Otherwise, select **No** to continue with Disk Defragmenter.

How Often Should I Defragment?

How often you defragment your hard disk depends on how often you use your computer. If you use it every day, you should run Disk Defragmenter about once a week. If your computer doesn't get heavy use, you probably only need to run Disk Defragmenter once a month or so.

Doubling Disk Space with DriveSpace

Although hard disks have been getting bigger over the years, they haven't kept pace with the ever-fatter programs developers have been throwing at us. As a result, we have a new corollary to Murphy's Law: No matter how huge your hard disk seems today, you'll wish it were twice that big six months from now.

But hey, why wait six months when you can nearly double the size of your hard disk right now? If you have Windows 95, you can do just that with the gnarly new DriveSpace program.

"Double the size of my hard disk?!" Well, okay, DriveSpace doesn't actually make your hard disk twice as big. Instead, it uses something called *disk compression* to make all the files on the disk take up less room. In most cases, DriveSpace can coerce the files into taking up about half the space they normally do. This means you can store twice as much data on the hard disk, so its size is effectively (if not actually) doubled.

The real trick, though, is that you can still use your files as though nothing has ever been done to them. They still have the same names, and they still appear in the same folders. They look the same, act the same, and, for all intents and purposes, *are* the same.

A Technical Aside: How Does Disk Compression Work?

Disk compression sounds like real pie-in-the-sky stuff, but it actually works. If you'd like to know how it performs its magic, here's a look at DriveSpace's inner workings.

Disk compression is based on an obscenely complex mathematical algorithm (called the Lempel-Ziv algorithm) that searches a file for redundant character strings and replaces them with small tokens. Let's look at a simple example. Consider the following phrase:

> *It was the best of times, it was the worst of times, it was the age of wisdom, it was the age of foolishness.*

To compress this quotation, the program starts at the beginning and looks for at least two consecutive characters that it has already seen. In this case, the first such match is the *t* and the following space at the end of the word *best*. This matches the *t* and the space that follows at the end of *It*. So the program replaces the match with a token, as shown here. (I've used an asterisk to represent the various tokens.)

> *I*was the bes*of times, it was the worst of times, it was the age of wisdom, it was the age of foolishness.*

Not very impressive so far. But the program chugs along finding small redundancies (for example, the *es* in *times* matches the *es* seen earlier in *best*), and then it hits the jackpot:

larger phrases such as *it was the, of times*, and *age of* are repeated and can all be replaced by tokens. In the end, you end up with something that looks like this:

I***b******wors******w*dom******fool*hn*s.

It looks weird, but it's less than half the size of the original. To decompress such data, all the program has to do is translate the tokens back to their original form. This is all handled by a mathematical formula, and it's quite safe.

Taking DriveSpace for a Test Drive

What DriveSpace does is complicated, but, fortunately, using the program isn't. As you did with Disk Defragmenter, you should do some preliminary chores before starting:

➤ Use Explorer or My Computer to toss out any junk files hanging around.

➤ Run a Thorough ScanDisk test to weed out any drive errors.

➤ Back up your important documents just in case some natural disaster occurs in the middle of the procedure. (For the basics of Backup, see Chapter 15.)

When you're all set, display the Start menu, open the **Programs** folder, open the **Accessories** folder, open the **System Tools** folder, and select **DriveSpace**. After a second or two, the DriveSpace window appears so you can pick out the drive you want to work with.

Use the Drives on this computer list to select the drive you want to compress; then pull down the **Drive** menu and select **Compress**. DriveSpace examines the drive and displays the Compress a Drive dialog box that gives you an estimate of what the drive's new capacity will be. The dialog box you see depends on the size of your hard disk.

If you have a hard disk with a capacity less than 1 gigabyte (that's 1,000 megabytes, abbreviated as GB), then you'll see the dialog box shown in the top figure on the next page. In this case, DriveSpace is going to increase the free space of your hard disk from about 210 megabytes to about 416 megabytes—yep, almost double.

On the other hand, if the size of your hard disk is greater than 1 gigabyte, DriveSpace gets a little more complicated. When DriveSpace compresses your hard disk, it doesn't just shrink each file separately. Instead, it combines all your files into one monster file and compresses that. This file is a *Compressed Volume File* (or CVF, for short). If you open up, say, Explorer, you won't see the CVF, however. Instead, you'll just see the normal contents of your hard drive.

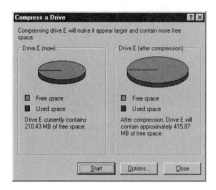

You'll see a dialog box like this one if your hard disk size is 1 GB or less.

If your hard disk is larger than 1 GB, however, DriveSpace has to divide the disk into a compressed part (the CVF) and everything else (the uncompressed part). In Explorer, the CVF appears as drive C, and the uncompressed part (the *host drive*) appears as drive H. (Actually, if the host drive has less than 2 megabytes of free space, it won't appear in Explorer at all.) In this case, you'll see a dialog box similar to the one in the next figure.

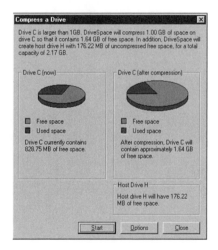

You'll see a dialog box like this one if your hard disk size is 1 GB or more.

Either way, select the **Start** button in the Compress a Drive dialog box, and another dialog box appears asking if you're sure you want to compress the drive. (This dialog box also gives you the option of backing up your files.) If you're sure, select **Compress Now**. DriveSpace checks the drive for errors (yours should pass with flying colors because you've already run ScanDisk) and then starts compressing. When it's done (it takes quite a while for larger hard disks), you're returned to the DriveSpace window.

The Least You Need to Know

This chapter showed you how to wield three of the Windows 95 system tools. You learned how to use ScanDisk to perform a checkup on your hard disk, you saw how Disk Defragmenter can keep your hard disk's hatches battened down, and you learned how to increase the capacity of your hard disk with DriveSpace.

The next chapter continues your look at the multitude of Windows 95 accessories as I tell you about Notepad, Calculator, Briefcase, and even a couple of games: FreeCell and Minesweeper.

Chapter 17

Everything but the Kitchen Sink: More Accessories

One of the first things I learned in my freshman Economics class (besides the fact that I was lousy at economics) was that there's no such thing as a "free lunch." So far, we've proved that the economists are wrong. Windows 95 users get a free lunch that's a multicourse meal. You've ingested WordPad, Paint, and Backup, as well as the system tools ScanDisk, Disk Defragmenter, and DriveSpace. That's a lot, but I hope you still have a little room for a few more treats. In particular, this chapter serves up seven—count 'em, seven—more accessories to whet your appetite: Notepad, Calculator, Date/Time, Briefcase, Solitaire, FreeCell, and Minesweeper. Bon appètit!

(Depending on how Windows 95 was installed on your machine, one or more of these programs may not appear on your Start menu. That's not a problem, though, because you can easily add them from your original Windows 95 disks. You can find the instructions for doing so in Chapter 23, in the section "Adding Windows 95 Components.")

Performing Text File Tasks with Notepad

Back in Chapter 13, you learned how to wield WordPad's word processing tools. But not all the documents you come across will have (or need) fancy character and paragraph formatting. Many documents are pure text files, which means they contain only the letters, numbers, and symbols you can peck out on your keyboard. Although you can use WordPad to work with these simpler document specimens, it's probably overkill. Therefore, Windows 95 comes with an accessory designed specifically for text files: Notepad.

Getting Notepad Up and Running

To get Notepad on the desktop, first select the **Start** button to display the Start menu. Then open the **Programs** folder and the **Accessories** folder; then select **Notepad**. The following figure shows the Notepad window that appears.

Notepad's window redefines "Spartan."

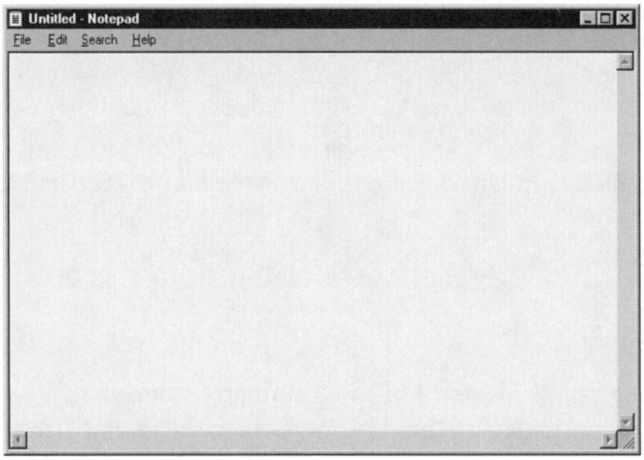

There's not much to see, is there? That's in keeping with Notepad's nature. It's just a simple tool for making quick edits to text-only documents. No one expects you to use it to write your next novel.

Some Notepad Notes

The austere layout of Notepad's window is matched by its frugal collection of commands and features. Check out the File and Edit menus, for example, and you'll see that, for the most part, they contain only the standard commands available in most programs: New, Open, Save, Save As, and Print on the File menu; Undo, Cut, Copy, Paste, and Delete on the Edit menu. Yawn. (I covered all of these commands back in Chapter 7.)

However, Notepad is not without its unique features and quirks, the most important of which I've summarized in the following list.

➤ Notepad assumes the documents you'll open are text files with names that end with .TXT. There are, however, lots of text files that don't have this extension. To see these other files in the Open dialog box, select the **All Files (*.*)** option in the **Files of type** drop-down list.

➤ One of Notepad's biggest limitations is that it chokes on documents that are over a certain size. If you try to open such a file, you'll see the dialog box shown next. In this case, you'll probably want to select **Yes** to open the file in WordPad.

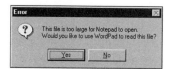

Some documents are too big for Notepad's britches.

➤ If you hit the right edge of the window as you're typing, Notepad may not wrap your text onto the next line. It'll just keep you on the same line for a thousand characters or so! To avoid this bizarre (and annoying) behavior, pull down the **Edit** menu and activate the **Word Wrap** command.

➤ The File menu's Print command doesn't display a Print dialog box. Instead, it just fires the document right to the printer without even so much as a how-do-you-do.

➤ The **File** menu's **Page Setup** command displays the dialog box shown in the following figure. You can use this dialog box to set various page layout and printing options, including the paper size and orientation, the size of each margin, and text that you want printed in each page's Header and Footer. (The **&f** thingy tells Notepad to print the name of the document, and the **&p** combo tells it to print each page number. You can also enter **&d** to print the current date, **&t** to print the current time, and **&l**, **&c**, or **&r** to align the header or footer text on the left, center, or right, respectively.)

Use the Page Setup dialog box to spell out various page layout and printing options for Notepad.

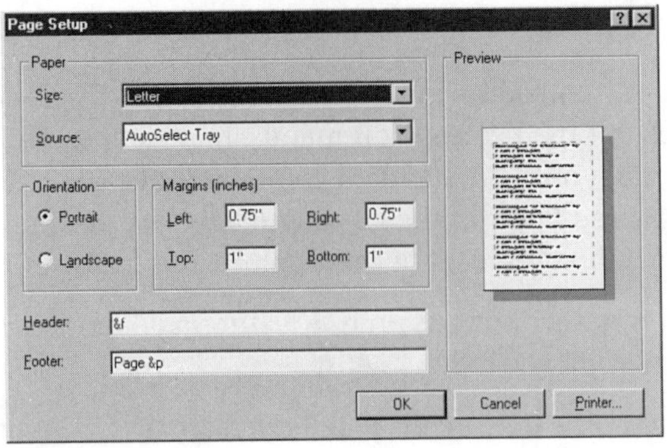

Figuring Out Calculator

Forget your fingers! Windows 95 gives you an easier way to add things up: the Calculator. To crank it up, display the **Start** menu, open **Programs**, open **Accessories**, and select **Calculator**. In no time flat, you see the Calculator window shown in the following figure. As you can see, Calculator looks just like your basic calculator. It won't do rocket science, but it's good for simple operations such as addition, subtraction, multiplication, and division.

The standard view of the Calculator window.

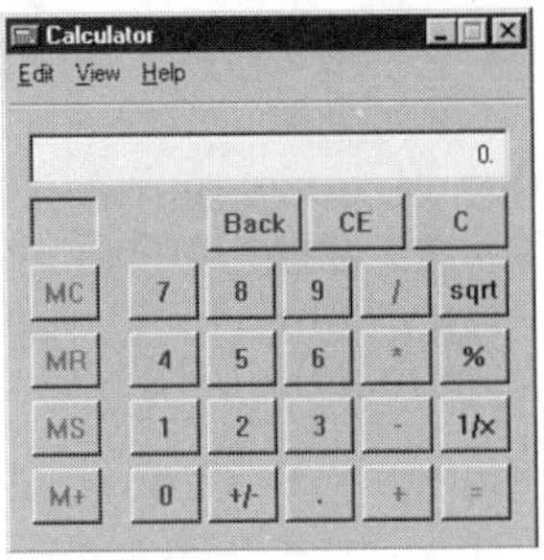

Working with Calculator

Using Calculator is a no-brainer. You just click the appropriate numbers and operators, and then click the equals sign (=) to see the answer in the readout below the menu bar. For example, to add 2 and 3, you do the following:

1. Click the **2** button. A **2** appears in the readout.

2. Click the **+** button.

3. Click the **3** button. A **3** appears in the readout.

4. Click the **=** button. A **5** appears in the readout.

You can even use your keyboard if you want. Simply use the numbers and operators from the numeric keypad (make sure you have Num Lock on, though). To see the results of a calculation, you can either press the equals sign (=) or the **Enter** key. The following table explains the other Calculator buttons.

Button	Description and Keyboard Equivalent
sqrt	Calculates the square root of the value that appears in the readout (press @ on your keyboard).
%	Calculates percentages (press %).
1/x	Calculates the reciprocal of the value that appears in the readout (press **r**).
+/-	Switches the sign of the value that appears in the readout (press **F9**).
C	Clears the current calculation (press **Esc**).
CE	Clears the value that appears in the readout (press **Delete**).
Back	Deletes the last digit entered (press **Backspace**).
MC	Clears the memory (press **Ctrl+L**).
MR	Recalls the current memory value and displays it in the readout (press **Ctrl+R**).
MS	Stores the value that appears in the readout to memory (press **Ctrl+M**).
M+	Adds the value that appears in the readout to the value stored in memory (press **Ctrl+P**).

Putting Your Results to Good Use

Once Calculator displays the result of a calculation in the readout, you can use it in another application by selecting the **Edit** menu's **Copy** command (or you can just press **Ctrl+C**), switching to the other application, and then selecting **Paste** in the application's **Edit** menu (or pressing **Ctrl+V**).

The Scary-Looking Scientific Calculator

Calculator also includes a Scientific calculator that you display by pulling down the **View** menu and selecting the **Scientific** command. As you can see in the next figure, this scary-looking thing is sure to warm the hearts of the tall forehead types who actually *enjoy* using things like hexadecimal numbers. The rest of us can simply shudder once or twice and then scurry back to the safety of the Standard calculator (by selecting the **View** menu's **Standard** command).

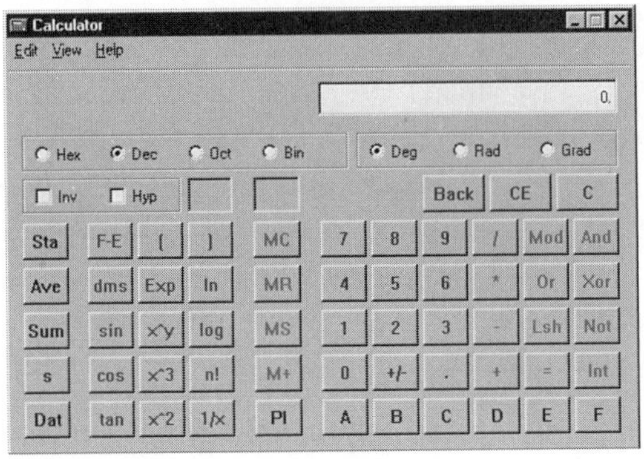

Calculator's egg-heads-only Scientific view.

Doing Time with Date/Time

As you know, Windows 95 displays the time on the right-hand side of the taskbar. But here are a couple of things you may not know:

➤ You can also use the taskbar to display the current date.

➤ You can adjust both the time and the date.

Displaying the date is a piece of cake: just point your mouse at the time on the taskbar, and a second or two later, Windows 95 pops up a banner that contains the date (see the following figure).

Point your mouse at the time to display the date.

Adjusting the time and/or date requires a bit more effort. For openers, display the Start menu, open the **Settings** folder, and select **Control Panel**. When the Control Panel window appears, double-click the **Date/Time** icon (or use the arrow keys to highlight the icon, and then press **Enter**). Windows 95 displays the Date/Time Properties dialog box shown in the next figure.

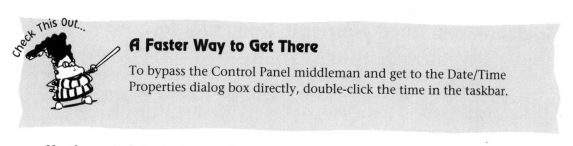

A Faster Way to Get There

To bypass the Control Panel middleman and get to the Date/Time Properties dialog box directly, double-click the time in the taskbar.

Use the controls in the **Date** and **Time** boxes to adjust the date and time, and then select **OK** to put the new settings into effect.

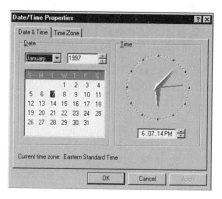

Use the Date/Time Properties dialog box to adjust the current date and time.

Taking Files on the Road with Briefcase

Previous versions of Windows refused to acknowledge the existence of notebook computers. They simply assumed a computer was a computer, and it really didn't matter if you could sling your computer over your shoulder and lug it home at night.

The reality, though, is that notebook computers *are* different from their desktop counterparts, and not just because you can toss them into cases. Beyond the obvious physical differences, most people *use* their notebooks differently than they use their desktops. That is, notebooks tend to be part-time machines, used only when your main computer isn't around.

Windows 95, however, recognizes this, and also recognizes another important fact of notebook computing life: your notebook often has to use documents from your desktop machine. Windows 95's Briefcase feature makes it a breeze to swap documents between a desktop and a notebook (provided, of course, that both machines are running Windows 95) because it keeps track of which files you change. Updating one system or the other takes only a couple of mouse clicks or keystrokes. This section introduces you to Briefcase and shows you how to use it to keep your desktop and notebook in perfect harmony.

Briefcase from Road Worrier to Road Warrior

Long gone are the days when professionals and other white collar types would do the 9-to-5 thing and then head home for some R-and-R. Doing work at home in the evenings, on the weekends, or while on a business trip, is rapidly becoming *de rigueur* for '90s executroids.

Nowadays, hip businessmen and women wouldn't be caught dead without a notebook computer at their side when they leave the office. And why not? The latest models are light as a feather, are no bigger than a sheaf of $8^1/_2$-by-11-inch paper, and are powerful enough to run any of the programs you have on your regular desktop computer. So working at home or on the road is just a matter of copying a document or two onto a floppy disk, and then copying the floppy files to the notebook, right? Hah, you wish!

Actually, it's no big whoop if you're only dealing with a single document. Here's the basic procedure:

1. Copy the document to a floppy disk.

2. Place the floppy disk in the notebook and copy the document to the notebook's hard drive.

3. While you're at home or traveling, work on the document using the notebook's software.

4. Copy the modified document back to the floppy disk.

5. Place the floppy disk in the desktop computer and copy the modified document back to the desktop's hard drive.

As you can see, keeping a single document in sync between the desktop and notebook isn't difficult. (A bit tedious, certainly, but not difficult.) However, things quickly get uglier when you start dealing with multiple documents. What if you only modify some of the documents when you work on the notebook? What if you create a *new* document on the notebook? What if the floppy disk you use contains other files? What if you make changes to the same document on both the desktop *and* the notebook?

These are thorny issues that until now required patience, careful planning, and often some knowledge of techno-esoterica (such as DOS batch files) to overcome. Now, however, these problems are a thing of the past because Windows 95 includes a feature that solves them all in one shot: Briefcase.

Some Terminology Clarifications

I'm throwing around the terms notebook and desktop a lot here, so make sure you know what you're dealing with. By a notebook, I mean any portable computer that's powerful enough to run Windows 95 (which eliminates all the so-called palmtop computers). By a desktop, I mean any computer that isn't readily portable, and so would normally be stationed as a semipermanent fixture on a desk. Also, don't confuse a desktop computer with the Windows 95 desktop (the screen area above the taskbar). In this chapter, desktop means a desktop computer; if I need to talk about the Windows 95 desktop, I'll say "Windows 95 desktop."

Briefcase is a special folder on your computer that you can use to hold the documents you transfer between your desktop and notebook computers. Instead of always copying individual documents back and forth, you usually just work with the Briefcase folder. The real advantage of using Briefcase, however, is that it synchronizes the documents on both machines automatically. If you work on a few documents on your notebook, for example, Windows 95 can figure out which ones are different and then lets you update the desktop machine by running a simple command. There's no guesswork and no chance of copying a file to the wrong folder; no muss, no fuss.

Okay, let's put Briefcase to work. The next few sections take you through the whole Briefcase show—from go to whoa.

Step 1: Load Up the Briefcase

Once you decide which documents you want to work with on your notebook, use Explorer or My Computer to copy the documents into the Briefcase folder:

An Easier Way to Cram Things into a Briefcase
A quick way to copy a document to the Briefcase is to right-click the document, select **Send To** in the shortcut menu, and then select **My Briefcase.**

➤ If you're using Explorer, either you can copy the files to the Briefcase folder in the folders list, or you can drag the files and drop them on the My Briefcase icon on the Windows 95 desktop.

➤ If you use My Computer, your only choice is to drag the documents and drop them on the My Briefcase icon on the Windows NT desktop.

When you copy a file to the Briefcase for the first time, the Welcome to Windows Briefcase dialog box appears. After you read the brief overview of Briefcase, select **Finish** to get rid of it.

Once you copy all your documents to the Briefcase, insert a disk into one of your desktop computer's floppy disk drives, and then use the **Copy** command to copy the Briefcase folder to the floppy disk. (I told you how to copy folders back in Chapter 12, in the "Copying and Moving Folders" section.) Here are a couple of points to keep in mind at this stage:

➤ Although you may be tempted to use the **Send To** command (as described in Chapter 11) to get the Briefcase onto the floppy disk, don't do it. Why not? Because Windows 95 will *move* the Briefcase to the floppy instead of just copying it, and that messes up Briefcase big-time.

➤ If you've used this disk to copy the Briefcase before, Windows 95 asks if you want to replace the Briefcase folder that already exists on the disk. In this case, it's cool to select **Yes** to replace it.

Step 2: Copy the Files to the Notebook's Hard Disk

Your next task is to get the files onto the notebook computer. Begin by inserting the disk containing the desktop Briefcase into the notebook's floppy disk drive. Using Explorer or My Computer, display the notebook floppy drive and open the My Briefcase folder. You'll see a window similar to the one shown here.

The floppy copy of the desktop Briefcase.

The My Briefcase folder has several columns, but three are of interest to us here:

Name   Tells you the name of the file.

Sync Copy In   Tells you the location of the original files. That is, it tells you the name of the desktop computer and the location in the desktop's hard drive where you can find the original files. (The copies of the files that reside inside a Briefcase folder are *sync copies*.)

Status   Tells you the current state of each document. At first, the status is **Up-to-date** because you haven't done anything to the files. The status changes after you make modifications to a file (as you'll see in a sec).

In the My Briefcase window, select the files you want to work with. (You'll usually want to work with all the documents in the Briefcase; if so, press **Ctrl+A** to easily select everything.) Finally, copy the files to whatever destination you like on the notebook's hard disk. (Make sure you don't *move* the files to the notebook, and don't move or copy the Briefcase folder from the floppy disk. If you do, you'll break the link between the Briefcase files and the original files.)

Step 3: Work with the Files on the Notebook

With the documents now safely stowed in the notebook's hard disk, you can go ahead and work on the files using the appropriate programs on the notebook computer. To make sure these files stay in sync with the files in the floppy Briefcase, don't move or rename the files.

Step 4: Update the Briefcase on the Floppy Disk

When you complete your notebook labors, the documents you worked with will be out of sync with the documents in the floppy disk Briefcase. So your next chore is to update the Briefcase on the floppy disk.

First, display the floppy disk's My Briefcase folder. You'll notice two things:

➤ The Sync Copy In column has changed to show the notebook folders in which you stored the files. This is perfectly normal.

➤ The Status column shows **Needs updating** for any files that you changed.

Now pull down the **Briefcase** menu and select the **Update All** command. Windows 95 examines the documents, compares them with the ones in the floppy disk Briefcase, and displays the Update My Briefcase dialog box to show you which documents need updating (see the following figure). Select the **Update** button, and Windows 95 updates the floppy disk Briefcase with the modified documents.

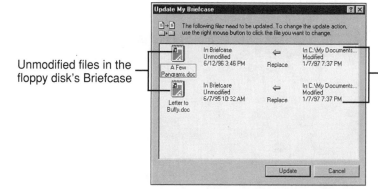

Unmodified files in the floppy disk's Briefcase

Briefcase shows you which files you modified.

Modified files on the notebook's hard disk

Step 5: Update the Files on the Desktop

When you get back to the office, slip the floppy disk into your desktop and open the disk's My Briefcase folder. Again, Briefcase shows you which documents you modified by displaying **Needs updating** in the Status column.

Pull down the **Briefcase** menu and select **Update All**. This time, Windows 95 compares the contents of the floppy disk Briefcase with the original files on your desktop computer. If it finds any discrepancies, it displays the Update My Briefcase dialog box again. Select **Update**, and Windows 95 perfectly synchronizes your desktop and notebook files.

Let the Good Times Roll: Windows 95 Games

You (or your company) didn't shell out the bucks for Windows 95 just so you could keep your nose grindstone-bound all day. Hey, you work hard, so why not play hard, too? Fortunately, playing is easier than ever because you get a fistful of games in the Windows 95 package, including Solitaire, FreeCell, and Minesweeper. The next few sections get your recreation off to a rousing start by introducing you to each of these games.

Kicking Back with Solitaire

Ever since Windows 3.0 was foisted upon an unsuspecting world in 1990, countless corporate citizens have frittered away untold hours of company time by playing a *very* addictive game: Solitaire. In fact, many people I know count themselves as devoted Windows fans only because they couldn't live without their daily dose of Solitaire!

To try it out, select the **Start** button, then **Programs**, **Accessories**, **Games**, and, finally, **Solitaire**. You'll see a window like the one shown in the following figure.

Solitaire: can you say "addictive?"

The idea behind Solitaire is simple: you have to transfer the cards from the card stacks to the suit stacks. Each of the suit stack rectangles holds an individual suit, and you place the cards in order, from Ace to King. To get to the cards beneath the upturned cards in the card stacks, you can move the cards to different rows. However, you can only move a card onto the bottom of a row if two conditions apply:

➤ The card currently at the bottom of the row is one higher than the card you're moving;

➤ The card currently at the bottom of the row is the opposite color of the card you're moving.

For example, if you're moving the 8 of Diamonds (which is red), you can only place it on a row where the bottom card is either the 9 of Clubs or the 9 of Spades (which are black). Here's a summary of the mouse actions you use to play the game:

➤ Click the deck to deal more cards.

➤ Drag the cards to move them between the card stacks.

➤ Double-click a card to place it on the suit stack.

Note, as well, that you can use the **Game** menu's **Options** command to change some game fundamentals (such as changing the number of cards that are drawn with each click of the deck: one or three). You can also change the current deck pattern by selecting the **Game** menu's **Deck** command.

While this little gem of a game is certainly one of the world's great timewasters, it can be frustrating if you don't win as often as you like. (The card "waterfall" that appears at the end of each successful game is, I'm sure, something we all enjoy seeing as much as we can.) To help out, Solitaire has a couple of built-in "cheat" features you can use to put a few more in the win column (how well you'll sleep at night is up to you):

➤ I'm sure many a Solitaire savant has pulled out a hair or two when, during a Draw Three game, the card you've been dying to get is drawn underneath one or two cards in the pile. To get at that pesky devil, pull down the **Game** menu and select **Undo** to reverse the draw. Now hold down the **Ctrl**, **Alt**, and **Shift** keys and click the deck. Solitaire draws only one card this time! Keep clicking until you turn over the card you want, and then resume the game normally.

➤ The quickest road to Solitaire defeat is to miss adding a drawn card to the card stacks. To prevent this from happening, pull down the **Game** menu and select **Options**. In the Options dialog box, activate the **Outline dragging** check box, and then select **OK**. Now drag each card you draw over the bottom card in each card stack. If one of the bottom cards turns black, you know you've found a match.

Filling Your Free Time with FreeCell

FreeCell is a variation on the Solitaire theme. You get several rows of cards, and the object is to arrange them in piles, where each pile represents one of the card suits arranged in order of rank. FreeCell differs from straight Solitaire in that you get four slots—called *free cells*—that you can use as temporary placeholders for your cards.

To start FreeCell, first select the **Start** button to display the Start menu. Then open the **Programs** folder, the **Accessories** folder, and the **Games** folder, and select **FreeCell**. When the FreeCell window appears, pull down the **Game** menu and select **New Game** (or you can bypass the menu by pressing **F2**). FreeCell deals out eight stacks of cards onto the desktop, as shown in the following figure.

Your goal in FreeCell is to move the cards from the card stacks into the home cells.

Free cells ———

——— Home cells

——— Card stacks

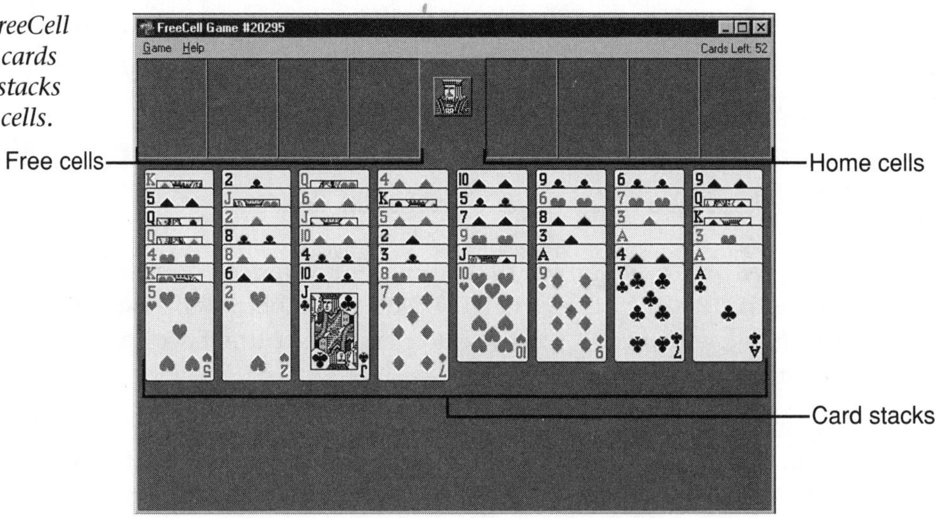

Your mission (should you decide to accept it) is to move these cards from the stacks into the home cells (the four boxes in the top-right corner of the window) while satisfying the following criteria:

➤ One card suit per home cell.

➤ The home cell stacks are arranged in order by rank, with the smallest card (the Ace) at the bottom and the highest card (the King) at the top.

You can use the free cells (the four boxes in the upper-left corner of the window) as temporary holding areas while you move the cards around. You move a card by first clicking it (this highlights the card) and then by clicking another card stack, on a free cell, or on a home cell. There are three basic moves:

➤ You can move a card from the top of a card stack into the free cells only if there's at least one empty free cell.

➤ You can move a card from the top of a card stack or from a free cell to the top of another card stack only if the card that's currently at the top of the other stack is a notch higher in rank and of the opposite color. For example, you can move the six of Hearts (red) to another stack only if the card at the top of that stack is the seven of Spades or Clubs (black).

Free Cell Tip
You can fire a card into the free cells quickly by double-clicking it.

➤ You can move a card from the top of a card stack or from a free cell to the home cells only if the home cell for the card's suit contains a card that is one lower in rank than the card you want to move. For example, if the card is the Queen of Diamonds, you can only move it onto the Diamonds home cell stack if the card currently on top of the stack is the Jack of Diamonds.

The overall strategy is to rearrange the card stacks to expose, at first, the lower ranked cards so you can get them into the home cells. Remember that Aces are low, so they're the first cards you want to expose. Once you place an Ace in a home cell, you can look for that suit's two and move it into the home cell, then the three, and so on. While you're rearranging, you can move cards into the free cells if you need to get them out of the way temporarily.

The Game of Living Dangerously: Minesweeper

Minesweeper is an extremely simple game to play, but it really gives your logic circuits a workout. To see what I mean, select the **Start** button to display the Start menu, open the **Programs** folder, the **Accessories** folder, and the **Games** folder; then select **Minesweeper**. Windows 95 displays the Minesweeper window.

To play Minesweeper, click the various squares you see to uncover what's underneath. Each square will either turn up nothing (which is good) or one of the following:

➤ A mine. When you click a mine, the game ends in disgrace.

➤ A number. The number tells you how many adjacent squares have mines under them. For example, if you click a square and the number 2 shows up, it means that two of the adjacent squares (left, right, top, bottom, or diagonal) have a mine lying in wait for a careless click.

In theory, by looking at the squares already uncovered and the numbers, you should be able to deduce which squares have mines. When you think you know, you can mark a square as mined by right-clicking it. Minesweeper places a flag on the square to remind you the square is (possibly) mined. (If you're not too sure about a square, you can right-click it again to change the flag to a question mark.) The figure below shows a game in progress. You win Minesweeper by successfully marking all the mined squares and uncovering all the unmined squares.

Mark a square that you think may be mined by right-clicking it.

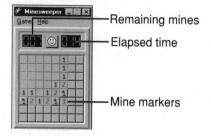

— Remaining mines

— Elapsed time

— Mine markers

The Least You Need to Know

This chapter added a few more courses to the free lunch of Windows 95 accessories. You looked at the Notepad text editor, the Calculator, Date/Time, Briefcase, and the games Solitaire, FreeCell, and Minesweeper.

Your next stop (assuming, that is, that you can drag yourself away from FreeCell or Minesweeper) is to check out some techniques for sharing info between Windows (and even DOS) programs.

Chapter 18

Sharing Info Between Programs

In This Chapter

➤ Copying information between Windows applications

➤ What OLE is, and how it can change your life

➤ Setting up links between the data in your Windows applications

➤ A treasure trove of techniques that'll help you get your programs to share and share alike

The mind is a strange thing. Take my mind, for example (please). I'm constantly forgetting important things like friends' birthdays, paying the mortgage, and doing the dishes. On the other hand, I vividly remember a commercial that was on TV, oh, about 20 years ago. It showed a father eating a chocolate bar and asking his daughter what she learned in school today. She replied, gazing longingly at the chocolate bar, "Shaaaring."

This chapter shows you what to do if one of your applications has the computer equivalent of a chocolate bar (a bar chart, perhaps?) that you want to share with another program.

The Clipboard: A Halfway House for Your Data

A friend of mine in the business world once told me a hilarious story about trying to work out a deal between two people who, for various reasons, refused to talk to one another (and were stubborn as mules, to boot). On one occasion, each person was hunkered down in a hotel suite (on different floors, of course), and both refused to meet on neutral ground. To get anything done, my friend was forced to shuttle back and forth between rooms, relaying curt messages and massaging obstinate egos.

This pigheaded behavior reminds me of DOS programs: trying to get them to share information with one another is at best painful and is usually impossible. Windows changes all that by acting, as my friend did, as a go-between for all your applications (Windows *and* DOS). Windows has a number of tricks up its electronic sleeve to accomplish this, but the two most common are the *Clipboard* and *object linking and embedding* (OLE). You'll examine the Clipboard in this section, and then the rest of the chapter will focus on the hocus pocus of OLE.

Any time you cut or copy something in an application, Windows stores the data in a special place called the *Clipboard*. The data then sits there, waiting patiently, maybe reading a magazine or two, until you issue a Paste command, at which time Windows then copies the information from the Clipboard to the current cursor position in the application. The important thing to note here is that, for the most part, Windows couldn't care less which application it's pasting into. In other words, you can cut or copy data from one application, and then paste the data into something completely different.

The Clipboard's Inconstant Contents

Keep in mind that the Clipboard is a bit fickle, so it'll jettison its contents as soon as something new comes along. If you copy some text and then, say, cut a piece of a Paint drawing a few minutes later, the Clipboard heartlessly discards the text and replaces it with the graphic. In other words, the Clipboard is only capable of storing the last thing you cut or copied. Not only that, but the Clipboard is emptied each time you turn off or restart your computer. (The Clipboard, apparently, has trouble handling commitment!)

Even though you already know how to cut, copy, and paste things (I showed you back in Chapter 7), it's worthwhile going through it again in this Clipboard context. So, for the sake of spelling all this out, let's go through the specific steps required to exchange data via the Clipboard:

1. Activate the application containing the data you want to share.

2. Select the data (by clicking and dragging with your mouse until it is all highlighted, or by using any of the other selection techniques described in Chapter 7, in the "Highlighting Text" section).

3. Pull down the **Edit** menu and select either **Cut** or **Copy**, as appropriate. Windows transfers the data to the Clipboard, as follows:

   ➤ If you cut, the data is deleted from its original location and moved to the Clipboard;

   ➤ If you copy, the data is left intact in its original position, and a copy of it is placed in the Clipboard.

4. Switch to the application into which you want to place the data.

5. Move the cursor (or whatever) to where you want the data to appear, pull down the **Edit** menu, and select the **Paste** command. The data is pulled from the Clipboard and pasted into the application. A copy of the data remains on the Clipboard, however, so you can paste it as many times as you need to.

The Clipboard sounds like some mysterious place, but it's actually just a special chunk of your computer's memory that Windows sets aside for all this cut-and-paste malarkey.

OLE: Can You See?

Now turn your attention to OLE—object linking and embedding. (In case you're wondering, you pronounce OLE as *"oh-LAY"*, like the bullfight chant.) This section attempts to knock some sense into this OLE business by explaining everything in terms we mere mortals can understand, and by placing OLE in its most practical, hands-on light.

The Clipboard method's greatest virtue is its simplicity, but it suffers from two major drawbacks. First, if the data is changed in the original application, the document containing the copy becomes out of date. This has two consequences:

➤ If you know the data needs to be updated, you have to repeat the whole copy-and-paste procedure to get the latest version of the data. And if you pasted it into several different files...you're talking major pain.

➤ If you don't know the data needs to be updated (for example, if someone else changes the original data without telling you), you're out of luck because you're stuck with an old version of the info.

Consider the following scenario: you have some spare time (hey, it could happen), and you decide to write a long-overdue letter to your mom. In fact, to show off your new skills, you decide to do it in WordPad and include some Paint drawings that the kids have done. So you write your letter, copy and paste the drawings, and then print everything out a few days later. When your kids see the letter, though, they're upset because they changed the drawings last night and the drawings in the letter don't show their updated artwork (as a parent, of course, you're *supposed* to know these things). You don't see what the big deal is, so they show you. As you can see in the following figure, the kids went to a lot of effort to finesse this masterpiece. How could you even *consider* sending that rudimentary attempt on the left?

The Paint drawing you pasted into WordPad doesn't change when the kids edit the original.

The original Paint picture pasted into WordPad

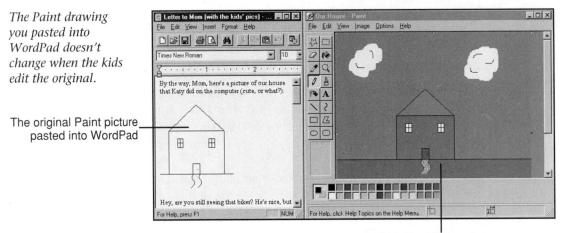

The edited Paint picture

As you can see, the Paint picture has been changed, but the older version you pasted into WordPad via the Clipboard just sits there, blissfully ignorant of the kids' careful coloring job.

The second drawback of the Clipboard becomes apparent when you want to make changes to the copied data. You may be able to edit the data directly (if it's just text, for example), but more often than not you need to crank up the original application, change the data there, and then do the Clipboard thing again. However, problems can arise if you're not sure which application to use or if you're not sure which file contains the original data.

These two drawbacks can create major roadblocks that slow you down when you try to share data between programs. Wouldn't it be great if you didn't have to worry about the updating of shared data? I know if I put together a wish list, it would probably contain two items:

➤ If the data changes in the original application, update the copied data automatically.

➤ If I want to make changes to the copied data, make it easy to find both the original application and the original data file.

Well, my friends, I'm here today to tell you that wishes *can* come true, because OLE addresses both of these issues. To see how, let's examine the three parts of OLE—objects, linking, and embedding.

Object   This is the data that's inserted into the receiving application (it could be text, graphics, sounds, or whatever). The basic Clipboard method sends raw data, but OLE is more sophisticated: it also sends information that enables you to update and work with the data easily.

Linking   This is one of the OLE methods you can use to insert an object into a destination document. When you link an object, OLE sets up and maintains a link between the source application and the object, which means that if the original data is changed, OLE updates the copy automatically. In the example I described earlier, suppose the copy of the picture in the WordPad document was linked to the original Paint file. When the kids made their changes to the Paint file, the WordPad document would have been updated right away, with no questions asked.

Check This Out...

OLE Lingo
To get through the rest of this chapter, you'll need some terminology for the application that creates the original data, and for the application that receives the copy. The official terms are *server* and *client*, respectively, but most people can never remember which is which. Instead, I'll use the terms *source* and *destination*.

Embedding   This is the other OLE technique you can use to insert an object into a destination file. When you embed an object, OLE copies not only the source data, but also all kinds of info about the source application. It's easy to make changes to the embedded object because OLE knows where it came from and can start the source application for you automatically. For example, you can make changes to a picture embedded in a WordPad document simply by selecting it (I'll show how to do this later on). OLE starts up Paint (the source application) and automatically loads the picture so you can make your changes. Note, however, that OLE maintains no connection between an embedded object and the original object. In particular, any changes you make to the embedded object have no effect on the original file.

Should I Link or Embed?

This question, while not quite up there with the major philosophical conundrums of our times, illustrates what is perhaps the most confusing aspect of OLE: under what circumstances should you link your objects or embed them? The answer lies in how OLE treats the source data. When you link an object, OLE doesn't even bother sending the data to the destination. Instead, it sends a "reference" that tells the destination application which file contains the source data. This is enough to maintain the link between the two applications. When you embed an object, however, the actual data is crammed holus-bolus into the destination document.

So you should link your objects if:

➤ You want to keep your destination documents small. The destination just gets the link info, and not the data itself, so there's much less overhead associated with linking.

➤ You're sure the source file won't be moved or deleted. To maintain the link, OLE requires that the source file remain in the same place (that is, the same disk drive and folder). If it's moved or deleted, the link is broken.

➤ You need to keep the source file as a separate document in case you want to make changes to it later, or in case you need it for more OLE fun. You're free to link an object to as many destination files as you like. If you think you'll be using the source data in multiple places, you should link it so you can maintain a separate file.

➤ You won't be sending the destination file via e-mail or floppy disk. Again, OLE expects the linked source data to appear in a specific place. If you send the destination file to someone else, they might not have the proper source file to maintain the link.

On the other hand, you should embed your objects if:

➤ You don't care how big your destination files get. Embedding works best in situations where you have lots of hard disk space and lots of memory.

➤ You don't need to keep the source file as a separate document. If you only need to use the source data once, embedding it means you can get rid of the source file and reduce the clutter on your hard disk.

➤ You'll be sending the destination file and you want to make sure the object arrives intact. If you send a file containing an embedded object, the other person sees the data, complete and unaltered.

Doing the Linking and Embedding Dance

If all this seems a bit confusing, don't worry; that's a normal reaction to all this High Geek techno stuff. If it's any consolation, however, deciding whether you want to link or embed is actually the hardest part of OLE. Once you know what you want to do, the rest is straightforward. However, just to keep us all on our toes, OLE gives us a few different methods to use to link or embed an object. The following two are the most common:

➤ You can copy the object from the source application and paste it in the destination application as a linked or embedded object.

➤ You can insert a new embedded object from within the destination application.

Linking or Embedding an Object by Pasting

If the object you want to link or embed already exists, you can place it on the Clipboard and then paste it in the destination document. If you think this sounds like what we did earlier...well, you're close. The difference, as the following steps show, is that you paste not with the Paste command, but with the Paste Special command:

1. Activate the source application, and open or create the document that contains the object.

2. Select the object you want to link or embed, pull down the **Edit** menu, and select the **Copy** command to place the data on the Clipboard.

3. Switch to the destination application and move to where you want the object to appear.

4. Pull down the **Edit** menu and select the **Paste Special** command. A Paste Special dialog box appears. The appearance of the Paste Special dialog box varies from application to application. The next figure shows the one that appears in WordPad.

   No Paste Special, No OLE If the destination application doesn't have a Paste Special command, it's bad news: it means the program doesn't support object linking and embedding.

   Alternatively, some applications (such as the old Cardfile program in Windows 3.1) have a Paste Link command on their Edit menus. If you want to link the object, you can use this command to bypass the Paste Special dialog box.

5. In the list of data types (the As list in the previous figure), select the first item (such as Microsoft Excel Worksheet).

6. To embed the object, activate the **Paste** option button; to link the object, activate the **Paste Link** option button.

7. Select **OK**. The destination application inserts the object.

WordPad's Paste
Special dialog box.

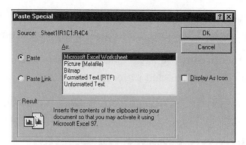

Inserting a New Embedded Object

If the object you want to embed doesn't exist, and you don't need to create a separate file, OLE lets you insert (that is, embed) the new object directly into the destination application. For example, suppose you want to embed a Paint drawing into a WordPad document, but the drawing doesn't exist and you don't need a separate Paint file for the drawing. In this case, OLE lets you embed a new Paint object in the WordPad document and create the drawing right from WordPad. Here's how it works:

1. In the destination application, move to where you want the new object to appear.

2. Either pull down the **Insert** menu and select **Object**, or pull down the **Edit** menu and select **Insert Object**. In either case, a dialog box appears. The next figure shows the Insert Object dialog box from WordPad.

WordPad's Insert
Object dialog box.

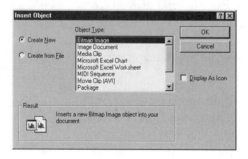

3. Make sure the **Create New** option is activated.

4. In the **Object Type** list, select the type of object you want to create. If you want to create a Paint drawing, for example, select the Bitmap Image object type.

5. Select **OK**. Windows 95 starts the source application for the object type you selected.

6. Create the object you want to embed.

7. Exit the source application. In most cases, you'll do this by pulling down the **File** menu and selecting the **Exit & Return to** *document* command, where *document* is

the name of the active document in the destination application. Otherwise, you exit just by clicking outside of the work area.

8. The source application may ask if you want to update the embedded object. If so, select **Yes**, and Windows 95 embeds the object.

Editing a Linked or Embedded Object

If you need to make changes to a linked or embedded object, you can start the source application and load the object automatically by using either of the following methods:

Updating Your Work In most source applications, you can embed the object without leaving the application by selecting the **File** menu's **Update** command. Since you won't be creating a separate file for the object, this is sort of like saving your work.

➤ Double-click the object in your document.

➤ Select the object, and pull down the **Edit** menu. Now either select the **Edit** *Type* **Object** command, where *Type* is the type of object you selected (for example, Bitmap Image or Document), or select the *Type* **Object** command, and then select **Edit**.

Working with OLE 2 Applications

The latest version of object linking and embedding—version 2—includes a fistful of new features that make creating and maintaining embedded objects even easier. Here's a summary of just a few of these features:

Drag and Drop Objects Between Applications You can move information from one open OLE 2 application to another simply by dragging selected data from one and dropping it in the other. If you want to copy the data, you need to hold down **Ctrl** while dragging.

In-Place Inserting If you insert a new OLE 2 object, Windows 95 activates *in-place* inserting. This means that instead of displaying the source application in a separate window, certain features of the destination application's window are temporarily hidden in favor of the source application's features:

➤ The title bar changes to tell you what kind of object you're now working with.

➤ The menu bar (with the exception of the File and Window menus) is replaced by the source application's menu bar.

➤ The toolbars are replaced by the source application's toolbars.

To exit in-place inserting and embed the object, click outside the object.

In-Place Editing   When you edit an OLE 2 object, the object remains where it is, and the destination application's window changes as it does with in-place inserting. Make your changes, and then click outside the object to complete the edit.

Let's look at an example to see OLE 2 in action. First off, the following picture shows the normal Microsoft Excel window.

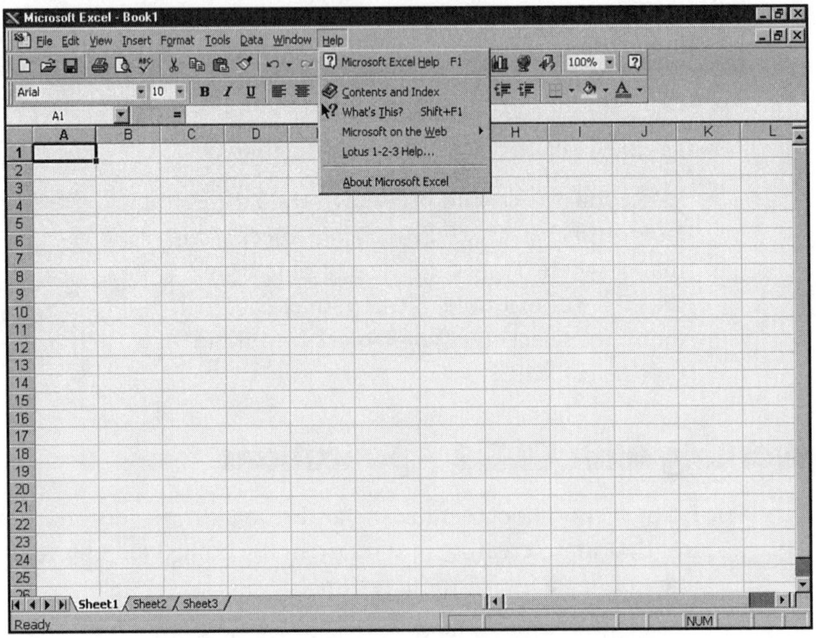

Your basic Microsoft Excel window.

Now I'll insert a Microsoft Word for Windows document into Excel. Word (versions 6.0 and later) is an OLE 2 application, so it supports in-place inserting. As the following picture shows, OLE 2 changes the menu bar and toolbars from Excel's to Word's. (For example, compare Excel's Help menu shown earlier with the Help menu shown in the following figure.)

228

Word's menu bar   Word's toolbars

With in-place inserting, the destination window (Excel) assumes many features of the source window (Word for Windows).

The Least You Need to Know

This chapter covered all kinds of fun stuff about exchanging information between Windows and DOS applications. It also took you on a tour of the strange and wonderful world of OLE.

You might think that text and graphics are about the only things you'd want to share between programs. But Windows 95 also enables you to link and embed sound recordings and even videos in some applications. First, however, you need to know how to work with these kinds of objects, which is just what I'll teach you in the next chapter as you explore Windows 95's multimedia capabilities.

Chapter 19

The Sights and Sounds of Multimedia

> **In This Chapter**
>
> ➤ Using a CD-ROM drive with Windows 95
>
> ➤ Playing with sounds
>
> ➤ Jammin' to audio CDs
>
> ➤ Trying out the Media Player
>
> ➤ Learn what this multimedia mania is all about

There was a time when our computers—big, dim-witted brutes that they are—would just sit there quietly and passively, letting out only an occasional beep to let us know someone was home. Now, however, they've turned into full-fledged entertainment centers capable of showing videos, making realistic burping noises, and even playing the latest audio CD from The Tragically Hip.

If you've heard about this multimedia hoopla, but you didn't know how to become part of the show yourself, step right up. This chapter gives you the basics of Windows 95's multimedia capabilities.

I'll talk about various Windows 95 accessories in this chapter, and you may find that one or more of them don't show up in the Start menu. If they don't, you need to install the missing components from your Windows 95 installation disks or CD-ROM. To find out how to install specific chunks of Windows 95, head for Chapter 23 and check out the "Adding Windows 95 Components" section.

Windows 95 and CD-ROM Drives

You'll be happy to know that Windows 95 and CD-ROM drives get along just fine, thank you. If you had a CD-ROM drive attached to your machine when you installed Windows 95, the Setup program almost certainly will have recognized the drive and automatically set it up for use with Windows 95.

If you add a new CD-ROM drive to your machine, how Windows 95 handles it depends on the type of drive you install:

➤ If the CD-ROM drive is "Plug and Play-enabled," Windows 95 recognizes it as soon as you plug it in.

➤ For all other CD-ROM drives, you need to tell Windows 95 to set it up for use. To find out how to install new hardware in Windows 95, make a beeline for Chapter 23's "Adding a New Piece of Hardware" section.

What's All This About Plug and Play?

Plug and Play is a new standard that should make life easier for anyone who adds new hardware to his computer or upgrades existing hardware.

In a system that doesn't support Plug and Play, installing hardware is often a hair-pulling exercise in frustration. Unless, of course, you actually *like* grappling with arcana such as DIP switches, IRQ settings, DMA channels, and other TLA (three-letter acronym) gobbledygook.

With Windows 95's Plug and Play, however, such primitive rituals become a thing of the past. You can, literally, just plug in a Plug-and-Play-enabled device, such as a sound card or CD-ROM drive, and Windows recognizes it immediately. How do you know if a device supports Plug and Play? Well, the box or manual will certainly tell you, or you can just install it, cross your fingers, and see what happens.

So how do you access a CD-ROM's contents from Windows 95? Easy: first open Explorer or My Computer and then look for the CD-ROM drive icon. (The drive icon that appears depends on the disc that's in the drive.) For example, in the Explorer window shown in the following figure, the CD-ROM is shown as drive D.

```
Exploring - Bookshelf96 (D:)
File  Edit  View  Tools  Help

Bookshelf96 (D:)

All Folders                          Contents of 'Bookshelf96 (D:)'
Desktop                              Name          Size  Type                  Modified
  My Computer                        Aamsstp             File Folder           2/27/96 2:59 PM
    3½ Floppy (A:)                   Books               File Folder           2/27/96 4:10 PM
    Hard drive (C:)                  Iexplore            File Folder           2/27/96 4:24 PM
    Bookshelf96 (D:)                 Mmcat               File Folder           2/27/96 4:25 PM
    Control Panel                    Office              File Folder           2/27/96 4:25 PM
    Printers                         Autorun       1KB   Setup Information     10/9/95 4:38 PM
  Network Neighborhood               Readme        38KB  Text Document         2/26/96 9:38 PM
  Recycle Bin                        Setup         72KB  Application           2/21/96 12:32 PM
  My Briefcase                       Setup         1KB   Configuration Settings 2/21/96 3:27 AM
  Online Services                    Setup.lst     3KB   LST File              2/21/96 12:18 PM
                                     Setup.tdf     1KB   TDF File              2/21/96 3:40 AM

11 object(s)          116KB (Disk free space: 0 bytes)
```

Explorer shows CD-ROM drives just like any other disk drive.

The CD-ROM drive

A CD-ROM drive looks and acts just like any other drive on your computer. Well, okay, I lied: it doesn't act *quite* like a regular drive. For example, you can't move or copy files to a CD-ROM, and you can't delete files from a CD-ROM. That's what the *ROM* in CD-ROM is all about: it stands for *Read-Only Memory*, which, translated from its native geekspeak, means you can only *read* the contents of a CD-ROM; you can't change them in any way. (Here, "reading" the contents means displaying text, viewing graphics, and running programs.)

Many CD-ROMs have setup programs that automatically install icons on the Start menu for easier access. Look for files named **Setup** or **Install** on the CD-ROM. Windows 95 also supports a CD-ROM feature called AutoPlay that promises to make CD-ROMs insanely easy to use. In a nutshell, a CD-ROM that supports AutoPlay automatically cranks up its setup program (if you haven't yet installed the disc) or the CD-ROM's program (if it is installed) as soon as you insert the disc! If you have the Windows 95 CD-ROM, you can give this AutoPlay thing a whirl. Just slap in the disc, and a few seconds later, you'll see the Windows 95 CD-ROM window appear, as big as life. You want goodies? This baby has goodies to beat the band. Just click any of the following icons to get in on the fun:

Don't Forget the Disc!
Some CD-ROM programs won't run unless the disc is in the CD-ROM drive. Once you install these kinds of CD-ROMs, you can avoid a stern warning from the Windows 95 police by making sure the disc is in the CD-ROM drive each time you try to run the program.

    Windows 95 Tour   Click this icon to get the 50-cent Windows tour.

    Microsoft Exposition   Clicking here starts the Microsoft Exposition program. This is a shameless Microsoft marketing ploy that tells you about other Microsoft products available for Windows 95.

233

Hover! Click this icon to start Hover!, a game that makes FreeCell and Minesweeper look about as exciting as watching paint peel. With Hover!, you drive a combination bumper car and hovercraft through a 3-D maze, trying to outrace and outbump your computer opponent. A major timewaster.

Cool Video Clips This icon displays the Videos folder, which contains a few short digital video clips. Some of them are way cool and you'll find yourself watching them over and over. (Deadlines, shmeadlines!)

Browse This CD Click this icon to use Explorer to view the contents of the disc.

Add/Remove Software Clicking this icon displays the Add/Remove Programs Properties dialog box. I talk about this dialog box in depth in Chapter 23 (see the "Adding Windows 95 Components" section).

Sound Advice: Working with Sounds in Windows 95

Take a stroll through any office these days and you're bound to hear all manner of boops, bips, and beeps emanating from cubicles and work areas. You might be excused for thinking the bodysnatchers have replaced your colleagues with R2D2 clones; what you're actually hearing is evidence that today's modern Windows 95 user is truly wired for sound.

If you're sick of carrying on a one-way conversation with your computer (if the yelling, cursing, and threatening that most of us direct at our digital domestics can be considered conversation), you can get into the sound thing by getting a sound card. This is a circuit board that you (or a nearby, easily-cajoled-with-flattering-comments-about-his-pocket-protector computer guru) attach to your computer's innards. Popular examples include the Windows Sound System and the Sound Blaster. Many sound cards not only play sounds, but also let you record your own. (I'll show you how to record sounds later on.) If you're shopping around for a sound card, make sure the card you get is both MPC-compatible (MPC sort of stands for Multimedia PC Marketing Council; look for an MPC logo on the sound card's box) and Plug and Play-compatible. For the best sound, you should also spring for a pair of external computer speakers.

The next few sections assume you have some sort of sound set up on your system and show you how to play sounds, adjust the volume, and record your own sounds.

Sounding Off: Playing Sounds

Sounds you play in Windows 95 come packaged as sound files (sometimes called *Wave* files, as in sound *wave*). Windows 95 comes with a small collection of sound files stored in your Windows folder (look inside the Media subfolder). However, there's no shortage of sound libraries on the market that contain dozens of sound effects (I call them CBS collections: chirpin', burpin', and slurpin') and clips from old movies and cartoons (so you can listen to Fred Flintstone say "Yabba dabba do" all day long).

Windows 95 gives you several different ways to play sounds, but the two most common are using the Sound Recorder and the Media Player. I talk about the Media Player later in this chapter, so let's check out the Sound Recorder method now. Here are the steps to follow:

1. Select the **Start** button to display the Start menu, open the **Programs** folder, open the **Accessories** folder, open the **Multimedia** folder, wipe the sweat from your brow, and then select **Sound Recorder**. The Sound Recorder window appears, as shown in the following figure.

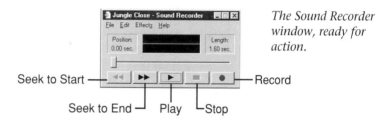

The Sound Recorder window, ready for action.

2. Pull down the **File** menu and select **Open**. Sound Recorder displays the Open dialog box.

3. Highlight the sound file you want to hear, and then select **OK**. (No sound files in sight? Try heading for your Windows folder and opening the Media subfolder to see the sound files that come with Windows 95.)

4. Select the **Play** button to play the sound from the beginning. For long files, you can drag the slider bar to any position in the sound file and then select **Play**. (The Seek to Start and Seek to End buttons move the sound to the beginning and end of the file, respectively.)

Keeping It Down to a Dull Roar: Adjusting the Volume

If your colleagues or family start complaining about the noise pollution drifting from your computer, you'll want to turn down the volume of your sound files to keep the peace. On the other hand, if you can hardly hear what Sound Recorder plays, you may need to pump up the volume a bit.

For either situation, Windows 95 comes with a Volume Control program that you can use to adjust the decibel level of the sounds you play. First, use either of the following methods to display the Volume Control on the desktop:

➤ Display the **Start** menu, open the **Programs** folder, open the **Accessories** folder, open the **Multimedia** folder, and select **Volume Control**.

➤ Double-click the **Volume** icon in the taskbar.

Techno Talk

blah blah blah blah

A Mini Look at MIDI What's this MIDI stuff all about? Well, MIDI enables computers and musical instruments (especially synthesizers) to talk to each other. With MIDI, a musician can crank out a tune on his instrument, and the notes are transcribed automatically on the computer. You can edit the resulting MIDI file note-by-note, or you can alter the pitch and tempo of certain sections to get the jingle just so.

Whichever method you choose, the Volume Control window appears. The setup of this window depends on what sound system you have installed. In most cases, though, you should see the following four sections (as shown in the next figure):

Volume Control This section controls the output of all the sounds you play.

Wave This section controls the output of normal sound files (Wave files) only.

MIDI This section controls the output of MIDI (Musical Instrument Digital Interface) files only. (See "Checking Out the Magical Media Player" later in this chapter to learn how to play MIDI files.)

CD Audio This section controls the output of any music CDs you play (see "Playing Audio CDs in Your CD-ROM Drive," later in this chapter).

Each section has two sliders: **Balance** adjusts the balance between the left and right speakers, and **Volume** adjusts the volume level (higher is louder). Use your mouse to drag the slider bars to the settings you want.

Note, too, that you can add more sections to the Volume Control window (or remove sections you don't use) by pulling down the **Options** menu and selecting the **Properties** command. In the **Show the following volume controls** list, activate the check boxes for the sections you want to see, and then select **OK**.

When your settings are just right, pull down the **Options** menu and select **Exit** to shut down the volume control.

Use the Volume Control program to adjust the volume for the sounds you play.

![Volume Control window screenshot showing Options and Help menus, with Volume Control, Wave, MIDI, and CD Audio sections, each with Balance and Volume sliders. SB16 Mixer [220]]

Rolling Your Own: How to Record Sounds

If you have a sound card capable of recording sounds (and you have a microphone attached to the sound card), you can have hours of mindless fun creating your own sound files. Preserving silly sounds for posterity is the most fun, of course, but you can also create serious messages and embed them in business documents. (Chapter 18's "Doing the Linking and Embedding Dance" section told you how to embed items in documents.)

To record a sound file, follow these steps:

1. Start the Sound Recorder, as described earlier.

2. If Sound Recorder already has a sound file opened and you want to start a new file, select the **File** menu's **New** command. If you'd prefer to add sounds to an existing file, open it, and find the position in the sound file where you want your recording to start.

3. If you want to adjust the quality of the recording, pull down the **Edit** menu and select **Audio Properties**. In the dialog box that appears, use the **Preferred quality** drop-down list to select the quality level of your recording, and then select **OK**. There are three levels to choose from:

    CD Quality   This level produces high-quality stereo sound, but it eats up disk space like nobody's business (a whopping 172 kilobytes per *second*!). Use this level only if you absolutely need the best sound possible and have a few acres of hard disk real estate to play around with.

    Radio Quality   This level gives you a lower-quality mono sound. As you might expect, though, its appetite for disk space is a lot less, clocking in at "only" 21 kilobytes per second. This is a good level for presentations and notes to colleagues.

    Telephone Quality   This level gives you the lowest-quality mono sound, but it usurps a mere 10 kilobytes for every recording second. Use this level for experimenting or creating "for-your-ears-only" sound files.

4. Grab your microphone, clear your throat, get your script, and do whatever else you need to do to get ready for the recording.

5. Select the **Record** button.

6. Speak (yell, groan, belch, whatever) into the microphone. Sound Recorder shows you the length of the file as you record. Note that you have a maximum of about 60 seconds (depending on the settings you use) to do your thing.

7. When you're done, select the **Stop** button.

8. Select the **Seek to Start** button and then the **Play** button to hear how it sounds. If you're happy with your recording, select the **File** menu's **Save** command, enter a name for the file in the Save As dialog box, and select **Save**.

As if letting you record your own sounds isn't enough, Sound Recorder also comes with a host of cool options for creating some really wild effects. Here's a summary:

Mixing sound files   You can mix two or more sound files so they play at the same time. So, for example, you can combine one sound file that contains narration with another that has some soothing music. To try this out, open one of the sound files and move to where you want the second file to start. Pull down the **Edit** menu, select **Mix with File**, highlight the other sound file in the Mix With File dialog box, and then select **Open**.

Changing the volume   If you recorded your sound file too loudly or too softly, pull down the **Effects** menu and select either **Increase Volume** (to make the sound louder by 25%) or **Decrease Volume** (to make the sound quieter by 25%).

Altering the playback speed   You can make your voice recordings sound like Alvin and the Chipmunks or Darth Vader by adjusting the speed of the playback. Pull down the **Effects** menu and choose either **Increase Speed** (to double the speed) or **Decrease Speed** (to halve the speed).

Adding an echo...echo...echo   The **Effects** menu's **Add Echo** command creates a neat echo effect that makes your sound files sound like they're being played in some cavernous location.

Reversing a sound   Playing a sound file backward can produce some real mind-blowing effects. To check it out, pull down the **Effects** menu and select the **Reverse** command.

Playing Audio CDs in Your CD-ROM Drive

Another advantage of having a sound card lurking inside your system is that you can use it to play audio CDs through your CD-ROM drive. That's right, whether you're into opera or alternative, classical or country, rock or rap, your favorite tunes are now only a few mouse clicks away.

The Windows 95 program that makes this possible is CD Player. Before you look at it, take a second to pop an audio CD into your CD-ROM drive. Once you do that, you can display the CD Player using one of the following techniques:

➤ Most likely Windows 95 will crank up the CD Player automatically and start playing the disc. In this case, click the CD Player's taskbar button.

➤ If Windows 95 doesn't start CD Player automatically, poke the **Start** button to get the Start menu on-screen, open the **Programs** folder, the **Accessories** folder, and the **Multimedia** folder, and select **CD Player**.

The CD Player window that appears is shown in the following figure. (If you don't see the toolbar in your window, pull down the **View** menu and activate the **Toolbar** command.)

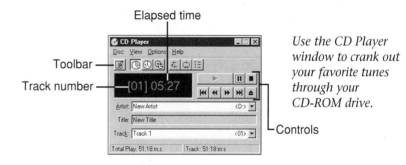

Elapsed time

Toolbar

Track number

Use the CD Player window to crank out your favorite tunes through your CD-ROM drive.

Controls

Operating the CD Player

The CD Player is set up to look more or less like a real CD player. The large black box shows the current track number in square brackets and (once the disc starts playing) the elapsed time for the track. Beside the box are the controls you use to operate the CD. The following figure shows the controls you have at your disposal.

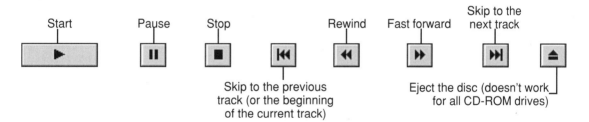

Start Pause Stop Rewind Fast forward Skip to the next track

Skip to the previous track (or the beginning of the current track)

Eject the disc (doesn't work for all CD-ROM drives)

CD Player also gives you a few more playing options, some of which you normally find only on mid- to high-end CD players:

If you want to play a specific track, select it from the Track drop-down list.

 To show the time remaining for the current track, click the toolbar's **Track Time Remaining** button, or select the **View** menu's **Track Time Remaining** command.

 To show the time remaining for the entire disc, click the **Disc Time Remaining** button, or pull down the **View** menu and select the **Disc Time Remaining** command.

239

To play the tracks in random order, click the toolbar's **Random Track Order** button, or pull down the **Options** menu and select the **Random Order** command.

 To play the disc continuously (that is, to start the disc over when the last rack is done), click the **Continuous Play** button, or select the **Options** menu's **Continuous Play** command.

To hear just the first 10 seconds of each track, click the **Intro Play** button in the toolbar, or pull down the **Options** menu and select the **Intro Play** command.

Becoming a Music Director: How to Create a Play List

When you first slip in an audio CD, the CD Player displays **New Artist** in the Artist box and **New Title** in the Title box. Because it's unlikely that these are the actual names of the artist and disc, you may want to fill in the correct information. Not only that, you can also enter a title for each track on the CD, and you can create a *play list*. A play list is a list of the tracks you want to hear, in the order you want to hear them. Amazingly, CD Player "remembers" this info and loads it automatically the next time you plop that particular CD into your CD-ROM!

To try this out, click the **Edit Play List** toolbar button, or pull down the **Disc** menu and select **Edit Play List**. CD Player displays the Disc Settings dialog box, shown in the next figure.

In the **Artist** text box, fill in the name of the group or singer, and in the **Title** text box, enter the disc's title. To enter the track titles, follow these steps:

1. Select a track in the **Available Tracks** list.

2. In the **Track** text box, enter the title.

3. Select the **Set Name** button.

4. Repeat steps 1–3 for the other tracks.

The Play List list box shows the current tracks in the disc's play list (which is every track, at first). To modify the play list, use the following techniques:

➤ To remove a track from the play list, select it in the **Play List** and click **Remove**.

➤ To add a track to the play list, select it in the **Available Tracks** list and click **Add**. (Yes, you can add your favorite tunes more than once.)

➤ To clear everything from the Play List, click **Clear All**.

➤ To change the order of the play list, use your mouse to drag the Play List tracks up or down.

➤ To revert to the original play list (all tracks, in disc order), click **Reset**.

When you're done, select **OK** to put your play list into effect. The following figure shows an example of a completed dialog box.

A sample CD Player play list.

Checking Out the Magical Media Player

One of Windows 95's best-kept secrets is the Media Player application. Depending on the hardware you've crammed into your system and the devices you've installed, this little gem can play sounds, MIDI (Musical Instrument Digital Interface) files, audio CDs, video files, and more.

To see what's what, follow these steps to use Media Player:

1. Select the **Start** button to display the Start menu, open the **Programs**, **Accessories**, and **Multimedia** folders, and then select **Media Player**. The Media Player window appears, as shown here.

The Media Player window.

2. Pull down the **Device** menu and select the type of device you want to use, such as **Video for Windows**. (If you want to select **CD Audio**, first make sure an audio compact disc is in your CD-ROM drive.) In most cases, Media Player displays the Open dialog box so you can select the file to play.

3. Select the file, and then select **Open**.

4. Select the **Play** button to start playing. The following figure shows Media Player's buttons and their uses. (As with the Sound Recorder, you can also use the slider to move to any position in the media.)

241

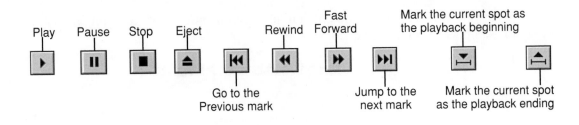

The Least You Need to Know

This chapter took you on a magical multimedia mystery tour. You looked at CD-ROMs, playing and recording sounds with Sound Recorder, adjusting the volume with Volume Control, playing audio CDs with CD Player, and playing MIDI files, videos, and more with Media Player.

Chapter 20

The Typology of Type: Working with Fonts

In This Chapter

➤ Font basics, including the lowdown on those newfangled TrueType fonts

➤ Selecting different fonts, and tips for using fonts like a pro

➤ Using the Character Map program to add cool symbols to your documents

➤ Adding new fonts to your system

➤ Some good maternal advice and fascinating tales of flying buttresses and cars as clothes

"The least you can do is *look* respectable." That's what my mother always used to tell me when I was a kid. My innate messiness meant I couldn't always follow that advice, but it's still something I keep in mind in these image-conscious times. If you don't look good up front (or if your work doesn't look good), you'll often be written off (and your work sent to the nearest trash bin) without a second thought.

When it comes to looking good—whether you're writing up a memo, slicking up a spreadsheet, or polishing up your résumé—fonts are a great place to start. This chapter gives you the skinny on what fonts are, how to use them, and how to add new ones to your system.

Just What the Heck Is a Font, Anyway?

Before I started using Windows, I didn't think too much about the individual characters that made up my writings. To me, an *a* was an *a*. End of story. Windows changed all that. Suddenly, it was easy to produce an *a* that looked, well, different. Suddenly, it was easy to make a really BIG *a*, if that was what I wanted, or an italic *a*, or a bold **a**. In other words, I discovered *fonts*.

Now, sad to say, it seems that I've become a sort of Prince Charles of fonts. No, I'm not having font-related marital difficulties. Instead, I like to look at fonts from an architectural point of view. That is, fonts are to characters what architecture is to buildings. In architecture, you look at certain features and patterns, and if you can tell a Doric column from a flying buttress, you can tell if the building is Classical or Gothic or whatever. Fonts, too, are distinguished by a unique set of features and patterns. You won't see any buttresses flying around, but font-spotters usually look out for the following four things: the typeface, the type size, the type style, and the character spacing.

The Typeface

Any related set of letters, numbers, and other symbols has its own distinctive design called the *typeface*. Typefaces, as you can see in the following figure, can be wildly different depending on the shape and thickness of the characters, the spacing, and the mood of the designer at the time.

Some example typefaces.

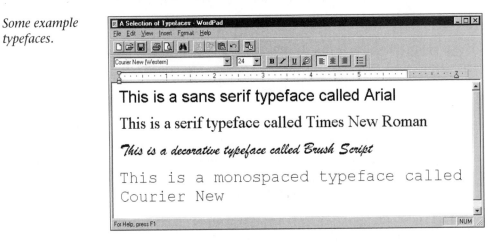

Typefaces come in three flavors: *serif*, *sans serif*, and *decorative*. A serif (it rhymes with *sheriff*) typeface contains fine cross strokes (typographic technoids call them *feet*) at the extremities of each character. These subtle appendages give the typeface a traditional, classy look. Times New Roman is a common example of a serif typeface.

A sans serif typeface doesn't contain these cross strokes. As a result, sans serif typefaces usually have a cleaner, more modern look (check out Arial in the previous figure).

Decorative typefaces are usually special designs used to convey a particular effect. So, for example, if your document really needs a classy, handwritten effect, something like Brush Script (shown in the next figure) would be perfect. Unfortunately, the Brush Script typeface doesn't come with Windows 95. However, lots of companies are selling font collections that include all kinds of strange and useful fonts that'll run you only a few cents per font.

Type Size and Style

The *type size* measures how tall a font is. The standard unit of measurement, just so you know, is the *point*, and there are 72 points in an inch. So, for example, the individual letters in a 24-point font would be twice as tall as those in a 12-point font.

The *type style* of a font refers to its attributes, such as **bold** and *italic*. Other type styles (often called type *effects*) are <u>underlining</u> and ~~overstrike~~ (sometimes called "strikethru" or "strikeout") characters. These styles are normally used to highlight or add emphasis to sections of your documents.

Techno Talk

The True Measure of a Font Technically, type size is measured from the highest point of a tall letter, such as "f," to the lowest point of an underhanging letter, such as "g."

The Character Spacing

The *character spacing* of a font can take two forms: *monospaced* or *proportional*. Monospaced fonts reserve the same amount of space for each character. For example, take a look at the Courier New font shown earlier. Notice that skinny letters such as "i" and "l" take up the same amount of space as wider letters such as "y" and "w." While this is admirably egalitarian, these fonts tend to look like they were produced with a typewriter (in other words, they're *ugly*). By contrast, in a proportional font, such as Arial or Times New Roman, the space allotted to each letter varies according to the width of the letter.

Okay, So How Does TrueType Fit In?

Imagine a world where individual cars, like clothes, can only fit people of a certain size. If you were 5'10", you'd be too big to fit into a car designed for a person who was 5'6" and too small for a car designed with someone 6'2" in mind. Dealers would need huge tracts of land to park all the models they'd need to keep in stock. If the land weren't available, you'd only see a minimal selection to cover the normal size ranges of society.

This bizarre scenario is actually a good description of font technology before the advent of TrueType and other font management programs. For any combination of typeface and type style, you had to have a separate file on your system for each type size. If you wanted to use, say, 8-point Courier italic, you'd have to have the appropriate file. Changing to 12-point Courier italic would require that your application load another file. Switching to Courier bold meant a whole new set of files. And these were just the fonts that you displayed on your screen. If you wanted to print anything, you had to have a completely separate collection of files. Ay caramba!

All these files, of course, took up acres of precious hard disk real estate. If you didn't have the room, you had to go without some fonts.

Scalable Fonts to the Rescue

But just as some genius came up with the idea of adjustable car seats, so, too, do we now have *scalable* fonts. Put simply, a scalable font is one that contains only one representation of each character. If you want a different size or style, a font management program kicks in and automatically *scales* the characters to the new size. It does this for both screen and printer fonts, so when the dust clears, you need only one file for each font family, which really cuts down on the hard disk space required by these fonts. Whew!

TrueType Is Scalable

TrueType, to get to the point, is a scalable font technology that's built right into Windows 95. You get not only a font manager program, but also a collection of TrueType fonts for the program to play with (the TrueType program has no effect on non-TrueType fonts). Here are a few other benefits of TrueType:

➤ It doesn't cost anything. Instead of spending your hard-earned money on a third-party type manager (such as Adobe Type Manager), you get TrueType free with Windows 95.

➤ Because they're scalable, TrueType fonts look good at large type sizes. Other fonts, while they may print okay, display ugly, jagged lines on your screen.

➤ You can exchange files with other Windows users without hassle. With other types of fonts, you never know if someone else can view or print your documents properly.

➤ TrueType fonts can print on any printer that Windows 95 supports. Other fonts are often printer-specific, so if you switch printers, you have to switch fonts.

Selecting Different Fonts in Applications

My mother also used to say that you'll never plow a field by turning it over in your mind—so that's enough theory. Let's get down to business and see how you go about selecting different fonts in your programs.

How you select a font depends on the application you use. Most programs that use fonts have a Format menu with a Font command. If you don't see a Format menu, look for Layout or something similar; if you don't see a Font command, look for a Text command or a Character command instead. (So much for Windows' consistent interface!) In any case, once you find the appropriate command, you see a dialog box that looks something like WordPad's Font dialog box shown here. To display this dialog box, pull down WordPad's **Format** menu and select the **Font** command.

The Font dialog box from WordPad.

From here, selecting the font you want is easy. First, use the **Font** list box to select the typeface. (Yeah, I know, it should be called the "Typeface" list. Ah, well....) Just so you know, the ones with the "double-T" symbol beside them are the TrueType fonts talked about in the previous section.

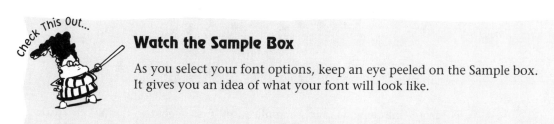

Watch the Sample Box

As you select your font options, keep an eye peeled on the Sample box. It gives you an idea of what your font will look like.

Once you settle on a typeface, you need to select a type style (in WordPad, use the Font style list), the type size (the **Size** list), and any extra effects (WordPad has two: Strikeout and Underline). (Note, too, that WordPad's Font dialog box gives you two other options.

Use the Color drop-down list to change the color of your text; use the Script drop-down list to work with different languages, if your system supports them.) Once you're done, select **OK** to return to the application.

If you highlight some text before starting, the application converts the text to the new font. If you don't select any text, the application displays anything you type from the current cursor position in that font. In the latter case, when you're done with the font, you can return to your regularly scheduled font by redisplaying the Font dialog box and turning off the options you selected earlier.

Getting Silly with the Character Map

A given typeface covers not only the letters, numbers, and symbols you can eyeball on your keyboard, but dozens of others besides. For example, were you stumped the last time you wanted to write "Dag Hammarskjöld" because you didn't know how to get one of those ö thingamajigs? I thought so. Well, hang on to your hats because I'm going to show you an easy way to get not only an ö, but a whole universe of strange and wondrous symbols.

It all begins with one of the accessories that comes with Windows 95: the Character Map. To check it out, select the **Start** button, open the Start menu's **Programs** folder and **Accessories** folder, and select **Character Map**. (Is Character Map missing in action? Then head for Chapter 23 and read the "Adding Windows 95 Components" section to learn how to install it.) The next figure shows the Character Map window that appears.

The layout is pretty simple: the squares show you all the symbols available for whatever typeface appears in the Font drop-down list box. If you select a different typeface, a whole new set of symbols appears.

The Character Map window gives you access to the full spectrum of Windows 95 characters.

To use a symbol from Character Map in an application, first select the symbol you want by double-clicking it with your mouse or by using your keyboard's arrow keys to highlight it and then pressing **Enter**. The symbol appears in the Characters to copy box. When you're ready, select the **Copy** button to copy the character to the Clipboard. (The Clipboard is Windows 95's temporary storage area for copied objects. I talk more about it in

Chapter 18.) Finally, return to your application, position the cursor where you want the character to appear, and select the **Edit** menu's **Paste** command.

A Cornucopia of Characters

Foreign characters are only the beginning of what you can get from Character Map. In the program's Font list, you should also check out typefaces such as Wingdings or Symbol for such exotica as astrological signs, currency symbols, and even clock faces! Note, as well, that some programs (such as Word for Windows and WordPerfect for Windows) have built-in commands for accessing these symbols.

Avoiding the Ransom Note Look

The downside to Windows 95' easy-to-use fonts is that they can sometimes be *too* easy to use. Flushed with your newfound knowledge, you start throwing every font in sight at your documents. The result, as you can see in this example, is usually a mess.

Overdone fonts can give even the most solemn text the dreaded "ransom note" look.

The problem, of course, is that there are just too many different fonts in one document, which turns even the most profound and well-written documents into a dog's breakfast (known in the trade as the "ransom note" look). Here are some tips you can use to avoid overdoing your fonts:

➤ Never use more than a couple of typefaces in a single document. Anything more looks amateurish and will only confuse the reader.

➤ If you need to emphasize something, bold or italicize it in the *same* typeface as the surrounding text. Avoid using underlining for emphasis because it's sophomoric, and some monitors don't display underlines very well.

➤ Use larger sizes only for titles and headings.

➤ Avoid bizarre decorative fonts for large sections of text. Most of those suckers are hard on the eyes after a half dozen words or so. Serif fonts are usually very readable, so they're a good choice for long passages. The clean look of sans serif fonts makes them a good choice for headlines and titles.

Adding New Fonts

Windows 95 comes with various fonts, including five TrueType font collections (Arial, Courier New, Symbol, Times New Roman, and Wingdings). This is usually fine for most people, but there are lots of inexpensive font collections on the market these days. If you buy one of these collections, here's how to add the fonts to your system:

1. Select the **Start** button to display the Start menu, open the **Settings** folder, and then select the **Control Panel** icon. Windows 95 displays the Control Panel window.

2. Select the **Fonts** icon. Control Panel opens the Fonts folder.

3. Pull down the **File** menu and select the **Install New Font** command. The Add Fonts dialog box appears.

4. Insert the disk containing the font files, and then select the appropriate disk drive from the **Drives** list. (You may also need to select a different folder using the **Folders** list.) Windows 95 reads the font names from the disk and displays them in the List of fonts box, as shown in the following figure.

Use the Add Fonts dialog box to add new fonts to your system.

5. To install all the fonts on the disk, choose the **Select All** button. Otherwise, in the **List of fonts** box, use either of these techniques to highlight the fonts you want to install:

Mouse users: hold down the **Ctrl** key and click each font.

or

Keyboard users: press **Tab** to move to the list of fonts. Then press **Shift+F8** and, for each font, move to it using the up and down arrow keys and press the **Spacebar**. When you're done, press **Shift+F8** again.

6. When you're ready to roll, select **OK** to return to the Fonts dialog box.

If you'd like to take a peek at some of your new fonts, you can do it right from the Fonts folder. Highlight the font you want to see and then select the **File** menu's **Open** command. (Or you can right-click the font and select **Open** from the shortcut menu.) Windows 95 displays some info and some samples for the font in a window like the one in the following figure. When you're done, select **Done**.

When you "open" a font, Windows 95 displays a window like this one.

The Least You Need to Know

This chapter introduced you to fonts in Windows 95. After a long-winded introduction on font nuts and bolts, you learned how to use fonts, how to extract symbols from the Character Map, and how to add fonts to your system.

This ends Part 4 and your tour of Windows 95's get-to-work features. In Part 5, I'll show you all kinds of fun techniques for customizing Windows 95 to suit your own, inimitable style.

Chapter 21

Windows Firefighting: Troubleshooting Common Problems

In This Chapter

➤ Handling startup woes

➤ Avoiding General Protection Fault errors

➤ Tackling low memory problems

➤ Mouse and keyboard conundrums

➤ Patching up printing problems

➤ A veritable cornucopia of computer complaints (and their solutions)

One of the biggest problems with computers is that it's so easy to become dependent on them. After having used one for a little while, most people wonder how they ever did without it (I know this may seem hard to believe for some of you, but it really does happen.) So it's all the more traumatic when your once trusty software sidekicks start doing strange and unpredictable things. Suddenly, in true codependent fashion, you find you can no longer function without your programs at your side. Write a letter by hand? How primitive!

So, in an effort to minimize the trauma associated with software problems, this chapter looks at a few of the ways your programs can go bad and offers nontechnical, relatively pain-free solutions.

Solving Startup Snags

Have you ever had problems starting your car? If so, you know only too well the subsequent emotional roller coaster ride: basic shock is the first to hit ("Oh no!"); then comes denial ("This *can't* be happening."); then anger ("@#$*&!"); and finally frustration ("Why me?"). To make matters worse, this only seems to happen on the coldest mornings when you're late for work (chalk up another one for Murphy's Law).

Windows 95 startup problems can be equally frustrating. When you have a deadline looming or an in-basket full of paper, the last thing you need is for your operating system to refuse to operate. This section lays out several strategies for dealing with Windows 95 startup problems.

Windows 95 Startup Options

If Windows 95 won't load when you turn on your computer, there are several options you can try to see if you can coax Windows 95 out of the starting blocks. For now, you need to restart your computer using any of the following methods:

➤ Hold down both **Ctrl** and **Alt**, and then tap the **Delete** key.

➤ Press your computer's **Reset** button.

➤ Turn the obstinate beast off, and then turn it back on again.

While your computer gets itself back to its feet, position a finger over the F8 key (but don't press it just yet) and keep a sharp eye out for the following line to appear on-screen:

Starting Windows 95...

As soon as you see this line, slam the **F8** key (you actually have about two seconds to do this). When you do, instead of starting normally, Windows 95 presents you with a menu similar to the following:

```
Microsoft Windows 95 Startup Menu
=================================
  1. Normal
  2. Logged (\BOOTLOG.TXT)
  3. Safe mode
  4. Step-by-step confirmation
  5. Command prompt only
  6. Safe mode command prompt only
  7. Previous version of MS-DOS

Enter a choice: 1
```

You select an option by pressing the number beside it and then pressing **Enter**. Here's a summary of what each of these options means:

Normal   Starts Windows 95 in the usual way.

Logged (\BOOTLOG.TXT)   Starts Windows 95 and logs the progress of the startup in a text file called BOOTLOG.TXT in the root directory of your hard drive (C:\>). If Windows 95 fails to start, BOOTLOG.TXT should tell you why. To check it out, restart your computer, press **F8** at the **Starting Windows 95_** message, and choose the **Safe mode command prompt only** option. At the C:\> prompt, type **edit bootlog.txt**. Keep your eyes peeled for a couple of lines that look something like this:

[000A94C1] Loading Device = C:\DOS\ATDOSHC.SYS
[000A94C1] LoadFailed   = C:\DOS\ATDOSHC.SYS

This tells you which file Windows 95 choked on. Other BOOTLOG.TXT keywords to look for are **Error** and **Fail**. You'll need to report the error to Microsoft Technical Support.

Safe mode   Starts Windows 95 with only a minimal configuration. Specifically, your mouse and keyboard will work, and your video display will be set to VGA. Other goodies such as your CD-ROM drive and networking are checked at the door. Always try Safe mode first to see if Windows will start with the minimal configuration. If it does (see the following figure), you can use Windows 95 to try to fix the problem (see "Some Safe Mode Diagnostics," later in this chapter).

Step-by-step confirmation   Starts Windows 95 and displays a prompt such as the following at each phase of the startup:

Process the system registry {Enter=Y,Esc=N]?

Press **Enter** to perform the action, and watch your screen for error messages. If you see an error, make a note of where it occurred. You may be able to get Windows 95 to start by rebooting your computer, selecting the **Step-by-step confirmation** option again, and, when you get to the spot where the error happened last time, pressing **Esc** to bypass the process.

Command prompt only   Displays the command prompt (C:\>) instead of the Windows 95 desktop. Once you're at the command prompt, try to start Windows 95 by typing one of the following commands and pressing **Enter**:

win /d:f
win /d:s
win /d:v
win /d:x

255

Windows 95 reminds you that you're in Safe mode by placing "Safe mode" signs in the four corners of the desktop.

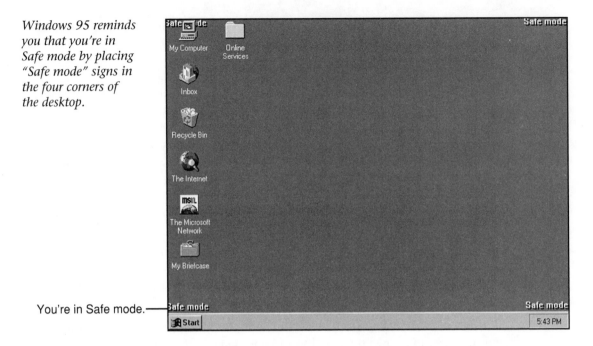

You're in Safe mode.

If one of these commands starts Windows 95 properly, contact Microsoft Technical Support and tell it which command worked. They'll let you know what to do from there.

Safe mode command prompt only   Starts Windows 95 in Safe mode and displays the command prompt instead of the desktop. Use this option if Windows 95 fails to start in Safe mode. Try starting Windows 95 using the commands outlined in the previous paragraph.

Previous version of MS-DOS   Starts the version of MS-DOS that was previously installed on your computer. You'll only see this option if you installed Windows 95 in a directory separate from the one used by your previous version of Windows. This is the if-all-else-fails option.

If you're running Windows 95 on a network, you'll also see a **Safe mode with network support** option that starts Windows 95 in Safe mode but enables networking.

Some Safe Mode Diagnostics

As I mentioned earlier, you should always try to start Windows 95 in Safe mode first. If you manage to get it up and running, Windows 95 has a few tools you can use to investigate the problem. Those tools include the Help system Troubleshooters, the Control Panel, the Device Manager, and ScanDisk.

Help system Troubleshooters   Windows 95's Help system comes equipped with several "Troubleshooters" that lead you step by step through specific problem-solving procedures. (Think of them as the Windows 95 cavalry, riding to your rescue.) To check them out, select the **Start** button and select **Help** on the Start menu. In the Help Topics window that appears, select **Troubleshooting**, and then select one of the topics that appears. For example, hardware conflicts are often a source of startup difficulties, so the **If you have a hardware conflict** topic might be a good place to start. Selecting this topic displays the Hardware Conflict Troubleshooter, shown in the following figure.

The modus operandi of most Troubleshooters is the same: they present some explanatory text and then pose a question. The possible answers appear at the bottom of the window. To select an answer, just click it (or, from the keyboard, press **Tab** until the answer is highlighted and then press **Enter**). If you need to reverse a step, select the **Back** button.

Click these buttons to answer the Troubleshooter's questions.

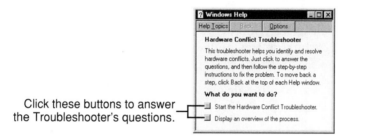

The Help system's Troubleshooters can help you diagnose and solve lots of Windows woes.

Control Panel   To use Control Panel to investigate a problem, select the **Start** button, open the **Settings** folder, and select **Control Panel**. The icons in Control Panel govern the settings for all kinds of devices on your system (such as your video display, your sound card, and your network adapter). Windows 95 may exhibit erratic behavior if these devices aren't set up correctly. Try selecting the icons for your equipment (most of which have been discussed elsewhere in this book) and checking to see if the settings are correct.

Device Manager   The third tool available, Control Panel's Device Manager, gives you a forest-instead-of-the-trees look at all the devices installed on your system. A conflict between these devices can cause all kinds of bad things to happen, so the Device Manager examines your system for conflicts and lets you know if there's a problem.

You get to the Device Manager by selecting Control Panel's **System** icon, and then selecting the **Device Manager** tab in the System Properties dialog box. If there's a problem, Windows 95 displays a yellow exclamation mark over the icon of the device that's stepping on another's toes (see the next figure). Use the Help system's Hardware Conflict Troubleshooter (previously discussed) to get things back in sync.

Device Manager uses icons to alert you to a hardware problem.

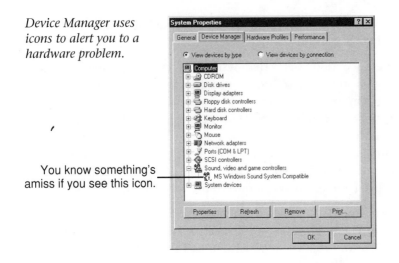

You know something's amiss if you see this icon.

ScanDisk The final investigative tool is ScanDisk. If your hard disk has some files or folders that need fixing, or if some tiny chunk of your hard disk has gone to seed, it could cause all kinds of problems for Windows 95. To make sure your system is fit as a fiddle, run the ScanDisk accessory regularly (as described in Chapter 16, in the "Avoiding Hard Disk Hard Times: ScanDisk" section).

If Windows 95 won't load even in Safe mode, you can run ScanDisk from the command prompt by following these steps:

1. Reboot your computer. When you see the **Starting Windows 95...** message, press **F8**.

2. Select the **Safe mode command prompt only** option.

3. Once you get to the command prompt (the **C:\>** thingy), type **cd\windows\command** and press **Enter**.

4. Type **scandisk** and press **Enter** to start the ScanDisk program. If ScanDisk finds an error, make sure you select **Yes** (or press **Y**) when it asks if you want to fix it.

5. When ScanDisk asks if you want to run a surface scan, select **Yes**.

6. When ScanDisk has completed its labors, select **Exit** (or press **X**) to return to the command prompt.

7. Reboot your computer and see if Windows 95 will start.

The Last Chance Saloon: The Startup Disk

If Windows 95 won't load in Safe mode, à la mode, or in any other mode, your hard disk likely has a problem that has corrupted the files Windows uses to get itself out of bed in the morning. In this case, your only hope is to boot your computer using your Windows 95 Startup disk. (I told you how to create a Startup disk back in Chapter 12, in the "Creating a Startup Disk" section.)

Place the Startup disk in drive A and reboot your computer. When you get to the A:\> prompt, type **scandisk c:** and press **Enter**. ScanDisk will check the integrity of your hard disk (I'm assuming here that you installed Windows 95 on drive C), let you know what the problem is, and (hopefully) fix it for you. Make sure you run the surface scan when ScanDisk asks.

Dealing with the Dastardly General Protection Fault

If you used Windows 3.1 regularly, you probably came across more than your share of General Protection Faults. These GPFs (as they were usually called) were particularly nasty errors that could ruin your data and cause your machine to lock up. Why did they occur? Well, applications, like people, have their own "personal space" in your computer's memory. GPFs occur, basically, when one application invades the personal space of another.

Windows 95 improves this situation by making it difficult, if not impossible, for Windows 95 applications to bump into each other. Oh sure, GPFs still exist (Windows 95 now calls them "illegal operations"), but they should appear far less frequently.

What to Do when a GPF Rears Its Ugly Head

When Windows 95 detects an illegal operation, all sorts of internal bells and alarms go off, and Windows 95 tries to minimize the damage wrought by the wayward program. When Windows has tidied things up as best it can, it displays a dialog box like the one shown in the following figure. Select the **Close** button to terminate the rogue program.

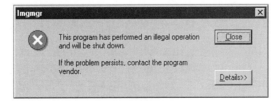

You'll see a dialog box like this when an application is caught trespassing.

If things are really ugly, however, the program may just freeze up solid—and nothing you do or say will make it go again. If that happens, press **Ctrl+Alt+Delete** to display the Close Program dialog box. Then highlight the offending application (it should say **Not responding** beside its name) and select the **End Task** button.

Windows 95 does a reasonable job of preventing programs from running amok and locking up your entire machine. So once you shut down a delinquent application, you can often get right back to work. However, because there's a chance your system may be unstable, it's a good idea to exit the rest of your programs and reboot your computer.

How to Avoid Those Nasty GPFs

This section looks at a number of ways to prevent illegal operations (or GPFs or whatever you want to call them).

If you're running an application written for an earlier version of Windows 95, upgrade to a newer version. As I've said, programs designed specifically for Windows 95 offer the most protection from debilitating crashes. If possible, you should upgrade your existing Windows software to the Windows 95 versions.

Use ScanDisk to weed out disk errors. Corrupted or damaged files on your hard disk are another common source of GPFs. To check for (and fix) these problems, use the Windows 95 ScanDisk accessory (as described in Chapter 16).

Keep an eye on your system resources. You can bet your bottom dollar that a GPF is just around the corner if your system resources drop below the 20% mark. Keep an eye on them if you're working with large applications.

Explorer Exasperations

Once you get the hang of Explorer (which won't take long if you read the three chapters in Part 3), you'll probably find it's one of the Windows 95 applications you use the most. But, of course, the more you use it, the more likely it is that some operation will go up in flames. The next few sections take you through some common Explorer complaints.

Explorer Isn't Showing You the Correct Information

Sometimes, whatExplorer *thinks* is in a folder or on a disk is not what's actually there. (Short attention span, I guess.) You can give Explorer a poke in the ribs by selecting the **View** menu's **Refresh** command, or by pressing **F5**.

You Have Problems Trying to Copy, Move, Delete, or Rename a File on a Floppy Disk

As explained in Chapter 11, Explorer makes it easy to copy or move files to and from a floppy disk. However, you might run into problems if the following scenarios exist:

The Disk Is Full

Explorer, rightly so, won't allow you to copy or move a file to a disk unless there's sufficient space. If the disk is full, delete any unneeded files or use another disk.

The Disk Is Write-protected

When a floppy disk is *write-protected*, you can't copy or move files to the disk or delete or rename files on the disk. Here's how to tell whether or not a disk is write-protected:

➤ When a 5^1/$_4$-inch disk is not write-protected, you see a small notch in the side of the disk. If the notch is covered with tape, simply remove the tape to disable the write-protection.

➤ For a 3^1/$_2$-inch disk, write-protection is controlled by a small, movable tab on the back of the disk. If the tab is toward the edge of the disk, the disk is write-protected. To disable the write-protection, slide the tab away from the edge of the disk.

You Can't Copy a Disk

As I mentioned back in Chapter 12, Explorer doesn't have a command to copy a floppy disk, so you have to head for the MS-DOS prompt and use the **diskcopy** command, instead. If Windows 95 *still* won't let you copy the disk, try these possible solutions:

Make sure the disk is inserted properly. If you're using 3^1/$_2$-inch disks, make sure they're inserted all the way into the drive. If you're using 5^1/$_4$-inch disks, make sure the drive's latch is closed.

Is the destination disk write-protected? Windows 95 won't copy files to a disk that's write-protected. Check the disk and disable the write-protection as described earlier in this chapter.

Are the two disks the same type? The **diskcopy** command is designed to work only with two disks that have the same capacity and are of the same type. (I explained disk capacity and disk types back in Chapter 12, in the section "Types of Floppy Disks".) If you have two different types of disk drives, you can still copy a disk, but you have to use the same drive for both the source and destination.

You Can't Tell Where the Current Folder Is Located

Once you've drilled down into several layers of subfolders, you may forget the name of the main folder, or even which disk drive you're working with. Although Explorer normally just shows you the name of the current folder, you can change that by pulling down the **View** menu and selecting the **Options** command. In the Options dialog box, activate the **Display the full MS-DOS path in the title bar** check box, and then select **OK**. The title bar and the top of the Contents list show the current drive and the folders leading to the current folder (this is called the current folder's *path*).

You Can't Tell How Much Free Space Is Left on Your Hard Disk

With applications growing by leaps and bounds, it doesn't take long for a hard disk to run out of room. If you're not sure how much hard disk acreage you have left, you can find out by using one of the following techniques:

➤ Highlight your hard disk in Explorer's All Folders list, and then select the **File** menu's **Properties** command.

➤ Right-click the hard disk and select **Properties** from the shortcut menu.

 ➤ Highlight the hard disk, and then click the **Properties** button in the Explorer toolbar.

In the Properties dialog box that appears, the General tab tells you how much free space is available (see the following figure).

A Handle for Your Hard Disk

Note that you can use the General tab to rename your hard disk. Why would you want to do this? Well, there's no good reason other than to give your hard disk a more interesting moniker. Just enter a name (11 characters or less) in the **Label** text box.

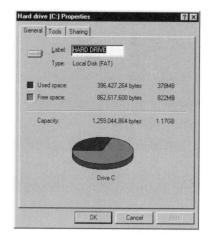

The General tab tells you how much room remains on your hard disk.

Windows 95 Tells You There Is Insufficient Memory to Run an Application

Memory is to Windows 95 what money is to an investor. The more you have, the more things you can do, but if you run out, well, you're out of luck. This section presents a few solutions for those times when money, er, memory is scarce.

Close down what you don't need   The most obvious (but the least convenient) solution is to close any running applications that you really don't need. The bigger the application, the more memory you'll save.

Delete the contents of the Clipboard   However, cutting or copying a graphic image can increase the size of the Clipboard (explained in Chapter 18) to several hundred kilobytes or more. If you run out of memory, a chubby Clipboard may be the culprit. To trim the Clipboard and release most of this memory, try one of the following methods:

➤ If you have an application running, highlight a small section of text (a single character or word will do) and select the **Edit** menu's **Copy** command. This replaces the current Clipboard with a much smaller one.

➤ Select the **Start** button, open the **Programs** folder, open the **Accessories** folder, and select the **Clipboard Viewer** icon. When the Clipboard Viewer window appears, select the **Edit** menu's **Delete** command.

Release some system resources Although Windows 95 has taken great leaps to improve the way it uses system resources, you may still run into problems with certain applications. If you do run into problems, try out these tips for preserving your system resources:

➤ When working with Windows 95 applications, don't leave open any unnecessary document windows.

➤ Turn off program features (such as status bars, rulers, and toolbars) that you don't use.

➤ Run DOS applications full screen instead of in a window.

➤ Turn off the wallpaper on your desktop. The "Wallpapering the Desktop? Why Not!" section in Chapter 22 tells you all about Windows wallpaper.

The Skinny on System Resources

System resources are small memory areas that Windows 95 uses to keep track of things such as the position and size of open windows, dialog boxes, and your desktop configuration (for example, wallpaper). You can have megabytes of free memory and still get **Insufficient Memory** errors if you run out of system resources! (Life can be so unfair.) How can you tell if your system resources are getting low? In Explorer, pull down the **Help** menu and select the **About Windows 95** command. As you can see in the following figure, the About Windows dialog box tells you what percentage of the system resource area is still available. You should start to be concerned if this number drops below 30%, and problems may start cropping up when this number dives under the 20% mark.

The About Windows dialog box tells you what percentage of system resources is still available.

Load larger applications first   Because of the way Windows 95 uses memory, you can often start more programs if you load your larger Windows 95 applications before your smaller ones.

Run the Help system's Memory Troubleshooter   The Memory Troubleshooter can help out with certain kinds of memory mishaps. Select the **Start** button and select **Help** to display the Help topics window; open **Troubleshooting**, and then select the **Memory troubleshooter** topic.

Shell out the bucks to buy more memory   The ultimate way to beat memory problems, of course, is simply to add more memory to your system. (Although, as you've seen, you still need to make sure that your system resources don't get too low.) Happily, memory prices have fallen over the past couple of years, so adding a megabyte or two shouldn't break your budget.

Mouse Mishaps

Using a mouse with Windows 95 is so easy that many people never learn how to work the program with the keyboard. This can present problems, though, if your mouse decides to go wacko on you. (I once saw an otherwise-composed individual panic badly when his mouse quit on him during a Windows presentation; he didn't have a clue about Windows keyboard techniques.) The next few sections show you how to respond to various mouse problems.

Your Mouse Pointer Is Doing Weird Things

Some people would say that the mouse pointer *always* does weird things, but some of the weirdness may not be your fault. If you find that your mouse isn't responding or that the pointer is racing all over the screen, you can usually fix it with one of these easy solutions:

Make sure the mouse is plugged in. Yeah, I know, this seems pretty simple-minded, but the Number One Rule when troubleshooting any device is to first ask, "Is it plugged in?" You'd be surprised how often the answer is a sheepish "No."

Try a mouse pad with a firmer feel. A nice firm mouse pad is essential for consistent mouse movements. If the pad is too soft, the roller sinks in too deep, which can cause it to stick.

Have you cleaned the little guy lately? If your mouse is behaving erratically, all you may need to do is clean its insides. A well-used mouse can take in quite a collection of dust, crumbs, and other alien substances that can play havoc on its delicate constitution. Your mouse documentation should tell you the proper cleaning procedure. If your mouse has a roller ball, you can also follow these steps:

1. Remove the cover on the bottom of the mouse.

2. Remove the roller ball.

3. Using a cotton swab dipped lightly in isopropyl alcohol or water, clean the rollers and other contact areas. (I also find a pair of tweezers or needlenose pliers comes in handy for pulling out the minidust bunnies that accumulate inside the rollers.)

4. Wipe off any excess liquid, and then replace the ball and cover.

Try a Different Mouse Driver

Windows 95 supports several kinds of mice, each of which uses its own device driver. If you're using the wrong driver, the pointer may not move at all or it may do some crazy things. To remedy this, you need to change to the correct driver by following these easy steps:

1. Select the **Start** button, open the **Settings** folder, and select the **Control Panel** icon. The Control Panel window appears.

2. Select the **Mouse** icon to display the Mouse Properties dialog box, and then select the **General** tab.

3. Select the **Change** button. Control Panel displays the Select Device dialog box (see the following figure).

Select your mouse from this list.

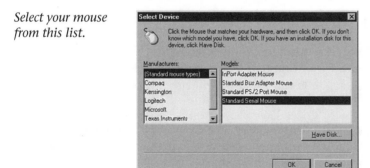

4. Activate the **Show all devices** option button.

5. In the **Manufacturers** list, highlight the name of the company that makes your mouse. Then, in the **Models** list, highlight your mouse.

6. Select **OK** to return to the Mouse Properties dialog box, and then select **Close**. A dialog box appears telling you that you need to restart Windows 95.

7. Select **Yes** to restart Windows 95.

If all else fails, you can often help your mouse regain its sanity by simply exiting and restarting Windows 95.

Windows 95 Doesn't Always Respond to Your Double-Clicks. If Windows 95 ignores some of your double-clicks, you probably need to slow down the *double-click speed*. Refer to Chapter 22 to learn how to do this.

You Have Trouble Seeing the Mouse Pointer. If you use a laptop or if your eyesight isn't what it used to be, you might have trouble keeping track of the little mouse pointer. You may be able to improve things a bit by telling Windows 95 to display "trails" as you move the mouse. You can find complete instructions by turning to Chapter 22 and reading the section "Controlling the Double-Click Speed."

The Mouse Pointer Moves Too Slowly or Too Quickly. The speed at which the pointer moves across the screen is governed by the *mouse tracking speed*. If this just doesn't feel right, you can change this setting to one that's more comfortable. Once again, check out Chapter 22 to get the nitty-gritty.

Persnickety Printing Perplexities

As I explained back in Chapter 8, Windows 95 makes printing easy because your applications get to pass their printing bucks to Windows 95, which then handles all the dirty work. This, unfortunately, doesn't mean that printing is trouble free. If you're having problems getting your printer to print, the next few sections tell you what to do.

Windows 95 Reports an Error While Printing

If Windows 95 can't communicate with your printer for some reason, it displays the dialog box shown in the following figure.

When this happens, try the following solutions.

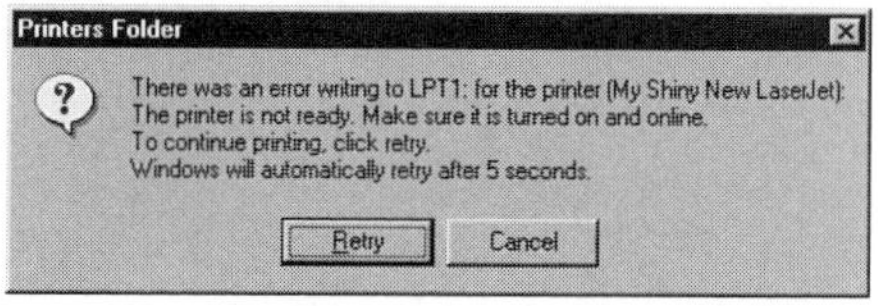

You'll see this dialog box if Windows 95 and your printer aren't on the same wavelength.

Make Sure Your Printer Is Powered Up and Online

Before you start any print jobs, verify that:

➤ Your printer is powered up.

➤ It's online (this means that it's ready to receive output). Most printers have an "Online" button you can select.

➤ The cable connections are secure.

➤ There's paper in the printer.

➤ There's no paper jam.

Tell Windows 95 to Be More Patient

Depending on the print job, some printers take an extra-long time to process the data Windows 95 sends them. If they take *too* long, Windows 95 assumes that the printer is "offline," and you get an error message. To fix this, follow these steps:

1. Select the **Start** button, open the **Settings** folder, and select **Printers**. Windows 95 displays the Printers window.

2. Highlight the printer you're using and select the **File** menu's **Properties** command (or right-click the printer icon and select **Properties** from the shortcut menu). Windows 95 displays the Properties dialog box for the printer.

3. Select the **Details** tab.

4. Increase the number in the Transmission retry box, select **Apply**, and then print your document again. Start with 120 seconds and, if you still get an error, increase the value in increments of 60 seconds.

5. Select **OK** to return to the Printers window.

You Can't Select the Print Command from an Application's File Menu

Most Windows 95 applications that can print include a Print command in the File menu. If this command is "dimmed" (that is, it appears in a light gray text and you can't select it), it means you have no printer installed in Windows 95. Skip back to Chapter 8, and read the "Telling Windows 95 About Your Printer" section to learn how to install a printer.

The Least You Need to Know

This chapter gave you solutions to some common Windows 95 problems, including difficulties with Windows 95's startup. I told you about the options you can use to start Windows 95, the Help system Troubleshooters, how to handle and (I hope) avoid General Protection faults, and how to solve a few Explorer errors. You also examined some simple solutions for memory mishaps, mouse maladies, and printer problems.

Part 5
Remaking Windows 95 in Your Own Image

When you install Windows 95 right out of the box, it comes in a basic, one-size-fits-all outfit. This off-the-rack approach is fine for some people, but the rest of us prefer a little more individuality to our Windows wear. We want our version of Windows 95 to reflect our impeccable tastes, our inimitable personality, and our charming quirks.

Windows 95, thankfully, is only too happy to oblige such rugged individualism. The program comes with a fistful of features that allow you to customize to your heart's content. The chapters here in Part 5 look at many of these features, including customizing the desktop, customizing the mouse and keyboard, adding new hardware and software to Windows 95, and removing detritus that you no longer need.

MORE ROUGE, SUGAR?

PLEASE.

Chapter 22

Makeover Time: Customizing the Desktop

In This Chapter

➤ Playing with Windows 95's colors

➤ Changing the desktop's background

➤ Setting up the Windows 95 screen saver

➤ Customizing the Start menu and taskbar

➤ Creating shortcuts for your programs and documents

➤ A veritable cornucopia of customization coolness

➤ Making your mouse more reliable

Fritterware is a nickname given to any option-ladened software program that makes you fritter away your time playing around with its bells and whistles. Windows 95, with its seemingly infinite number of customization options, is the undisputed fritterware champ. To prove it, this chapter looks at all the different ways you can spruce up the Windows 95 desktop.

Renovating the Desktop

In its default incarnation, the Windows 95 desktop is a rather barren expanse. While this does have the virtue of making icons and other desktop fauna easy to see, it's not very inspiring. If you prefer something with a little more pizzazz, why not go for the gusto and use any of Windows 95's umpteen methods for remaking the desktop in your own image?

For starters, you need to get the Display Properties dialog box on-screen by using either of the following methods:

The easy way: Right-click an empty area of the desktop and click **Properties** in the shortcut menu.

The hard way: Select the **Start** button to display the Start menu, open the **Settings** folder, and then select **Control Panel**. In the Control Panel window, launch the **Display** icon.

Whichever method you choose, the Display Properties dialog box appears, as shown in the following figure. The next few sections take you through most of the tabs in this dialog box. (Note that while you work in this dialog box, you can select the **Apply** button at any time to leave the dialog box open and yet still see what kind of mess the choices you made will make of your desktop. When you're done fiddling with all of the options, select **OK**—or possibly **Close**, depending on what mood Windows is in—to put your changes into effect.)

Use the Display Properties dialog box to customize the look and feel of the desktop.

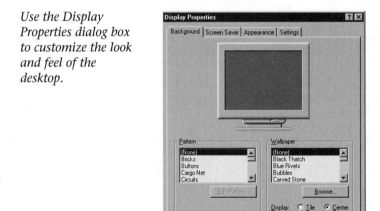

Doing Windows 95's Colors

The scene outside my window on this chilly April morning is not a pretty one. I see leafless, lifeless trees that haven't yet answered the call of spring; I see rain drizzling down in one of those April showers that, allegedly, bring May flowers; and I see a sky covered with colorless, foreboding clouds that promise, for a while anyway, uninterrupted irrigation for all the would-be buds. Yuck!

Believe me, the *last* thing I want to see on my computer screen is Windows 95's usual teal-and-steel, the-bland-leading-the-bland, I'd-rather-go-to-a-yawning-festival-thank-you colors. Teal, schmeal, I say. If you, too, feel like giving Windows 95 a makeover, the screen colors are a good place to start.

The easiest way to change Windows 95's colors is to select one of the predefined color schemes. These schemes control the colors of just about everything you see in Windows, including the desktop background, the pull-down menus, and all the window nuts and bolts (the title bars, borders, scroll bars, and so on).

To choose a scheme, begin by selecting the **Appearance** tab in the Display Properties dialog box (see the following figure).

Watch these fake windows to see what effect your scheme will have.

Use the Appearance tab to select a different Windows 95 color scheme.

The items in the Scheme drop-down list affect two things:

➤ The color of Windows 95 components.

➤ The font used in those elements that contain text (such as title bars).

Stop Squinting!

If your eyesight isn't what it used to be, Windows 95's title bar and dialog box text may be a strain on your peepers. If so, try out any of the Scheme items that have (large) in their names—such as **Rose (large)** or **Windows Standard (extra large)**.

The box above the Scheme list contains a couple of phony windows—one active and one inactive—and a pretend dialog box. By looking at the way your color choices affect these objects, you can see what havoc each scheme will wreak on your desktop, without actually changing anything. Use the **Scheme** list to try out some other schemes until you find one that strikes your fancy. Perhaps the Red, White, and Blue scheme, if you're feeling patriotic, or maybe you prefer something sillier, such as Eggplant or Pumpkin? (No, I did *not* make up those last two!)

If you feel really brave, you can create your own color scheme. To do this, use the **Item** drop-down list to select the element you want to work with (such as Desktop or Active Title Bar), and then use the **Color** list to change its color. (In some cases, you can also change the element's Size and Font.) When you're done, select **Save As**, enter a name for the new scheme in the dialog box that appears, and then select **OK**.

Trying Out a Desktop Pattern

Like the color schemes you saw in the previous section, Windows also comes with a selection of desktop patterns (and some of these have silly names, too). To pick out one of these patterns, first select the **Background** tab. (I showed the controls on this tab in a figure earlier in this chapter.) Then use the **Pattern** list box to select a pattern. The sample computer screen above the list shows you what each pattern looks like.

Wallpapering the Desktop? Why Not!

In the real world, wallpapering is a chore that, for most people, ranks right up there with grouting the bathtub and shampooing the cat. Fortunately, this isn't the real world, and wallpapering the Windows 95 desktop is actually quite entertaining.

On the **Background** tab, use the **Wallpaper** list to browse through the selection of wallpapers. When you see one that sounds like fun, highlight it and check out the sample computer screen. (Note that most of the wallpapers are just tiny squares; to get the full effect, you need to make sure to select the **Tile** option.)

Screen Saver Silliness

In olden times (say, five or six years ago), monitors weren't as good as they are today, and most of us struggled along using ugly DOS screens. One of the problems people faced was leaving their monitors on too long and ending up with some DOS hieroglyphics burned permanently into the screen (this is usually referred to, not surprisingly, as *burn-in*). To prevent this from happening, some genius came up with the idea of a *screen saver*: a program that automatically kicks in after the computer is idle for a few minutes. The screen saver displays some kind of moving pattern on the screen that helps prevent burn-in. However, with a simple touch of a key or jiggle of a mouse, the normal screen returns, unharmed and none the worse for wear.

Nowadays, it's pretty tough to burn an image into your screen. Improvements in monitor quality and the graphical nature of Windows 95 have made such a fate virtually impossible. Curiously, though, screen savers are still around and are, in fact, flourishing. The reason: most of them are just plain cool. Who cares about preventing burn-in when you can watch wild, psychedelic patterns or your favorite cartoon every few minutes?

There are scads of commercial screen savers on the market, and Windows 95 comes equipped with some of its own. To try them out, select the **Screen Saver** tab in the Display Properties dialog box (see the next figure), drop down the **Screen Saver** list, and select a screen saver.

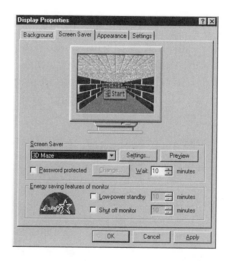

Use the Screen Saver tab to pick out a Windows 95 screen saver.

You can also choose the following options:

Wait This spinner controls the amount of time your computer must be inactive before the screen saver starts doing its thing. You can enter a number between 1 and 60 minutes.

Preview Select this button to give the screen saver a trial run. To return to the dialog box, move your mouse or press any key.

Settings Select this button to set various options for the screen saver. The Setup dialog box that appears depends on which screen saver you chose. Choose the options you want, and then select **OK** to return to the Display Properties dialog box.

Password protected Activate this check box if you want Windows 95 not to stop the screen saver unless the correct password is entered. (You specify a password by clicking the Change button and entering the password—twice—in the dialog box that appears.)

Depending on the monitor you have, you may also see a group named Energy saving features of monitor. You can use these settings to save energy when your computer isn't used:

Low-power standby Activate this check box to have Windows 95 put your monitor in "standby mode" after the number of minutes specified in the spinner. This means your monitor screen turns black, but that a simple mouse jiggle or keystroke will bring it back to life.

Shut off monitor Activate this check box to have Windows 95 turn off your monitor altogether after the number of minutes specified in the spinner. In this case, you have to punch the monitor's "On" button to get the screen back.

Customizing the Taskbar and Start Menu

As you've seen throughout most of this book, the taskbar and the Start menu are two of Windows 95's truly indispensable features. So it's nice to know that, handy as they are, there are ways to make both the taskbar and the Start menu even handier. It's all done through the Taskbar Properties dialog box, which you can plop onto the desktop using either of the following methods:

➤ Select the **Start** button, open the Start menu's **Settings** folder, and select **Taskbar**.

➤ Right-click an empty part of the taskbar and select **Properties** from the shortcut menu.

Windows 95 displays the Taskbar Properties dialog box, shown next. The next couple of sections give you the scoop on the options available in this dialog box. When you complete your labors in this dialog box, select **OK** to put your changes into effect.

Use the Taskbar Properties dialog box to renovate the taskbar and Start menu.

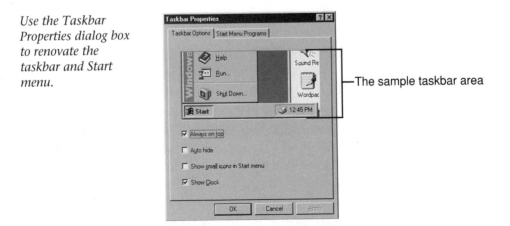

The sample taskbar area

Some Taskbar Tidbits

The Taskbar Options tab presents several check boxes that control the behavior of the taskbar. Here's a rundown:

Always on top   As you saw back in Chapter 9, when you maximize a program's window, it enlarges to consume all of the screen *except* for the taskbar. If you want to eke out a little bit of extra screen acreage for your programs, deactivate the **Always on top** check box. Then, when you maximize a program, its window takes up the entire screen, taskbar and all. The taskbar is still there, but the window now sits "on top" of it, which means, of course, that you lose all the convenience of the taskbar. Pitsville. However, all is not lost: you can get the taskbar back on-screen by pressing **Ctrl+Esc** to display both the taskbar and Start menu, and then pressing **Esc** by itself to close the Start menu.

Watch the Sample Taskbar   The Taskbar Options tab displays a sample taskbar and Start menu in a box above the check boxes. As you play with the various settings, keep an eye on this area to see what effect each option has on the taskbar.

Auto hide   This check box gives you a better way to create more room for your programs to roam. When you activate **Auto hide**, Windows 95 reduces the taskbar to a thin, gray line at the bottom of the screen whenever you work in a program's window. This gives you, effectively, the entire screen to work with. The trick, though, is that you can redisplay the full taskbar simply by moving your mouse pointer to the bottom of the screen. Move the mouse back up again, and the taskbar retreats to its gray line.

Show small icons in Start menu   Activating this check box reduces the icons used for each item in the Start menu to smaller, cuter, versions of themselves. Although this makes each icon a little harder to see, it reduces the overall size of the Start menus, which makes them a bit easier to navigate.

Show Clock   This check box toggles the Clock in the bottom-right corner on and off. If you're not into time, man, deactivate this check box.

Adding Items to the Start Menu

When you install a program, it's usually decent enough to add an icon for itself to your Start menu. However, most DOS-based programs wouldn't know the Start menu from a

Denny's menu, so they won't create Start menu icons for themselves. DOS programs, Windows-ignorant savages that they are, have an excuse, but you may come across a few ornery Windows-based programs that won't do it, either. That means you have to add these programs to the Start menu (ugh) manually. To give it a go, follow these steps:

1. Select the **Start Menu Programs** tab in the Taskbar Properties dialog box, and then select the **Add** button to display the Create Shortcut dialog box, shown on the next figure.

Why Is It Called a "Shortcut"?

Well, because the icons you select on the Start menu aren't the programs themselves. You simply use them to tell Windows 95, "Yo, I want to start this program. *You* do all the hard work of finding the file and cranking it up." So, in that sense, a Start menu icon is a shortcut because it's a faster way for you to start your programs.

Use the Create Shortcut dialog box to fire a program onto the Start menu.

2. If you happen to know the name of the file that starts the program, and if you know the drive and folder where it resides, type all that in the **Command line** text box. For example, suppose the file that starts your program is WP51.EXE, and it's on drive C in the WP51 folder. Then enter the following in the **Command line** box: **c:\wp51\wp51.exe**.

    If you're not sure about any of this, select the **Browse** button to display the Browse dialog box, hunt down the file that starts the program, highlight it, and then select **Open**.

3. Select **Next >**. Windows 95 displays the Select Program Folder dialog box, shown in the following figure.

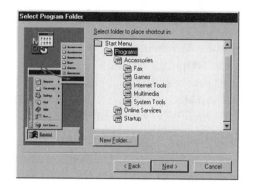

Use the Select Program Folder dialog box to pick out a Start menu home for your program.

4. Highlight the folder where you want the program's icon to appear. Note that if you highlight Start Menu, the icon appears on the main Start menu (the one that appears when you select the Start button). If you highlight Desktop, the program's icon appears right on the Windows 95 desktop. (For the latter, however, you can only start the program by double-clicking it; for more about desktop shortcuts, see the section "Easy Program Access: Creating Shortcuts on the Desktop," later in this chapter.)

5. Select **Next** >. The Select a Title for the Program dialog box appears.

6. Use the **Select a name for the shortcut** text box to enter the name you want to appear on the Start menu.

7. Select **Finish** to, well, finish.

Starting Programs Automatically When You Start Windows 95

Windows 95 has a slick feature that makes starting programs a breeze: the Startup folder. The icons you stuff into this folder load automatically each time you start Windows 95. This is great for applications that you use constantly, such as WordPad or Explorer, or for documents (such as a to-do list) that you start up first thing every day.

Use the same technique I outlined in the previous section to create a Start menu icon for the program or document. When you get to Step 4, highlight the **Startup** folder. When you're done, you can see what's in your Startup folder by selecting the **Start** button, opening the **Programs** folder, and then opening the **Startup** folder.

279

Removing Items from the Start Menu

As you'll see in Chapter 24, Windows 95 has a feature that enables you to "uninstall" some programs. (See the "Wiping a Program Off Your Computer" section.) One of the chores this feature takes care of for you is to expunge any traces of the program from the Start menu. If it misses something, however, or if you need to get rid of a Start menu shortcut that you added manually, you need to clean up the Start menu yourself.

To try it, select the **Start Menu Programs** tab in the Taskbar Properties dialog box, and then select the **Remove** button to display the Remove Shortcuts/Folders dialog box Open the folder containing the shortcut, highlight the shortcut, and then select **Remove**. Select **Close** to head back to the Taskbar Properties dialog box.

Making More Room to Maneuver on the Taskbar

Although you'll probably only work with, at most, a few programs at once, Windows 95's multitasking capabilities sure make it tempting to open a boatload of applications. The problem, though, is that it doesn't take long for the taskbar to become seriously over-populated. As you can see in the following figure, with ten programs on the go, the taskbar buttons become all but indecipherable. ("Hey, Vern! What's this here 'Ph...' program supposed to do?") If you can't figure out what a particular taskbar button represents, point your mouse at the button you're puzzling over, and after a couple of seconds a banner appears telling you the full name of the program.

An example of taskbar overcrowding.

If you'd prefer to take in everything at a glance and you don't mind giving up a little more screen area, you can expand the taskbar to show two or more rows of buttons. To give 'er a go, point your mouse at the top edge of the taskbar (when it's positioned properly, the pointer changes to a two-headed arrow). Then drag the edge of the taskbar up until you see the dotted line above the taskbar. When you release the mouse button, Windows 95 expands the taskbar (see the following figure). You can enlarge the taskbar to include as many as ten (!) rows.

With two rows, the buttons have some breathing room.

Easy Program Access: Creating Shortcuts on the Desktop

For our final desktop customization trick, I'll show you some other methods for creating shortcuts directly on the Windows 95 desktop. Why would you want to do that? Well, anything on the desktop is accessible with a simple double-click, so there are lots of good reasons for such convenience.

A Desktop Shortcut Bonus As an added bonus, if you have a folder or disk drive shortcut on the desktop, you can move or copy files by dragging them from Explorer or My Computer and dropping them on the shortcut.

➤ If you have a favorite program buried under interminable Start menu folders, placing a shortcut for it on the desktop lets you crank it up lickety-split.

➤ If you have a document you use regularly (such as a to-do list or, like me, a never-put-off-until-tomorrow-what-you-can-put-off-until-the-day-after-tomorrow list), you can create a shortcut for the document to keep it within easy reach.

➤ If you do a lot of work in a particular folder, you can create a shortcut for the folder. Double-clicking the folder's shortcut icon opens the folder right away. (No more wading through windows in My Computer, or tracking down the folder in Explorer.)

➤ You can also create shortcuts for disk drives. So, for example, you might want to add a shortcut for your CD-ROM drive or for a floppy disk drive.

➤ Printers are shortcut candidates, too. If you create a printer shortcut, you have quick access to your printer's folder so you can watch the progress of your print jobs. You can also drag a document from Explorer or My Computer, drop it on the printer, and Windows 95 will print it for you, no questions asked!

As you saw earlier, you can use the Taskbar Properties dialog box to add shortcuts to the desktop. But Windows 95, of course, never gives you just one way to do anything. So, as a public service (it's a tough job but, hey, somebody's gotta do it), here are three other methods you can use:

➤ Right-click an empty part of the desktop, select **New** in the shortcut menu, and select **Shortcut**. Follow the instructions given earlier to fill out the Create Shortcut dialog box that appears.

➤ In Explorer, highlight **Desktop** at the top of the All Folders list, select the **File** menu's **New** command, and then select **Shortcut** (or right-click **Desktop**, select **New**, and select **Shortcut**). Again, fill out the Create Shortcut dialog box.

281

➤ Drag the program, document, folder, drive, Control Panel item, printer, or whatever from Explorer (or My Computer) and drop it on the desktop. If Windows 95 asks if you want to create a shortcut for the item, select **Yes**.

Drag-and-Drop Warning! If you drag a file or folder onto the desktop, Windows 95 moves it there. To create a shortcut, instead, right-drag the file or folder and then, when you drop it on the desktop, select **Create Shortcut(s) Here** from the menu.

The following figure shows my desktop with a random sampling of shortcuts. Notice that each shortcut icon has a small arrow in the lower-left corner; this is Windows 95's way of telling you that an icon is a shortcut.

Are you wondering how I got my shortcuts to line up in apple-pie order? It's easy: just right-click on an empty part of the desktop, select **Arrange Icons** from the shortcut menu, and then select **by Name**, **by Type**, **by Size**, or **by Date**, by Jove. Neat freaks can also activate the **Auto Arrange** command to tell Windows 95 to keep the desktop spic-and-span all the time.

Desktop shortcuts give you easy double-click access to programs, files, folders, drives, printers, and more.

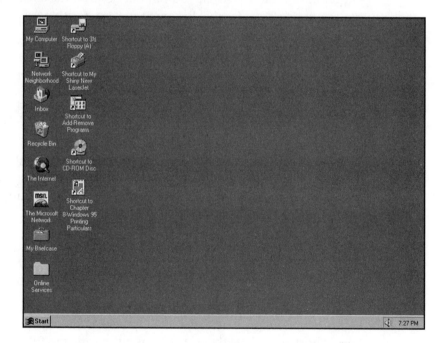

To delete a shortcut, either right-click it and select **Delete** from the menu, or drag the shortcut into the **Recycle Bin**. (If you use the right-click method, a dialog box appears asking if you're sure you want to delete the shortcut. In this case, select **Yes**.) Note, however, that deleting a shortcut does *not* delete the program, file, folder, or whatever, only the shortcut icon.

Sharing Your Computer? Here's How to Avoid Fistfights

Do you share your computer with other people either at work or at home? Then you've probably run smack dab into one undeniable fact: people are individuals with minds of their own! One person prefers Windows in a black-and-purple color scheme; another person just loves that annoying "Bubbles" wallpaper; yet another person prefers to have a zillion shortcuts on the Windows 95 desktop; and, of course, *everybody* uses a different mix of applications. How can you possibly satisfy all these diverse tastes and prevent people from coming to blows?

Well, it's a lot easier than you might think. Windows 95 enables you to set up a different *user profile* for each person who uses the computer. Each profile includes all the customization stuff covered in this chapter, such as colors, patterns or wallpapers, shortcut icons, the screen saver, and the programs that appear on the Start menu.

This means that each person can customize Windows 95 to his or her heart's content without foisting their tastes on anyone else. To set up a user profile, follow these steps:

1. Select the **Start** button, open the **Settings** folder, and select the **Control Panel** icon. Windows 95 throws the Control Panel window on the screen.

2. Select the **Passwords** icon and, in the Passwords Properties dialog box that appears, select the **User Profiles** tab.

3. Activate the **Users can customize their preferences and desktop settings** option button, activate the two check boxes in the **User Profile Settings** box, and then select **OK**. Windows 95 asks if you want to restart your computer.

4. Select **Yes**.

When Windows 95 reloads (and each subsequent time you crank up Windows 95), you see the Welcome to Windows dialog box. The idea here is that each person who uses the computer will have his or her own user name, which Windows will use to save his or her settings. So when you log on, you type your user name in the **User name** field, type an optional password in the **Password** field, and then select **OK**. If this is the first time you've entered your password (even if you leave it blank), the Set Windows Password dialog box appears. In the **Confirm new password** text box, enter the password again and select **OK**.

A Faster Way to Log On

If someone else logged on to Windows 95 and you prefer to use your settings, you don't have to restart Windows. Instead, select the **Start** button and select the **Shut Down** command. In the Shut Down Windows dialog box that appears, activate the **Close all programs and log on as a different user?** option and then select **Yes**.

If this is the first time you've logged on, the Windows Networking dialog box appears to ask if you want Windows 95 to save your settings. Select **Yes**. Windows 95 loads normally, and you can start customizing willy-nilly.

The Made-to-Measure Mouse

In *Star Trek* and other sci-fi stories, the computers of the future are operated by voice commands. You simply say, "Computer!" and a couple of high-tech-sounding beeps tell you the computer is ready to obey your commands. In one of the *Star Trek* movies, the crew of the Enterprise travels back in time to modern-day Earth. There, Scotty (the engineer) has to use a late '80s-vintage PC (a Macintosh, I think). So, of course, he says "Computer!" and is disappointed when nothing happens. Then one of the locals hands the mouse to Scotty who puts it in front of his mouth and yells "Hello Computer!" as though he were speaking into a microphone!

I'm sure few of you have mistaken your mice for microphones (there's an idea for you budding entrepreneurs: micerophones!), but a mouse isn't an obvious tool to wield. For many new users, the biggest obstacle to overcome when learning Windows 95 is learning how to use a mouse for the first time. The problems range from controlling it, to getting double-clicks to work properly, to just finding the darn pointer! For the most part, these problems resolve themselves as people get used to the little rodent. However, the Windows 95 programmers were thoughtful enough to include some mouse customization features so you can set up the mouse just the way you likes it.

To see these options, select the **Start** button, open the **Settings** folder, and select **Control Panel**. In the Control Panel window, open the **Mouse** icon. The Mouse Properties dialog box appears, as shown here. The next few sections take you through using most of the controls in this dialog box. When you're done, select **OK** to put your new mega-mouse settings into effect.

Use the options in the Mouse Properties dialog box to customize your mouse.

Setting Up the Mouse for Left-Handers

Most mice and the applications that use them are "handists": they assume the user is right-handed. Southpaws, if you're tired of this politically incorrect discrimination, you can get a small measure of revenge by swapping the left and right buttons on your mouse. All you have to do is select the **Buttons** tab in the Mouse Properties dialog box and activate the **Left-handed** option button. This affects your mouse movements in the following ways:

➤ You now click and double-click with the right mouse button.

➤ To drag something, you press and hold down the right button.

➤ To display a shortcut menu (or a *context menu* as it's called in the Mouse Properties dialog box), left-click an object.

➤ To perform the "special drag" in Explorer (the one that displays a shortcut menu when you drop a file or folder), you use the left mouse button.

Controlling the Double-Click Speed

One of the things that a mouse-aware program must do is distinguish between two consecutive single clicks and a double-click. For example, if you click once, wait five seconds, and then click again, that qualifies as two single clicks in most people's books. But what if there's only a second between clicks? Or a half second? This threshold is called the *double-click speed*: anything faster is treated as a double-click; anything slower is treated as two single clicks.

You can adjust this threshold using the **Double-click speed** slider on the Buttons tab of the Mouse Properties dialog box. You have two options:

➤ If you find that Windows 95 doesn't always recognize your double-clicks, set up a slower double-click speed by moving the slider bar to the left.

➤ If you find that Windows 95 is sometimes interpreting two consecutive single clicks as a double-click, set up a faster double-click speed by moving the slider bar to the right.

To test the new speed, double-click the **Test area**. If Windows 95 recognizes your double-click, a Jack-in-the-box pops up. (Yes, you read that correctly: a Jack-in-the-box. Obviously, some of the Windows 95 designers had *way* too much time on their hands!)

Trying Different Pointers On for Size

As you trudge through Windows 95, you notice that the mouse pointer busies itself by changing into different icons depending on what you do. There's the standard arrow for selecting everything from check boxes to files and folders; there's the two-headed arrow for sizing window borders; and there's the dreaded hourglass icon that appears whenever a program or Windows 95 is too busy to bother with your petty concerns right now.

Surprisingly, the pointers used by Windows 95 in these and other situations aren't set in stone. To see how you can specify different pointers, select the **Pointers** tab in the Mouse Properties dialog box (see the following figure).

Use the Pointers tab to change the look of the Windows 95 mouse pointers.

Some of the pointers you get in the selected scheme

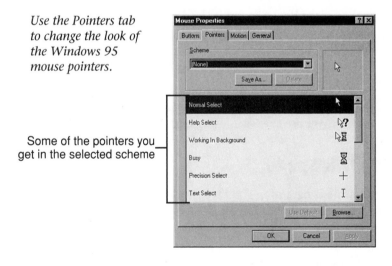

The easiest way to try out different pointers is to choose one of the pointer schemes that come with Windows 95. To do so, select a scheme from the **Scheme** drop-down list, and then take a look at the sample pointers in the box below the list to see what they look like. For example, the following figure shows the pointers you get when you select the Windows Standard (extra large) scheme (which is handy for anyone who has trouble picking out the pointer in a maze of windows).

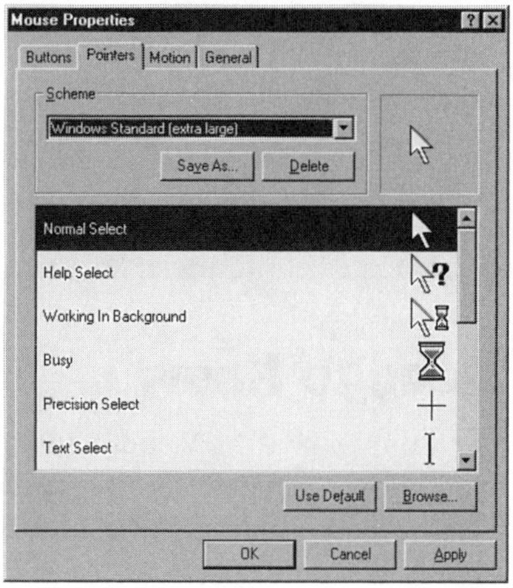

Try the extra-large pointers if you're having problems seeing the mouse pointer on-screen.

Controlling the Tracking Speed

When you move the mouse on its pad, Windows 95 translates this movement and tracks the mouse pointer on your screen accordingly. How quickly the mouse moves across the screen is the *tracking speed*. If this speed is out of whack (for example, if you move the mouse furiously but the pointer just creeps along or, on the other extreme, if the slightest hand tremor causes the pointer to go racing across the screen), your mouse is likely to end up in the nearest garbage can.

The good news is that adjusting the tracking speed is a snap. In the Mouse Properties dialog box, select the **Motion** tab (shown in the following figure) and take a look at the **Pointer speed** slider. You can do two things with this control:

➤ If your mouse pointer is flying around the screen, slow it down by dragging the slider bar to the left.

➤ If the pointer is too slow, drag the slider bar to the right.

If you want to test the new setting, select the **Apply** button and move the mouse around.

The Motion tab controls the mouse tracking speed and mouse trails (see the next section).

```
Mouse Properties                           ? X
 Buttons | Pointers | Motion | General |
 ┌─Pointer speed──────────────────────────┐
 │                                         │
 │  ≡     Slow ──────────┤───────── Fast   │
 │                                         │
 └─────────────────────────────────────────┘
 ┌─Pointer trail──────────────────────────┐
 │        ☑ Show pointer trails            │
 │                                         │
 │   Short ──────────────────┤ Long        │
 │                                         │
 └─────────────────────────────────────────┘



         OK      Cancel      Apply
```

The Least You Need to Know

This chapter showed you how to give the Windows 95 desktop a makeover to make it look its best. I showed you how to change colors, cover the desktop with a pattern or wallpaper, set up a screen saver, customize the taskbar and Start menu, and add shortcuts to the desktop. Wow! Now *that* was a chapter!

Your Windows 95 customization fun is only just beginning, though. In the next chapter, I'll show you how to set up your mouse and keyboard to your liking.

Chapter 23

Adding New Stuff to Windows 95

In This Chapter

➤ Installing chunks of Windows 95

➤ Installing new programs in Windows 95

➤ Telling Windows 95 about your new hardware

➤ A treasure trove of techniques for adding on to your Windows 95 house

You know that old saying that "The only difference between a man and a boy is the price of his toys"? Well, they got *that* right! In the transition from little kid to big kid, we go from Hot Wheels to hot cars, from tiny transistor radios to full-blown stereo systems, and of course, from scrawny, pint-sized calculators to brawny, king-sized computers.

For many people (even non-geeks), a computer is the ultimate toy because you can always add new gadgets and doodads to make your machine better, faster, smarter, or just plain more fun. The problem, though, is installing all these hardware and software gizmos. I'm convinced that Murphy must have just finished setting up some kind of computer doohickey when he formulated his famous Law ("If anything can go wrong, it will").

I suppose the makers of Windows 95 must have become fed up dealing with installation irritations, because they built several features into Windows 95 that make setting up both hardware and software practically painless. This chapter checks out these features and shows how they can make your life easier.

Adding Windows 95 Components

Like a hostess who refuses to put out the good china for just anybody, Windows 95 doesn't install all of its components automatically when you run the Windows Setup program. Don't feel insulted, though, because Windows is just trying to go easy on your hard disk. The problem, you see, is that some of the components that come with Windows 95 are software behemoths that will happily usurp acres of your precious hard disk land. So, in a rare act of digital politeness, Windows bypasses these programs (as well as a few other nonessential tidbits) during a typical installation. If you want any of these knickknacks on your system, you have to grab Windows 95 by the scruff of its electronic neck and say "Yo, bozo! Install this for me, will ya!"

That's all well and good, Author Boy, but this is the first I've heard about Windows 95 having a neck. Don't I just rerun the installation program?

Nope. The good news about all of this is that Windows 95 comes with a handy "Windows Setup" feature that enables you to add any of Windows 95's missing pieces to your system without having to trudge through the entire Windows installation routine.

To get to Windows Setup, select the **Start** button, open the **Settings** folder, and select **Control Panel.** In the Control Panel window, launch the **Add/Remove Programs** icon to display the Add/Remove Programs Properties dialog box, and then select the **Windows Setup** tab. You see a dialog box like the one shown here.

The Windows Setup dialog box lets you add the bits and pieces that come with Windows 95.

The **Components** box lists the various chunks of Windows 95 that you can add (or remove, which I'll discuss in the next chapter). Note that some of these "components" actually consist of several programs (which I guess we could call "component components"); the Accessories component, for example, includes WordPad, Paint, Calculator, and more.

If you examine this dialog box, you'll see three varieties of check boxes:

Unchecked: This means that the component is not installed. If the component comes in several pieces, none of those pieces are installed.

Checked with a gray background: This means that the component is partially installed. That is, the component has multiple chunks, but only some of those chunks reside on your system.

Checked with a white background: This means that the component is installed. If the component comes in several pieces, all of those pieces are installed.

Check This Out...

How Much Is Installed?

To find out how many of the component's programs are installed, check out the Description box; below the component description, you'll see something like **18 of 19 components selected.** This tells you that the component consists of 19 programs and only 18 of them are installed on your system.

Okay, it's time to bring out your brass tacks and get down to the nitty-gritty of adding some of these component things. If you're in a devil-may-care, you-only-go-around-once kind of mood, you can install an entire component by activating the check box next to it. To install just one or more pieces of a component, highlight the component and select the **Details** button. A list of the programs in the component appears, as shown in the following figure. Again, activate the check box for each program you want to install. When you're done, select **OK** to return to the Windows Setup tab.

Choose individual pieces of a component you want to install.

When you finish making your selections, select **OK**. Windows 95 will likely ask you to insert one or more of your original Windows disks (or your Windows CD-ROM). Insert the disk it asks for and select **OK** to continue. Depending on the components you add, Windows 95 may ask you to restart your computer. If it does, select **Yes** to let Windows 95 handle this for you. When the restart is complete, the new programs are ready to roll.

Great: A New Program! Not So Great: Installing the Darn Thing!

Most new PCs come stocked with a few programs, but it's a rare computer owner who's satisfied with just these freebies. Most of us want something better, faster, *cooler*. Unfortunately, the other definition of "computer user" is "sucker for software marketing hype." So all you have to do is read some breathless package copy ("Most programs offer you everything but the kitchen sink. Well, our new *CodeBloat* suite of applications comes with a brand new kitchen sink, right in the box! Free!") and five minutes later you walk out of the software store with some new-fangled program tucked under your arm.

Before Windows 95 came along, you were on your own when it came time to install the program on your system. Now, however, that's all changed. In your program's journey from floppy disk to hard disk, you can bring along Windows 95's Add/Remove Programs Wizard, which will walk you through a series of dialog boxes to get the program's installation show on the road.

Windows Setup Versus Add/Remove Programs Wizard

Don't get confused by the similarities between Windows Setup (discussed earlier in this chapter) and the Add/Remove Programs Wizard. Windows Setup only deals with the accessories and programs that are native to Windows 95 itself; the Add/Remove Programs Wizard handles everything else.

Installing the Program Without the Wizard

Before I show you the "prestidigital" tricks the Add/Remove Programs Wizard has up his sleeve, there's a chance you might not have to bother with any of that hocus-pocus. Why? Well, if you read Chapter 19, "The Sights and Sounds of Multimedia," you may recall that I mumbled something about Windows 95's new AutoPlay feature. If a CD-ROM disc supports AutoPlay, it means that the disc runs its application automatically as soon as you plop the disc in the CD-ROM drive.

But what if you have to install the application first? Ah, in this case, most AutoPlay CDs will crank up their installation programs automatically once you insert the disc. For example, when I insert my Microsoft Bookshelf 1996-97 CD, a few seconds later I see the following dialog box. All I have to do is click one of the buttons and the installation proceeds without further ado.

CD-ROMs that support AutoPlay are often kind enough to launch their installation programs automatically when you insert the disc.

So, if your program comes on CD-ROM, your first task is to insert the disc and see if anything happens. If not, don't sweat it because you can always fall back on the Add/Remove Programs Wizard.

Installing the Program with the Wizard

To work with the wizard, first crank up the Add/Remove Programs dialog box as described earlier. Then click the **Install/Uninstall** tab (if it isn't visible already), and select the **Install** button. The dialog box that appears asks you to insert the first installation disk or the program's CD-ROM. When you've done that, select **Next >**.

The wizard checks all your floppy and CD-ROM drives, searching desperately for any installation program it can find. When it locates a likely candidate, it displays it in the **Command line for installation program** text box, as you can see in the following figure.

If the wizard was successful in tracking down the setup program, select **Finish** to continue. How do you know the wizard isn't giving you a bum steer? There are three ways to tell:

➤ The first letter in the text box represents the letter of the disk drive where the wizard found the program. In the previous figure, for example, the drive letter is **A**. This letter should be the same as the letter of the disk drive into which you inserted the disk.

➤ The part after the backslash (\) is the name of the installation program. It should say something like **INSTALL.EXE** or **SETUP.EXE**.

➤ Many installation disks tell you the name of the program to run (or it may appear in the manual that comes with the program). This name should match the text box text.

The Add/Remove Programs Wizard can hunt down your software's installation program automatically.

If the wizard didn't find the program properly, select the **Browse** button, find and highlight the installation program in the Browse dialog box that appears, select **Open** to return to the wizard, and *then* select **Finish**. In either case, the software's installation program runs automatically.

If you're installing a program designed to run with Windows 95, the installation program will probably set up an icon (and maybe even a whole submenu) on the Start menu, from which you can run the program. If you install a DOS program or a Windows program that doesn't set itself up on the Start menu, head back to Chapter 22 and read the "Adding Items to the Start Menu" section.

Submenus Versus Program Groups

If the application you're dealing with was designed specifically to work with Windows 95, the installation program will probably ask you to choose a Start menu location (that is, a submenu or folder) in which to display the application's icon. No big whoop there. On the other hand, if the program was designed for Windows 3.1, you'll be asked which *program group* you want to use.

As you know by now, Microsoft replaced the old Windows 3.1 program groups with Start menu folders, so this is really a six-of-one-half-a-dozen-of-the-other deal. That is, whether you're choosing a submenu or a program group, you're really choosing the Start menu home for the application.

Adding a New Hunk of Hardware

Playing around with your computer's hardware is usually a job best left to serious geeks. This is especially true if the hardware is part of your computer's delicate and not-to-be-messed-with-lightly innards. Having said that, however, there are a few external hardware upgrades that are well within the abilities of all but the most dedicated technophobes. For example, you can install most external devices—such as a mouse, modem, CD-ROM drive, printer, and scanner—simply by connecting a cable to the appropriate *port* in the back of the computer.

In the prehistoric age of computing (before Windows 95), getting a lump of hardware attached to your computer was the easy part. The real challenge occurred afterward when you had to configure the hardware to ensure that it wouldn't conflict with any of the other devices in your system. This was rarely a simple task. In most cases, it required settings to be tweaked, switches to be flipped, hair to be pulled, moons to be howled at, and hardware deities to be placated with the appropriate sacrifices.

Thankfully, you can now move beyond these arcane rites into an era of easy and painless hardware installation. The reason is that Windows 95 now supports a wonderful initiative called *Plug and Play*. This means that, in most cases, once you add a new device to your system, turn it on (if necessary), and then restart the computer, Windows 95 recognizes the device automatically and makes the appropriate adjustments. (The latter may require you to insert your Windows 95 CD-ROM or one of the floppy disks.)

Happy Hardware Trails

For best results, make sure you buy hardware that's Plug and Play-compatible. It will tell you this somewhere on the box. If you don't see anything about Plug and Play (or PnP, as Plug and Play is usually abbreviated), chances are the device doesn't support it. (You may want to ask the salesperson, just to be safe.) Getting a Plug and Play device ensures that Windows 95 will "communicate" with the device and grill it for the info that Windows 95 needs for proper setup.

If Windows 95 doesn't recognize the device, you have two ways to proceed:

➤ Windows 95 comes with an Add New Hardware Wizard that will lead you step-by-step through the installation process. The next section shows you how to work with this wizard.

➤ Most devices come with a disk that has an installation program that will set up the hardware appropriately. Try this route if the Add New Hardware Wizard doesn't work out, for some reason.

Wielding the Add New Hardware Wizard

To give the Add New Hardware Wizard a go, first fire up the Control Panel by selecting the **Start** button, opening the **Settings** folder, and selecting the **Control Panel** icon. In the Control Panel window, open the **Add New Hardware** icon to display the first of the Wizard's dialog boxes. This first dialog box merely displays a couple of not-very-useful sentences, so go ahead and select **Next >** to continue. The wizard then displays the dialog box shown in the following figure.

To avoid gut-wrenching hardware upgrades, let the Add New Hardware Wizard lead you step by step through the installation process.

This wizard dialog box asks you whether you want Windows to detect your new hardware automatically. This is the best way to go, so make sure to activate the **Yes (Recommended)** option and then select **Next >**. (See the next section to learn how to specify hardware yourself.)

When Windows 95 tells you it's ready to look for new hardware (and gives you a scary-sounding warning about how this process "could cause your machine to stop responding." Yikes!), select **Next >** once again to continue. Your computer will now make some strange crickets-on-speed noises for a few minutes. This is perfectly normal and it just means that Windows 95 is scouring every nook and cranny of your system to look for new devices.

If the Add New Hardware Wizard doesn't find any new hardware, it tells you so. If that happens, select **Cancel**, shut down your computer (make sure you use the Start menu's **Shut Down** command), check to see if you attached the new device correctly, and then try again. If it's still a no-go, try installing the hardware using the instructions in the next section.

More likely, however, the wizard will tell you it's finished detecting and is ready to install the support files for the device. To make sure the wizard was successful, select the **Details** button to eyeball what the wizard found. As you can see in the following figure, the wizard gives you a list of all the new devices it tracked down.

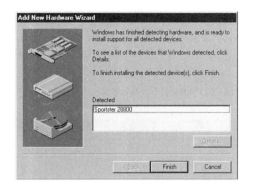

The Add New Hardware Wizard is usually pretty good at picking out the new hardware on your system.

Now select **Finish**. You'll likely be prompted to insert your Windows 95 CD-ROM or a floppy disk, so just follow the instructions that show up. You may also be asked to restart your computer to put the changes into effect.

Specifying New Hardware by Hand

The Add New Hardware Wizard has a special gift for identifying devices. However, it's far from perfect, especially for older and more obscure devices (such as that digital dog polisher you got for Christmas). So what do you do if the wizard falls down on the job? Well, Windows 95 maintains a huge list of devices that it can work with. So all you need to do is pick out your device from this list.

To do this, launch the Add New Hardware Wizard once again. When you get to the second dialog box (the one that asks if you want Windows to detect your hardware automatically), make sure to activate the **No** option, and then select **Next >**. As you can see in the following figure, the wizard displays an impressive list that includes every kind of hardware under the sun; and just in case you have an extraterrestrial device, there's even an Other devices selection you can go with. Use the **Hardware types** list to highlight the hardware category that's appropriate for your new device, and then select **Next**.

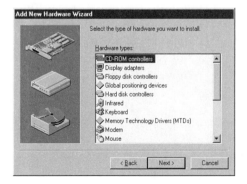

This dialog box lists all the hardware types that Windows 95 can work with.

In most cases, the wizard then displays another dialog box that lists various devices in the category you chose. For example, the next figure shows the dialog box that appears if you selected Mouse in the list of hardware types. Use the **Manufacturers** list to choose the company that made your device, and then highlight the name of the device in the **Models** list. When you're done, select **Next >**.

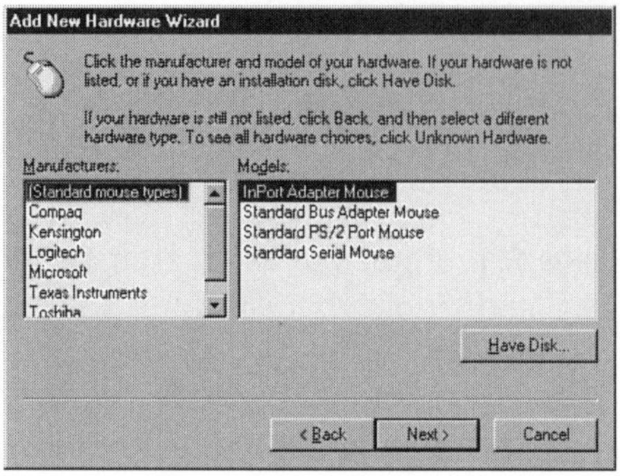

For most hardware types, the Add New Hardware Wizard provides a list of manufacturers and models so you can choose your device.

The route from here depends on the device you're working with. Here are some things to expect:

➤ You may see another dialog box that asks you for info about the new device. Provide the requested data as best you can (you may have to—shudder—crack open the manual that came with the device).

➤ You may be asked to insert your Windows 95 CD-ROM or a floppy disk or two.

➤ If you can't find your device in Windows 95's list, click the **Have Disk** button, insert the disk that came with the device, and follow the instructions that come your way.

The Least You Need to Know

This chapter continued your look at Windows 95 customization by shifting your emphasis from renovating the Windows 95 house to constructing new additions. You learned how to add Windows 95 components, how to use Windows 95 to install software, and how to tell Windows 95 about your new hardware. The next chapter takes the opposite tack as you learn how to remove stuff from your computer.

Removing Stuff from Windows 95

In This Chapter

➤ Saying sayonara to Windows 95 components

➤ Saying adios to programs you no longer need

➤ Saying au revoir to hardware devices

➤ Your guide to saying good-bye to those pesky applications and devices that you want out of your life

One of my favorite sketches from the old *Saturday Night Live* shows was called "The Thing That Wouldn't Leave!" It featured John Belushi as a late-staying party guest who wouldn't take any of the hosts' hints about leaving. Instead, he kept hanging around, watching TV, eating their food, downing their drinks, and even making long-distance phone calls!

If you have a Windows component, an application, or a hardware device that has worn out its welcome, forget the hints: this chapter shows you various techniques for giving digital deadbeats the heave-ho.

Removing a Windows 95 Component

In the last chapter, you saw how the Windows Setup feature made it easy to bring Windows 95 components in from the cold of the CD-ROM or floppy disk to the warmth of your hard drive. What happens, though, if you grow tired of a particular component's company? For example, the artistically challenged may want to get rid of that Paint program they never use, or the hopelessly unwired may be itching to expunge HyperTerminal from their systems.

Happily, with Windows Setup, giving these and other Windows 95 components the bum's rush is even easier than installing them. And as an added bonus, lopping off some of Windows' limbs serves to free up precious hard disk space, so you'll have more room for *really* important games, uh, I mean, applications.

As you might expect, removing Windows 95 components is the opposite of adding them. Your first chore is to slap the Windows Setup tab on-screen. Begin by slamming the **Start** button, selecting the **Settings** command, and then selecting **Control Panel**. When the Control Panel window shows up, launch the **Add/Remove Programs** icon, and then select the Windows Setup tab.

From here, deactivate the check boxes for the components you want to blow away. For multiprogram components, select **Details** to see the individual programs, deactivate the check boxes for those you want to nuke, and then select **OK** to return the Windows Setup tab.

When you're done, select **OK**. Windows 95 removes the components you specified without further delay. Note that, depending on the component you removed, Windows 95 may ask to restart your computer. If so, select **Yes** to make it happen.

Putting the Boot to an Application

Windows applications, like the people you meet, fall into three categories: friends for life, acquaintances you deal with occasionally, and those you hope you never have to speak to again. Avoiding people you dislike is usually just a matter of avoiding contact with them, and they'll get the hint after a while. Unlikable Windows applications, however, just don't seem it get it. They keep hanging around like the proverbial party guests that won't leave. If you have a Windows application that has worn out its welcome, this section shows you a couple of methods for uninstalling the darn thing so it's out of your life forever.

If you wonder whether all of this is really necessary, here are just a few of the benefits you can reap by obliterating unneeded applications:

Extra hard disk space   Some of today's behemoth Windows applications can chew up 10, 20, or even 30 megabytes of precious hard disk property. With hard disk space at a premium these days, you can't afford to waste even half a megabyte on some dog of a program (much less 20 or 30).

Easier navigation   The Start menu will be easier to navigate if you get rid of extraneous icons and submenus.

Faster performance   Sending an application packing can also sometimes improve your computer's performance. Depending on the type of program, you can end up

with more memory, a faster loading time for Windows, and faster execution of your other programs.

The sheer thrill of nuking stuff You spend most of your Explorer and My Computer time being careful not to accidentally delete important files. What a guilty pleasure it is, then, to blow away entire folders stuffed with formerly important files and subfolders.

Method I: The Automatic Uninstall

When it comes to uninstalling unwelcome applications, the good news is that Windows 95 has a feature that enables you to vaporize any application with a simple click of the mouse. The bad news is that this feature is only available for some programs.

To check, first display your old buddy the Add/Remove Programs Properties dialog box (as described earlier in the chapter). As you can see in the following figure, the bottom half of the Install/Uninstall tab displays a list of the programs that Windows 95 knows how to remove automatically.

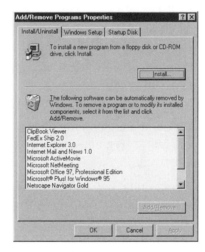

The Install/Uninstall tab maintains a list of programs that you can annihilate automatically.

If the program you want to blow to kingdom come is on this list, highlight it and then select the **Add/Remove** button. What happens from here depends on the program. You may see a dialog box asking you to confirm the uninstall, or you may be asked if you want to run an "Automatic" or "Custom" uninstall. For the latter, make sure you select the **Automatic** option. Whatever happens, follow the instructions on the screen until you return to the Install/Uninstall tab, and then select **OK** to wrap things up.

Method II: Uninstalling a Program Manually

For those applications that can't be uninstalled automatically, you need to turn up your sleeves and do the whole thing by hand. You may be wondering why the heck I need to devote so much verbiage to something as simple as blowing an application to smithereens. After all, isn't it just a matter of deleting a file or two and getting rid of a Start menu icon? Hah, you wish! Windows applications seem to enjoy scattering files left, right, and center over your hard disk. To make sure no piece of an old application ever rears its ugly head (usually as some kind of impenetrable error message), you need to disinfect your system by removing any and all files associated with the program.

To make the whole chore easier, I've divided it up into three steps that cover everything from deleting files to deleting Start menu icons. The next few sections take you through, step by step.

Step 1: Delete the Application's Files

The first stage of your uninstalling tour involves rubbing out any files and folders created by the application's installation program. To do this, you need to know the name of the program's main folder. If you can't remember, here are three ways to find out:

➤ In Explorer or My Computer, open your Windows folder and then open the Start Menu folder. Keep opening folders until you see the application's icon. Right-click the icon, click **Properties** in the menu that appears, and then click **Shortcut** to display a dialog box similar to the one shown here. In most cases, the Target text box contains the name of the folder in which the application resides.

➤ In Explorer or My Computer, look for a folder name that closely resembles the name of the application. Many programs install themselves in the Program Files folder, so be sure to check there.

➤ Load the application, pull down its **File** menu, and select the **Open** command. The Open dialog box that appears may display the name of the program's main folder.

Now that you know where the application's files are hiding, use Explorer or My Computer to highlight the folder. Before pounding the Delete key, though, take a quick look at the displayed files. Can you see a date and time common to most of them? (To get a true picture, you may need to do two things: activate the **View** menu's **Details** command, and pull down **View**, select **Arrange Icons**, and then select **by Date**.) If so, make a note of both the date and time; you'll need them later on when hunting down the application's other files.

Right-click the application icon and then click Properties to display this dialog box.

This box tells you where the application resides.

Open the Start Menu folder.

Next, you should also check to see if the folder contains any data files you want to preserve. If you spent any time at all creating documents (or whatever) in the application, it's a wise precaution to save them for posterity. For one thing, you may want to use them in another application; for another, you may change your mind six months from now and decide to reinstall the application. If you want to save your data, highlight the files and then move (not copy) them to another folder, or to a floppy disk. With that out of the way, go ahead and delete the application's folder (as described back in Chapter 12 in the "More Recycle Bin Fun: Deleting Folders" section).

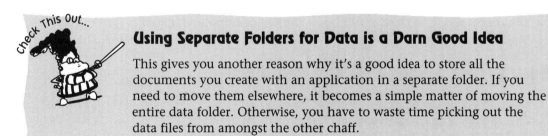

Using Separate Folders for Data is a Darn Good Idea

This gives you another reason why it's a good idea to store all the documents you create with an application in a separate folder. If you need to move them elsewhere, it becomes a simple matter of moving the entire data folder. Otherwise, you have to waste time picking out the data files from amongst the other chaff.

Step 2: Delete Other Files Installed by the Application

Your file deletion chores aren't quite done yet. As I mentioned earlier, many applications scatter a few of their files in various places. To give your hard disk a thorough cleaning, you need to seek out these rogue elements. Rather than trekking through every single folder, though, you can narrow your search somewhat. In the vast majority of cases, you'll find any extraneous files lurking in your main Windows folder (usually WIN-DOWS), Windows' SYSTEM subfolder, and your hard drive's root folder (usually C:\).

The bad news is that the WINDOWS and SYSTEM folders often contain hundreds of files. How can you tell which files belonged to the application? There's no foolproof method, but there are some clues you can keep an eye out for:

➤ Look for file names that suggest the original application. For example, you can be reasonably confident that a file name beginning with WP is probably a WordPerfect file.

➤ Look for files with dates and times that match the common date and time you observed earlier in the application's main folder.

Not Sure About a File? Try Moving It

If you're not sure about a particular file, especially one in your WIN-DOWS or SYSTEM folder, try moving it to another folder or to a floppy disk instead of deleting it outright. This way, if Windows or some application displays an error message complaining about the missing file, you can easily restore it.

When your detective work is done, go ahead and delete the files.

Step 3: Delete Start Menu Icons and Submenus

Your next chore is to erase any traces of the program from your Start menu. You learned how to do this in Chapter 22 (see the "Removing Items from the Start Menu" section).

"Your Program Has Left the Building"

Okay, that's all she wrote. The program is now completely expunged from your system. The only thing left to do is exit and then restart Windows.

Handing Hardware Its Walking Papers

Our computer's software guests aren't the only interlopers who can wear out their welcome. Hardware devices, too, can become tiresome, boring, or simply outdated. Unlike software, however, there is no tried-and-true method for exiling a device from your computer. That is, once you've physically removed the hardware from the computer, how you let Windows 95 know depends on a number of factors. Here are a few general notes on how you go about this:

Plug and Play stuff   If the device supports the Plug and Play standard mentioned in the last chapter, then you probably don't have to do much of anything. Windows 95 will likely recognize that the device has bailed out of your system and will make the appropriate adjustments automatically.

Printer   If the device is a printer, select the **Start** button, select **Settings**, and then select **Printers**. In the Printers window that appears, delete the icon for the printer you removed.

Monitor   If the device is a monitor, I assume you have a replacement. Therefore, you need only tell Windows about the new monitor by following these steps:

1. Right-click an empty patch of the desktop, click **Properties** in the menu that appears, and then click **Settings** in the Display Properties dialog box.

2. Click **Advanced Properties** to display the Advanced Display Properties dialog box, and then activate the **Monitor** tab.

3. Click the **Change** button to display the Select Device dialog box.

4. Activate the **Select all devices** option (see the next figure), use the **Manufacturers** and **Models** lists to highlight your new monitor, and then click **OK**.

5. If you're asked to insert your Windows 95 CD-ROM or a floppy disk, follow the instructions that appear.

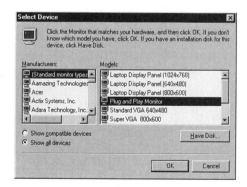

Use the Select Device dialog box to pick out your new monitor.

Modem   I'll show you how to set up a modem in the next chapter. For now, though, you can tell Windows 95 that you no longer have a modem by selecting the **Start** button, selecting **Settings**, and then selecting **Control Panel**. Launch the **Modems** icon, highlight your modem in the list, and then click **Remove**.

305

Other devices   For most other devices, here are the steps to plow through to tell Windows 95 a chunk of hardware is no longer connected to your system:

1. Select the **Start** button, select **Settings**, and then select **Control Panel**.

2. Open the **System** icon and, in the System Properties dialog box that appears, activate the **Device Manager** tab.

3. In the list of device types, open the type that corresponds to the device (by clicking the plus sign) and then highlight the device.

4. Click the **Remove** button. Windows 95 asks you to confirm the renewal.

5. Click **OK** and then follow the instructions on the screen (if any).

The Least You Need to Know

This chapter showed you how to rid your life of unwelcome software and hardware guests. This concludes your look at customizing Windows 95. From here, you head into Part 6 in which you'll explore how to get the most out of a particular piece of hardware: your modem.

Part 6
Modems and More: Communicating with Windows 95

It wasn't all that long ago that the people were mourning the demise of letter writing. The evil twin influences of reduced leisure time and overexposure to television were usually cited as the reasons for the passing of a once-popular pastime. Now, however, letter writing is making a big comeback. That's not to say that you'll see mail carriers' mailbags groaning under the weight of epistles, postcards, and billets-doux as folks try to catch up on their correspondence. No, the real force behind this resurgence of the written word is e-mail. In corporations and colleges, at home and on the road, people who would never even consider putting pen to paper are exchanging electronic missives and messages in staggering numbers. Not only that, but faxes, bulletin boards, networking, and the ever-ubiquitous Internet have created a veritable communications frenzy. The six chapters here in Part 6 show you how to get on this bandwagon using Windows 95.

Chapter 25

Basic Modem Fun

In This Chapter

➤ What's a modem, and what can you do with the darn thing?

➤ Telling Windows 95 about your modem

➤ Getting Windows to dial your phone

➤ HyperTerminal: the pumped-up communications program

➤ Everything you need to get your modem's mojo working

Over the years, desktop PCs have stoutly resisted any and all attempts to gussy them up. Although we've seen a few machines in recent months that look almost stylish, the vast majority of today's monitors and cases still look basically the same as they did fifteen years ago: squat, rectangular, and unremittingly beige.

So, to inject our machines with some individuality, we've had to resort to accessorizing: plugging in peripherals and attaching add-ons. The popularity of some of these electronic adjuncts has waxed and waned in accordance with the trends of the day as dictated by the digital powers-that-be. The ubiquitous mouse, for example, was once a fashion statement that declared oneself to be "non-DOS." Other recent PC fashion accessories have included ergonomic keyboards (especially the curvaceous Microsoft Natural Keyboard with its Dali-esque design) and CD-ROM drives.

Check This Out...

The Internet Scoop
Looking for Internet information? This chapter is, of course, a prerequisite. From here, check out Chapter 27, "Reach Out and Touch Some Net: Dial-Up Networking," and Chapter 28, "Windows in Cyberspace: Getting on the Internet."

These days, however, the *de rigueur* accessory for PC fashion plates is the modem. *Everyone*, it seems, is flocking online like so many swallows to Capistrano. The Internet, of course, is the Big Thing, but folks are connecting to commercial services, bulletin boards, and other online locales in record numbers. And we're not only talking about the extroverts of the world who just want to reach out and modem someone, *anyone*. No, people of all walks of life, temperaments, and levels of expertise are surfing like there's no tomorrow.

Windows 95 has jumped on this modem bandwagon in a big way with a totally revamped communications system, easier modem setup, and some decent communications accessories. This chapter shows you how to get your modem up and surfing, and then shows you how to use your modem and Windows 95's HyperTerminal accessory to tap into existing online services (such as bulletin board systems and large-scale data marketplaces such as CompuServe). And, believe it or not, you can even teach your modem to dial your phone when you're making regular phone calls! Stay tuned for the details.

What's All This About Modems?

Although *modem* sounds like a way to ask for seconds ("Hey, Wilbur, gimme mo' dem black-eyed peas!"), it's actually a little piece of hardware that attaches to your computer. This handy device makes it possible for two or more computers to communicate through telephone lines—which are known as POTS to the online cognoscenti: Plain Old Telephone Service. Phone lines aren't built to carry computer data, though; they're built to carry sounds. So the modem's job is to convert computer data to sounds that can be sent across the phone lines. On the receiving end, the other modem then captures the incoming sounds and converts them back to computer data.

There are three types of modems:

➤ An *internal* modem is a circuit board that resides inside the computer.

➤ An *external* modem is a plastic or metal box that squats on your desk and connects to one of the ports in the back of the computer.

➤ A *PC Card* modem is a credit card-sized wafer that plugs into a PC Card slot in a notebook computer.

Within each of these species, modems are also characterized by how quickly they can squirt data from here to there and back again. The speed of modem transmissions is measured in *bits per second*. (A *bit* is the fundamental unit of all computer data; to give you a frame of reference; it takes 8 bits to make up a single character, such as the letter *A* or the number *2*.) Older modems trickle along at a measly 1,200 or 2,400 bits per second (bps). Newer modems, however, offer more impressive velocities ranging from 14,400 bps to 33,600 bps. (And, according to the tall forehead types in the lab, we'll soon see new-fangled modems that can pump out data at even faster rates.)

Modem Etymology

In case you're wondering, the word *modem* is a blend of the words *modula-tor* and *demodulator*. Translated from its native geekspeak, the modulator part converts computer data into sounds and the demodulator part converts sounds into computer data.

But how in the name of Alexander Graham Bell can sounds represent a spreadsheet or a picture of Cindy Crawford?

The techniques developed by modem nerds to shuffle data along a phone line are obscenely complex. However, the basics are easy enough. Remember that every last piece of data in your computer is nothing more than a collection of 1s and 0s (see the "What's a Byte?" sidebar in Chapter 12). So, at least theoretically, you could send any file along a phone line by converting the 1s into a particular tone and by converting the 0s into a different tone.

A Modem Buyer's Guide

If you're in the market for a modem, the good news is that buying a modem has never been easier. Most name brand modems use the same set of internal commands, so they'll work well with just about any communications software. (The big names in the modem biz are Boca Research, Cardinal, GVC, Hayes, Megahertz, Motorola, Practical Peripherals, Supra, U.S. Robotics, and Zoom.) With that in mind, here are a few notes to consider when purchasing your link to the online world:

➤ If you have a desktop computer, you'll probably want to buy an external modem because they're super easy to install. Internal modems require minor surgery inside your computer, so they're not for the faint of heart. However, if you know someone who can install an internal modem for you, they have three significant advantages: they don't require a separate power supply; they don't take up any room on your desk; and you don't have to remember to turn them on.

➤ If you have a notebook computer, it's likely you'll need to buy a PC Card modem. (Check your computer manual to make sure your system has a PC Card slot. Note that on older machines this might be called a PCMCIA slot.)

➤ Modems aren't hard to install, but for foolproof installations, make sure you get a modem that supports Plug and Play.

➤ As far as speed goes, get the fastest modem that you can afford. The slower the modem you use, the more frustrating your online experiences will be, and the more hair you'll pull out.

➤ Most new modems comes with fax capabilities built in. However, if you plan on doing some faxing (as described in Chapter 30, "More on Exchange: Some Fast Fax Facts"), double check to make sure the modem can do the fax thing.

➤ External modems require a "serial cable" to connect to your computer. Unfortunately, most of these modems don't come with the cable so you'll need to purchase one, as well. (Ask the salesperson if you're not sure what to get.)

What Can You Do with a Modem?

A modem's purpose in life is to enable you to establish a connection between your computer and another computer: it can be a friend's machine across town, a bulletin board service (BBS for short), your local library, a commercial online service like the Microsoft Network, or even the Internet.

However, modems also have a few other tricks up their electronic sleeves. For example, they can dial your telephone if you want to make a regular phone call. Also, as I mentioned in the last section, fax/modems can send and receive faxes. I'll teach you how to get your modem to perform all of these tricks in this chapter and in the other five chapters here in Part 6.

Modem Installation Made Easy

Before you can use any communications software, you need to tell Windows 95 what kind of modem you have. After you do that, you need to configure the modem to suit the types of online sessions you plan to run. To that end, the next few sections take you through the rigmarole of installing and configuring your modem.

Getting the Modem Ready for Action

For starters, makesure your modem is properly installed. If you have an external modem, here's a checklist to run through:

➤ Attach the power supply.

➤ Attach one end of the serial cable to the port in the back of the modem, and then attach the other end of the cable to the appropriate COM port in the back of your computer. (You may have to decipher your computer manual to figure out the correct port.)

➤ Run a telephone cable from the wall jack to the jack in the back of the modem. If the modem has two jacks, use the *line* jack.

➤ Make sure you turn the modem on.

If you have an internal modem installed, the part of the card that you can see in the back of your computer will contain one or two telephone jacks. To get this type of modem ready, all you need to do is run a telephone cable from the wall jack to the *line* jack in the back of the card.

If you have a PC Card modem, slide the card into one of your notebook's PC Card slots, and then attach the telephone cable.

Telling Windows 95 About Your Modem

The next item on the agenda is to let Windows 95 know that you have a modem. Begin by cracking open the **Start** menu, selecting **Settings**, and then selecting **Control Panel**. Once the Control Panel window appears, launch the **Modems** icon. The Install New Modem Wizard appears, as shown in the following figure. This wizard will attempt to detect your modem automatically. Assuming you installed the modem correctly (as described in the last section), select **Next >** to begin the detection process.

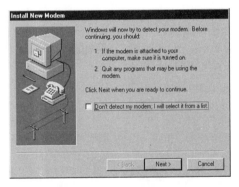

The Install New Modem Wizard takes you through your modem installation.

Once the wizard completes its work, you see a dialog box similar to the one shown here if it found your modem successfully. In this case, select **Next >** to continue.

If the wizard fails in its quest to find your modem, all is not lost. In this case, click **Next >** to get a list of all the modems that Windows 95 knows about. Use the **Manufacturers** and **Models** lists to highlight your modem, and then click **Next >**. (If you don't see your modem, select (Standard Modem Types) in the Manufacturers list, and then choose the standard model that corresponds to your modem's speed.) In the next wizard dialog box, highlight the port to which your modem is attached, and then select **Next>**.

You'll see this dialog box once the wizard locates your modem.

With your modem now installed in Windows 95, the wizard tosses the Location Properties dialog box at you, as shown in the next figure. The purpose of this dialog box is to enable Windows 95 to dial your modem properly. To do this, it requests four chunks of information from you:

What country are you in now?   Use this list to choose your country (this determines the country code used with long distance calls).

What area (or city) code are you in now?   Use this text box to enter your area code. This helps Windows 95 determine whether or not a call you place is a long distance call.

If you dial a number to access an outside line, what is it?   Use this text box to enter the number (or numbers) you have to dial to get an outside line. If you don't have to dial a number, leave this box blank.

The phone system at this location uses   Select either **Tone** or **Pulse**, depending on the type of dialing your phone uses.

Click **Next >** and then click **Finish** in the last of the wizard's dialog boxes.

Now the wizard pesters you for information about your current location.

The Modems Properties Dialog Box

When the Add New Modem Wizard completes its labors, it displays the Modems Properties dialog box shown next. This dialog box also appears the next time you launch the Modems icon in Control Panel. Once inside this dialog box, you can do any of the following:

➤ To install a second modem, click **Add** to use the Add New Modem Wizard once again.

➤ To delete a modem you don't use, highlight it and then click **Remove**.

➤ To change how Windows 95 dials the modem, click **Dialing Properties** and then use the dialog box that appears to make your changes. (I'll discuss the options in this dialog box in depth in Chapter 27, "Reach Out and Touch Some Net: Dial-Up Networking.")

When you're done, click **OK** to return to Control Panel.

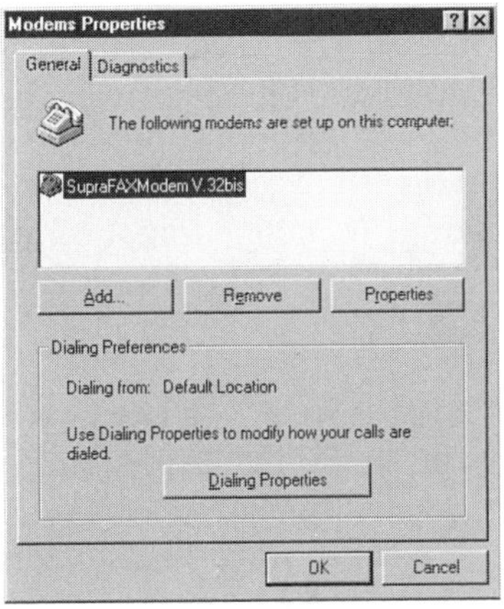

This dialog box shows you the modem you installed.

A Note About Online Services

The easiest way to get online is to subscribe to an *online service* such as CompuServe, America Online, or Prodigy. These online services are really just a collection of computers that you can dial up using your modem. These services offer lots of useful and interesting attractions (and, of course, a few useless and dull ones, too) assembled by the company that owns the service. You normally have to pay a monthly fee (and sometimes additional hourly charges) to hook up to an online service.

In most cases, the connection to the service is handled by special software supplied the company, so you need to contact them to get everything you need. However, later

315

versions of Windows 95 boast an Online Services icon on the desktop. Double-clicking this icon displays the window shown in the following figure. From here, you have a couple of ways to proceed:

➤ Double-click the **About the Online Services** icon to find out a bit more about the services.

➤ Double-click one of the other icons to set up a trial account with a service.

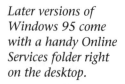
Later versions of Windows 95 come with a handy Online Services folder right on the desktop.

Too Busy to Dial Your Phone? Let Windows 95 Do It!

If you don't have one of those fancy-schmancy speed-dial phones on your desk, Windows 95 can provide you with the next best thing: Phone Dialer. This is a simple program whose only mission in life is to accept a phone number from you and then use your modem to dial the number for you automatically.

Starting Phone Dialer

To take advantage of Phone Dialer, you need both a phone (duh) and a modem. In addition to attaching the modem cable to a serial port in the back of your computer (if you use an external modem), you also need to rearrange your phone cables:

➤ Run one phone cable from your phone to the "Phone" jack on your modem.

➤ Run a second phone cable from your modem's "Line" jack to the phone jack on your wall.

After you do all that malarkey, you can get into Phone Dialer by selecting the **Start** button, opening the **Programs** folder, opening the **Accessories** folder, and selecting the **Phone Dialer** icon. You'll see a window that looks suspiciously like the one shown in the following figure.

Looks just like a telephone keypad, doesn't it? To dial a number, just type it in the **Number to dial** text box (or click the appropriate numbers with your mouse) and then select the **Dial** button. After a couple of seconds, you'll hear the number being dialed through your modem's speaker. Pick up the receiver and, after the modem has completed dialing, click the **Talk** button in the dialog box that appears. If you want Windows 95 to keep a log of the call (who you called and for how long), type the person's name in the dialog box that remains on-screen. When the call is done, click the **Hang Up** button.

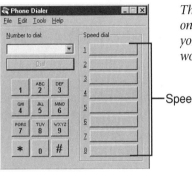

The Phone Dialer is only too happy to do your dialing dirty work.

Speed dial buttons

If you want to dial the same number again later, don't bother retyping it. Instead, simply select the number you want from the **Number to dial** drop-down list. (Note that Windows 95 automatically saves these numbers between Phone Dialer sessions.)

Quick Connections with Speed Dial

Phone Dialer is certainly handy, but it becomes downright useful when you take advantage of the speed dialing feature. You can program the eight buttons arranged down the right side in the Speed dial group with frequently called numbers. You just click a programmed button, and Phone Dialer dials the number for you automatically.

To program a speed dial button, click it to display the Program Speed Dial dialog box, shown next. Use the **Name** text box to enter the name you want associated with the number, and use the **Number to dial** text box to enter the number itself. Then click the **Save** button to save the info, or click **Save and Dial** to save it and dial the number right away. With all that done, you can launch any of your speed dial numbers simply by clicking the appropriate button in the Phone Dialer window.

Use this dialog box to program an empty speed dial button.

If you want to change the name or number associated with one of the speed dial buttons, you can't just click it, because that will dial the number. Instead, select the **Edit** menu's **Speed Dial** command. In the Edit Speed Dial dialog box that shows up, click the button you want to change, and then use the **Name** and **Number to dial** text boxes to edit the information. Click Save when you're done.

Getting Wired with HyperTerminal

The Phone Dialer is a handy tool, but it's almost certainly not why you bought your modem. Instead, your modem's true *raison d'être* is to connect to other modems and thus propel you into the world of online services and bulletin board systems. (Although, as I've said, many online services have their own software that you must use to establish a connection.) To do this, you need a communications program (or *terminal* program, as modem geeks like to say) that can operate your modem and handle the behind-the-scenes dirty work of dialing, connecting, downloading, and uploading.

In Windows 3.x, modem communications were handled by the Terminal accessory, a homely, Spartan program that proved to be merely adequate in everything it did. Few people liked Terminal, and even fewer actually used it, but the Windows 95 replacement—a program called HyperTerminal—should please all but the most discriminating modem jockeys. The next few sections show you how to use HyperTerminal to set up, dial, and work with online connections.

Setting Up HyperTerminal for Modem-to-Modem Connections

To start HyperTerminal, choose the **Start** button, open the **Programs** folder, the **Accessories** folder, and then select **HyperTerminal**. This opens a folder that contains four icons, as you can see in the following figure. Three of these icons—AT&T Mail, CompuServe, and MCI Mail—are predefined HyperTerminal connections. The fourth icon—Hypertrm—is the HyperTerminal program itself. Once you create your own HyperTerminal connections down the road, they'll show up in this window, as well.

HyperTerminal enables you to connect to remote computers with your modem.

Here are the steps to follow to define your own HyperTerminal connections:

1. In the HyperTerminal folder, double-click the **Hypertrm** icon. HyperTerminal displays the Connection Description dialog box.

2. Use the **Name** text box to enter a descriptive name for the connection, use the **Icon** list to highlight an icon for the connection, and then click **OK**. The Phone Number dialog box, shown here, appears.

The Phone Number dialog box is where you enter (you guessed it) the phone number.

3. Use the **Phone number** text box to enter the phone number you'll call (the dash is optional). If the call is long distance, enter the area code in the **Area code** text box. If the call is *really* long distance (outside North America), use the **Country code** drop-down list to select the appropriate country code.

4. If you have more than one modem installed, select the one you want to use from the **Connect using** drop-down list.

5. Click **OK**. HyperTerminal displays the Connect dialog box, shown here.

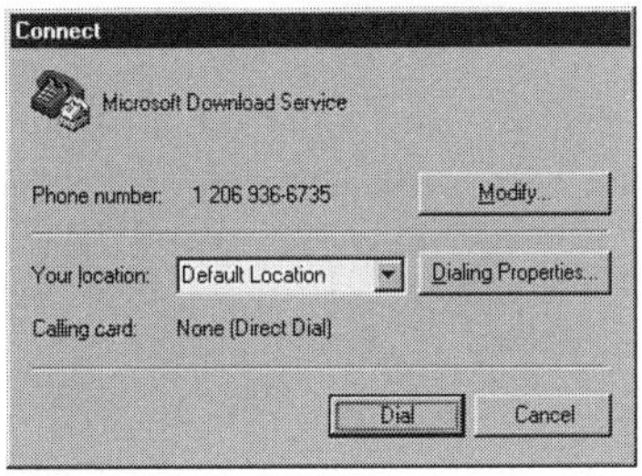

You can use the Connect dialog box to establish the connection or modify the dialing properties.

If you need to dial a number to get an outside line, if you'd like to dial using a calling card, or if you need to disable Call Waiting, select the Dialing Properties button, fill in the appropriate info in the Dialing Properties dialog box, and select **OK**. You're returned to the Connect dialog box, and you're ready for action. Make sure your modem is turned on, and then click **Dial** to dial the number.

What Happens Now?

When you select Dial, the modem dials the number, and your computer connects to the other computer, just like that! If you're calling a BBS, directions appear on-screen telling you how to work with the computer you're calling (see the example screen in the following figure). Just follow along with whatever it tells you. If you connect to a friend's computer, you won't see anything fancy: what you type simply appears on his screen, and vice-versa. You can send and receive files to and from each other, too.

A typical screen in a typical Hyper-Terminal session.

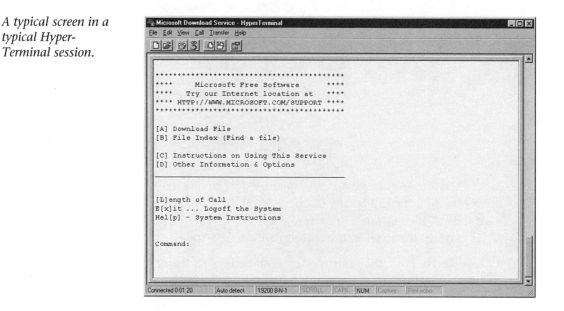

The File Transfer Thing

If you need to receive a file from a BBS or online service (or, more rarely, send one of your own files to the service), you generally need to slog through the following steps:

1. Move to the appropriate file transfer area. All services have different sections you can move into and out of. For example, there might be sections for browsing information, getting help, leaving messages, and so on. You usually get a menu of choices; look for a menu item such as Download (if you're receiving), Upload (if you're sending), or Files. If you want to transfer files to a friend, skip to step 4.

2. Tell the service you want to receive or send a file (how you do this depends on the service). You'll be asked to enter the name of the file. If you're receiving a file and you're not sure of its name, you can usually browse through a list of the service's files to find the one you want.

3. You'll also be asked which "transfer protocol" you want to use. This isn't as scary as it sounds because HyperTerminal can only use a few of these protocol things, and there are one or two you'll use almost all the time (I explain everything you need to know a little later).

4. Tell HyperTerminal you want to perform a file transfer (I'll discuss this in detail in a sec).

5. When the transfer is complete, you usually have to press **Enter** or some other key to let the service know you're back.

The next couple of sections take a closer look at steps 3 and 4.

Transfers Between Friends Are Easier

If you want to exchange a file with a friend, the two of you first need to decide which protocol you want to use. Then you pull down the **Transfer** menu and select either **Send File** or **Receive File** (as needed), while your friend issues the appropriate "receive" or "send" command in her program at the same time. For example, suppose you want to send a file to your friend. You select the Transfer menu's Send File command, and your friend selects the "receive" command in his or her communications program.

Following Protocol

In diplomacy, *protocol* defines the rules and formalities that smooth communications between nations. Just to get two modems *talking* to each other requires perfect synchronization of various communications settings (most of which, thankfully, HyperTerminal handles for you automatically). If you now want to actually exchange data, that just adds a whole new level of complexity.

The good news is that this complexity is something you can safely ignore because the world's modem nerds have worked out various solutions. These solutions are *protocols,* and, in the same way that diplomatic protocols make cultural exchanges easy, communications protocols are designed to make it easy for two modems to exchange data. The only thing you have to do is make sure both modems use the same protocol. Otherwise, you'll end up like two diplomats trying to perform different ceremonies at the same time: things just won't mesh properly.

Here's how it works. When you let the BBS know you want to receive or send a file, it eventually displays a list of the protocols it can use and asks you to select the one you want to use during the transfer. Which one should you choose? Well, HyperTerminal supports six different protocols, but two are the most common: Zmodem and Xmodem. Zmodem is better because it's faster, but not all BBSs support it. I've yet to encounter a BBS that doesn't support at least XModem, so that's a good fallback choice. (I'll tell you how to select a protocol in the next section.)

Receiving and Sending Files

Once you tell the online service the name of the file you want to receive or send and the protocol to use, the service says something like **Ready to send/receive file. Please initiate file transfer.** At this point, pull down the **Transfer** menu and select either the **Receive File** command (if you want to receive a file) or the **Send File** command (if you want to send a file). Note that, in some cases, HyperTerminal selects the appropriate command for you automatically.

If you selected Receive File, the Receive File dialog box appears (see the following figure). In the **Place received file in the following folder** text box, enter the name of the folder in which you want to store the file. If you're not sure of the folder's name, select the **Browse** button, pick out a folder in the Select a Folder dialog box that appears, and select **OK** to return to the Receive File dialog box. To select a protocol, activate the **Use receiving protocol** list and pick out the same protocol you selected in the BBS. When you're done, select the **Receive** button to proceed with the transfer.

Use the Receive File dialog box to select a folder to store the file and a protocol.

If you selected Send File, the Send File dialog box appears. In this case, enter the name of the file to send in the **Filename** text box (or use the **Browse** button to select the file), use the **Protocol** drop-down list to choose the same protocol you selected in the BBS, and select **Send** to make it so.

In either case, HyperTerminal displays the progress of the transfer in a dialog box. If, for any reason, you need to abort the transfer in midstream, you can select the **Cancel** button.

When the transfer is complete, HyperTerminal returns control to the service, and you can continue with other service options or log off.

Closing the Connection

When you finish using the service, issue the command to disconnect. This command varies depending on what service you call, but it's usually something like L for logoff, Q for Quit, or E for Exit. You should log off in whatever manner it expects; don't just hang up! If you call a friend, there won't be any special command to issue; you have to manually disconnect by selecting the **Call** menu's **Disconnect** command, or your friend must issue a similar command in her communications software.

When you're done using HyperTerminal, exit the program in the usual way (by selecting the **File** menu's **Exit** command). When HyperTerminal asks if you want to save the "session," select **Yes**. Notice that now the HyperTerminal window displays the icon you selected to represent the connection you just set up! To call this same number again, you can just select that icon instead of selecting HyperTerminal itself.

The Least You Need to Know

This chapter got your look at communicating with Windows 95 off to a rousing beginning. You learned all kinds of semi-useful info about modems and computer communications, and I showed you how to wield the Phone Dialer and HyperTerminal tools.

For your next communications trick, Chapter 26 shows you how to connect your computer to your network.

An Introduction to Windows 95 Networking

In This Chapter

➤ Setting up your computer for networking

➤ Accessing folders and printers on other computers

➤ Sharing your folders and printers with others

➤ A brief networking primer that'll have you surfing your "net" in no time flat

Back in the high-flying '80s, *networking* was the buzzword du jour. Although to the innocent observer networking appeared to be a social skill designed to augment business contacts, it was really just a high-falutin' euphemism for unabashed *schmoozing*.

Nowadays, though, the meaning of networking has changed from cocktail party conversations to computer system connections. Everywhere you turn, people are hooking computers together to see what happens. If you're a budding network administrator and you've connected a couple of machines at home or at the office, this chapter looks at some simple network stuff: setting up your computer, sharing files, sharing printers, accessing other computers, and other networking know-how.

Networking for Novices

If you'd like to take the networking plunge and connect a couple of computers for sharing files and printers (which is the simple definition of a network), Windows 95 is probably your best way to go. Why? Well, it takes most of the pain out of connecting computers, and you can share stuff with others in your network using the familiar Explorer tools you looked at in Part 3.

When most people think of networks (if, in fact, they ever think of them at all), the image that springs to mind is one of a central, monolithic computer that contains all the data and applications and has dozens or even hundreds of "terminals" attached to it. *Workgroups*, however, are different. A workgroup is a small group of computers connected by some kind of network cable. Each computer has its own applications and data, but the other computers in the workgroup can share these resources. In this egalitarian setup, all the computers in the workgroup are treated equally; no one machine is "better" or more important than any other. In most workgroups, the computers are related to each other somehow. For example, all the computers in a company's accounting department could form one workgroup, while the marketing department might have its own workgroup.

Some Net-Words

Networks in which all the machines have their own programs and data and can share these with the other computers are *peer-to-peer* networks.

A networked computer's *resources* include the disk drives, folders, programs, documents, and printers associated with that computer. The purpose of a network is to share these resources among several computers.

Each workgroup has a name (Accounting, for example), and each computer in the workgroup has its own name (this is usually the name of the person using the computer, but it can be just about anything you like). You specify the workgroup name and computer name when you set up Windows 95. In my case, I have five computers set up as a workgroup. My group name is *Olympus*, and the five computer names are *Apollo*, *Hermes*, *Mercury*, *Selene*, and *Zeus* (don't ask).

The whole point of setting up a workgroup is so the members of the group can share their resources. For example, if you have five computers in the group but only one printer (as I do), you can set things up so that each machine can print from that one printer. Cool. Similarly, you can share files, applications, and even CD-ROM drives. Does this mean that other people in the group can just play with your machine willy-nilly? Heck no, not if you don't want them to. *You* decide which resources on your computer are shared, and for extra safety, you can set up passwords to prevent undesirables and other members of your family from accessing sensitive areas.

Getting Your System Network-Ready

A single chapter is, of course, a pitifully small amount of space to devote to a large topic like networking. Because I can't cover everything, I'm going to assume that you have (or some cajolable networking sage has) installed the necessary network hardware on your computers.

With that disclaimer out of the way, I can show you how to set up Windows 95 for network use. The next two sections take you through the two main steps: installing the network software and identifying your computer for network purposes. (If you see the Network Neighborhood icon on your Windows 95 desktop, you can skip both steps because—lucky you—it means networking is already installed on your computer.)

Setting Up the Network Software

Most network noodling is done via a *network adapter*, which is a component that sits inside your computer. You plug the network cables into the adapter, and the adapter takes care of the dirty work of sending data out to the network and receiving data coming in from the network. For all this to run smoothly, you have to tell Windows 95 what kind of adapter you're using. Here are the steps to follow:

1. Select the **Start** button, open the **Settings** folder, and select **Control Panel**. Windows 95 displays the Control Panel window.

2. Select the **Network** icon, and the Network dialog box appears.

3. Select the **Add** button. Control Panel displays the Select Network Component Type dialog box.

4. Select **Adapter** and then select **Add**. The Select Network adapters dialog box appears, as shown in the next figure.

5. Use the **Manufacturers** list to highlight the manufacturer of your network adapter; use the **Network Adapters** list to highlight the adapter (you should find both things either on the box the adapter came in or in the adapter's manual); and then select **OK**.

6. You may now be asked to insert your Windows 95 CD-ROM or floppy disks. If so, follow the instructions on the screen until Control Panel returns you to the Network dialog box.

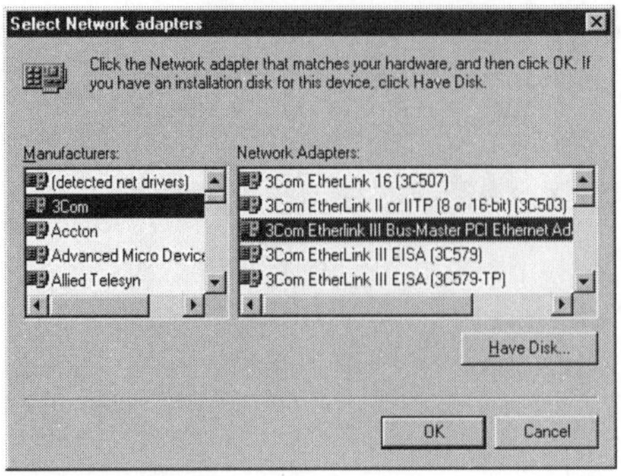

Use this dialog box to specify the type of network adapter you're using.

Setting Up Sharing

If you want to be a good network citizen and share stuff on your computer with your net friends (which I'll show you how to do later in this chapter), follow these steps to activate sharing:

1. In the Network dialog box, select the Configuration tab (if needed), and then select the **File and Print Sharing** button. The File and Print Sharing dialog box appears (see the following figure).

2. Activate the two check boxes.

3. Select **OK**.

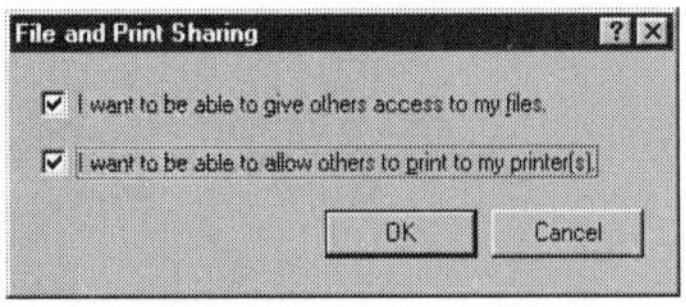

Activate these check boxes to share your stuff with other folks on your network.

Establishing Your Computer's Network Identity

Your next task is to give your computer a name and address on the network. The name is what appears in Explorer when you hang out in the Network Neighborhood (which I'll talk about later). The "address" is actually the name of the workgroup that your computer is a member of.

To do this, select the **Identification** tab in the Network dialog box (see the next figure). Then fill in the fields as explained next.

Use the Identification tab to establish a network name for your machine.

Computer name   Enter a network name for your computer (15 characters maximum). Ideally, you should enter a name that'll make it easy for others on the network to figure out which computer they're working with.

Workgroup   Enter the name of your network workgroup. If you set up your own network at home or in the office, you can enter any name you like (again, use a maximum of 15 characters). Just be sure to use the same name for each computer you include in your network. If you hook into a larger network at the office, the network system administrator assigns you a workgroup name.

Computer Description   Use this text box to enter a description for your computer (up to 48 characters). Windows 95 shows this description in some networks' lists to help others figure out which computer they're working with. This doesn't have to be anything fancy; a simple "Biff's Computer" or "Buffy's Honkin' Pentium Beast" will do.

When all that's done, select **OK** to put your changes into effect. When Windows 95 asks if you want to restart your computer, select **Yes**.

Logging In to Your Network

After you set up your network and restart Windows 95, eventually you'll be pestered to enter a "user name" and a password. Here are the steps to follow to get through this:

1. The default name shown in the **User name** text box is the computer name you entered during setup. If you want, you can change the logon name to something different (such as, say, your first name).

2. Use the **Password** text box to enter a password if you want to prevent others from getting into your copy of Windows 95. If your network is at home, you may not want to bother with a password (you *do* trust those kids of yours, don't you?), in which case, you can leave the Password text box blank.

   If you do use a password, make sure you enter one that's easy for you to remember but hard for others to figure out. When you enter the password, the letters appear as asterisks (*) for security reasons (you never know who might be peeking over your shoulder!).

3. Select **OK**. The Set Windows Password dialog box appears.

4. Reenter your password in the **Confirm new password** text box, and then select **OK**. Windows 95 finishes loading.

When you start Windows 95 in the future, all you have to do is enter your password. If, however, you change your user name, you have to repeat the whole process.

A Tour Around the Network Neighborhood

Okay, you can now do some networking! Windows 95 calls your workgroup and network the "Network Neighborhood," which certainly sounds friendly enough. Here's how to see what's in your Network Neighborhood:

➤ Double-click the desktop's **Network Neighborhood** icon.

➤ Open Explorer and select **Network Neighborhood** in the All Folders list.

The next figure shows the Network Neighborhood folder, which shows two things:

Entire Network   Open this folder to see all the workgroups that are part of the full network to which your computer is attached. (If you're just hooked up to your own workgroup, Entire Network shows only that workgroup.) Opening these workgroup folders displays the names of all the computers that comprise each workgroup.

Some computer names   The computer names shown in Entire Network are the names of the computers in your workgroup (including your own). Note that the Comment column contains the computer descriptions you entered earlier. (If you don't see this column, pull down the **View** menu and activate the **Details** command.)

The Network Neighborhood: your computer's community.

These are the computers in my workgroup.

Because each Network Neighborhood computer is really just a folder, you can use the usual My Computer or Explorer techniques to check out what's on the various machines. For each computer, you'll see those resources that the owner of the computer has chosen to share with the network. (I'll tell you how to share your resources later in this chapter.) For example, the following figure shows the window that appears when I open the folder for the computer named Hermes. Notice that this computer is sharing two hard disks (drives C and D), a CD-ROM drive (drive E), and a printer. The other computers in the workgroup can access these resources as though the hardware is part of their own systems.

If you open the folder for a Network Neighborhood computer, Windows shows the computer's shared resources.

Actually, the level of access available for a shared resource depends on the *access rights* the sharer has granted the sharees. As you'll see later on, you can prevent others from messing with your resources by giving them *read-only* access. If you run into, say, a shared folder that's read-only, you won't be able to change any of the folder's files. If you try, you'll see a curt error message telling you that **Network Access is denied**. Bummer.

It's also possible to tailor access to a shared resource by using passwords. For example, if you try to view a shared disk drive that has been password-protected, Windows 95 displays the Enter Network Password dialog box, shown in the following figure. You won't be able to access the drive until you enter the correct password in the **Password** text box. (Note, too, that unless you want to reenter the password every time you access this resource, you should leave the **Save this password in your password list** check box activated.)

Windows 95 displays this dialog box if a resource is protected by a password.

Working with the Resources in Your Workgroup

As I've said, one way to play with the shared resources in your workgroup is to head into the Network Neighborhood and "open" the computers you see listed. Here are two other ways to work with these resources:

➤ You can "map" a network disk drive so that it appears to be a disk drive on your computer. For example, let's say your system has two floppy disk drives (drives A and B) and a hard disk drive (drive C). You can map a network drive, and it will appear as drive D on your computer. This makes it easier to copy and move files to and from the network drive; it makes it easier to open files on the drive and it makes the drive accessible from the MS-DOS prompt.

➤ You can install a network printer and use it (more or less) just like a printer attached directly to your computer. (Why "more or less"? Well, there are some things you won't be able to do, such as purging other people's print jobs.)

Mapping a Network Drive

Mapping a network drive is easier done than said. For starters, display the Network Neighborhood folder and open the computer that contains the drive you want to work with. Now try either of the following techniques:

➤ Highlight the network drive, pull down the **Tools** menu, and select the **Map Network Drive** command.

➤ Right-click the network drive and select **Map Network Drive** from the shortcut menu.

Whichever method you choose, the Map Network Drive dialog box appears, as shown in the following figure. (Unless, that is, the drive is protected by a password, in which case, you'll see the Enter Network Password dialog box so you can enter the appropriate password.) The Drive box shows you the drive letter that Windows 95 will use to map the network drive. If you'd like this drive to be mapped every time you log on to Windows 95, activate the **Reconnect at logon** check box. When you're ready, select **OK** to map the drive. After a few seconds, the new drive appears in Explorer's All Folders list as part of the My Computer folder. (For those of you who have been paying attention: yes, the mapped drive also appears in the My Computer window.)

This dialog box tells you the drive letter that Windows 95 will assign to the mapped network drive.

To disconnect a mapped drive, use either of the following techniques:

➤ Highlight the mapped drive, pull down the **Tools** menu, and select the **Disconnect Network Drive** command.

➤ Right-click the network drive, and select **Disconnect** from the shortcut menu.

Either way, the Disconnect Network Drive dialog box appears. Make sure to highlight the drive you want to disconnect , and then select **OK**. If Windows 95 asks if you're sure you want to disconnect, select **Yes**.

Installing a Network Printer

One of the big advantages of setting up a workgroup in your workplace or home is that you can share expensive items (such as printers) among all your computers. You don't need to get a separate printer for each machine or put up with the hassle of swapping printer cables around. Here are the steps to follow to install a network printer for use on your computer:

1. Display the Network Neighborhood, open the computer that has the shared printer, and then highlight the printer.

2. Select the **File** menu's **Install** command.

3. You may see a Connect to Printer dialog box mumbling something about the "server" not having "a suitable printer driver." If so, ignore the geekspeak and select **OK**.

4. If you were subjected to the Connect to Printer dialog box in Step 3, you'll next see a dialog box from the Add Printer Wizard. Use the **Manufacturers** and **Printers** lists to highlight the printer you want to install, and then select **OK**.

5. From here, you follow the same steps that I outlined for installing a printer in Chapter 8, in the "Telling Windows 95 About Your Printer" section.

Playing Nicely with Others: Sharing Your Resources

Networking is, literally, a two-way street. It's fine to play around with the resources on other people's machines, but only a real greedy-guts would refuse to share his own computer's resources. To avoid being shunned by your peers, you need to designate a resource or two that can be shared. Read on to learn how.

Part I: Sharing Disk Drives and Folders

If you have a CD-ROM drive or perhaps some data in a folder that the others in your workgroup are lusting after, you should put your coworkers out of their misery by sharing the drive or folder with them.

The first thing you need to decide is how you want to share your resources. For each drive or folder you share, Windows 95 gives you three choices (called *access rights*):

Read-Only   At this level, someone else accessing one of your shared drives or folders can only copy, open, and view files. They can't move files, modify them, rename them, delete them, or add new ones.

Full   This anything-goes level gives others complete access to the files in the shared drive or folder. They can move, copy, open, view, modify, rename, and delete files, and they can even create new files.

Depends on Password   This level enables you to assign separate passwords for read-only and full access. At home, for example, you might want to give the kids read-only access to certain folders, but give yourself and your spouse full access. That's no problem; you simply assign a read-only password and tell it to the kids, and you assign a separate full-access password for you and your spouse.

Here are the steps you need to follow to share a disk drive, CD-ROM drive, or folder:

1. In Explorer or My Computer, highlight the disk drive or folder you want to share.

2. Pull down the **File** menu, select the **Properties** command, and select the **Sharing** tab in the Properties dialog box that appears (see the following figure). Alternatively, you can right-click the drive or folder and select **Sharing** from the shortcut menu.

3. Activate the **Shared As** option button.

4. The **Share Name** text box shows either the letter of the disk drive or the name of the folder. Because this is what appears in Explorer's Name column when other people access your computer, it's probably best that you leave the name as is. You should, however, enter a brief description of the resource in the **Comment** text box. (Something like "Hard disk" or "CD-ROM drive" or "Crucial workgroup files" is sufficient.)

5. Select the type of access you want for this resource: **Read-Only**, **Full**, or **Depends on Password**.

6. If you want others to be required to enter a password in order to access the shared drive or folder, enter the appropriate password in either the **Read-Only Password** or the **Full-Access Password** text box. If you selected **Depends on Password**, you need to enter a password in both text boxes. (If you do enter a password, don't forget to let the other people in your group know what it is!)

7. Select **OK**. If you entered a password, you're asked to confirm it. In this case, reenter the password and select **OK**. When you return to Explorer or My Computer, you see a little hand under the folder's icon. This reminds you that you've shared the folder.

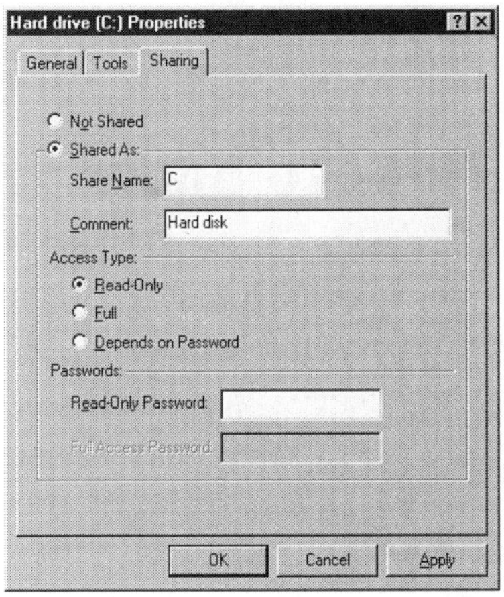

Use the Sharing tab to share a drive or folder with your workgroup pals.

Part II: Sharing Printers

Sharing a printer among several computers in a workgroup is similar to sharing folders. First, you need to open the Printers folder either by highlighting it in Explorer's All Folders list or by selecting **Start**, opening the **Settings** folder, and selecting **Printers**.

Highlight the printer you want to share, and then select the **File** menu's **Sharing** command (or right-click the printer and select **Sharing** from the shortcut menu). Windows 95 displays the printer's Properties dialog box and selects the **Sharing** tab (see next figure). Activate the **Share As** option, enter a comment, and then enter an optional password. Select **OK** to enable sharing. (If you entered a password, the Password Confirmation dialog box appears. Reenter the password and select **OK**.)

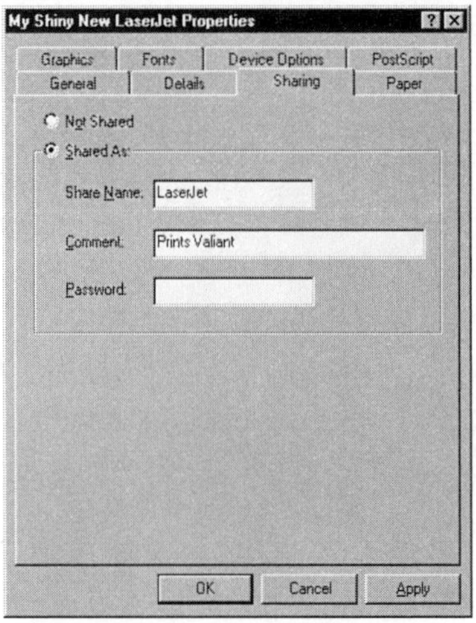

*The Sharing tab in a
printer's Properties
dialog box.*

The Least You Need to Know

This chapter taught you how to set up your computer for networking, how to access the shared resources on other network machines, and how to share your own resources with your workgroup peers.

This chapter assumed that you'll connect your computer to the network in the usual way: by adding a network adapter to the computer and then running some cable from the adapter to the network. However, Windows 95 also lets you connect to a network remotely by using a modem. I'll show you how this works in the next chapter.

Chapter 27

Reach Out and Touch Some Net: Dial-Up Networking

In This Chapter

➤ Setting up Windows 95 for Dial-Up Networking

➤ Creating a new Dial-Up Networking phonebook entry

➤ Connecting to the remote network

➤ Working with different dialing locations

The networking techniques that you saw in the last chapter assumed some kind of physical connection between machines. What do you do, however, when a physical connection just isn't physically possible? For example, suppose you're on the road with your notebook computer and need to access a file on your network server. Or suppose you're working at home and need to send a file to your office machine. Is there any way to access a network in the absence of a physical connection?

The answer is that, for these remote predicaments, you *can* connect to a network and use its resources just like you can with a physical connection (albeit more slowly). The solution is Windows 95's Dial-Up Networking feature. With Dial-Up Networking, you can establish a connection and log on to a network over phone lines by using your modem.

Not only that, but Dial-Up Networking is also your ticket to the wild and wacky world of the Internet because you can use it to create a connection to your Internet service provider (ISP). (I'll show you how this works in the next chapter. Note, as well, that this chapter assumes you don't connect to the Internet via your local area network.) This chapter shows you how to configure and use Dial-Up Networking.

What Is Dial-Up Networking?

In Chapter 25, "Basic Modem Fun," I showed how your computer can exchange data with remote machines by attaching a modem to the serial port and by running a phone line to the modem. In Chapter 26, "An Introduction to Windows 95 Networking," I showed you how your computer can exchange data with machines on a network by inserting a network adapter inside the computer and by running a network cable to the card.

Dial-Up Networking is an amalgam of these two technologies. It gives you access to a network, but a modem and phone line replace the adapter and cable. Your network access is identical to that of a machine attached directly to the network: you log on with your user name and password; you can browse and use shared resources; you can share your local resources; you can access the Internet if your network has the appropriate connection; you can retrieve mail; and so on. The main difference is that, because you use a serial port and modem as the network connection point, data transfers will be much slower.

Install a Modem First!

To save yourself a step down the road, you should make sure that you installed your modem in Windows 95. I showed you how to do this in Chapter 25, in the "Modem Installation Made Easy" section.

Setting Up Windows 95 for Dial-Up Networking

With that blather out of the way, you can dive right into the deep end of Dial-Up Networking. To get the show off the ground, you need to do two things:

➤ Install and configure Dial-Up Networking.

➤ Create a Dial-Up Networking phonebook entry.

Configuring Your First Connection

Begin by opening the **Start** menu, selecting **Programs**, **Accessories**, and then **Dial-Up Networking**. (No sign of the Dial-Up Networking icon? Don't worry: you just need to install it from your Windows 95 disks. Trudge back to Chapter 23 and read the "Adding Windows 95 Components" section to find out how to install it.) A dialog box appears with a brief description of Dial-Up Networking. Select **Next** > to continue.

Windows 95 starts the Make New Connection Wizard so you can specify the particulars of your Dial-Up Networking session. Windows 95 calls these particulars a *connection* and each connection contains, among other things, a name, the modem to use, and the phone number to dial.

For starters, Windows 95 then displays the dialog box shown in the following figure. You need to fill in two things:

> **Type a name for the computer you are dialing:** Use this text box to enter a name for the new Dial-Up Networking connection.

> **Select a modem:** If you installed multiple modems, use this drop-down list to select the modem you want to use for this connection.

Select **Next** > when you're done.

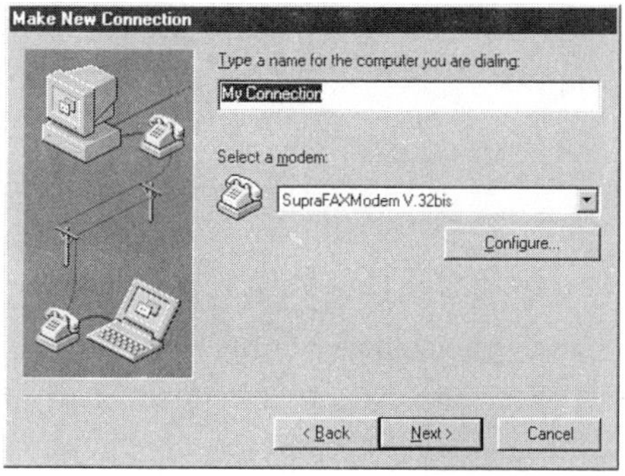

Use this dialog box to enter a connection name and choose the modem to use with Dial-Up Networking.

Check out the next Make New Connection Wizard dialog box shown here. You use this dialog box to enter the area code, phone number, and country code for the computer you'll connect to. When you're done, select **Next** >.

That'll do it: your new connection is ready to roll. In the final dialog box, select **Finish** to shut down the wizard.

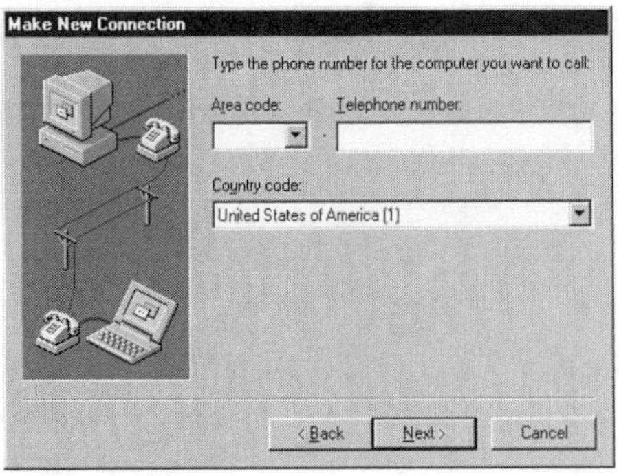

Use this dialog box to specify the phone number for your connection.

Creating More Connections

After you finish creating your initial connection, each time you start Dial-Up Networking, you'll see the Dial-Up Networking window, as shown in the following figure. If you need to create another connection, double-click the **Make New Connection** icon to launch the Make New Connection, and then follow the same routine that I outlined in the last section.

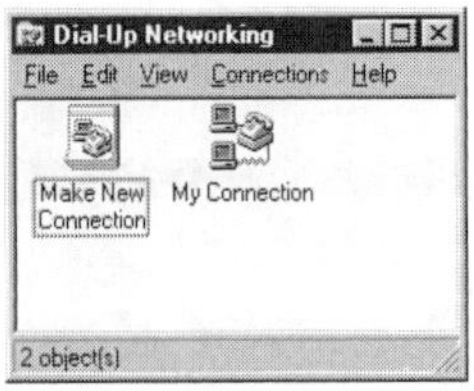

Double-click the Make New Connection icon to, well, make a new connection.

Connecting to the Remote Network

Okay, you're finally ready to make the connection. If you haven't done so already, get the Dial-Up Networking window on board by selecting **Start**, **Programs**, **Accessories**, and then **Dial-Up Networking**. (This is a good time to make sure your modem is hooked up properly and, if you have an external modem, that it's turned on.) Now just double-click the connection icon to get the show on the road.

Windows 95 displays the Connect To dialog box in which you enter your user name and password (see the following figure). Also, if you activate the **Save password** check box, Dial-Up Networking will remember your password for future calls.

Dial-Up Networking dials the modem and then negotiates your logon with the remote system. (Depending on the connection you're using, you may see a terminal window appear so you can enter more information. More on this in the next chapter.) When you're safely connected, a dialog box appears to confirm the connection and to track the duration of your session (see the next figure). Clicking the **Details** button in this dialog box shows you the server type and protocols being used.

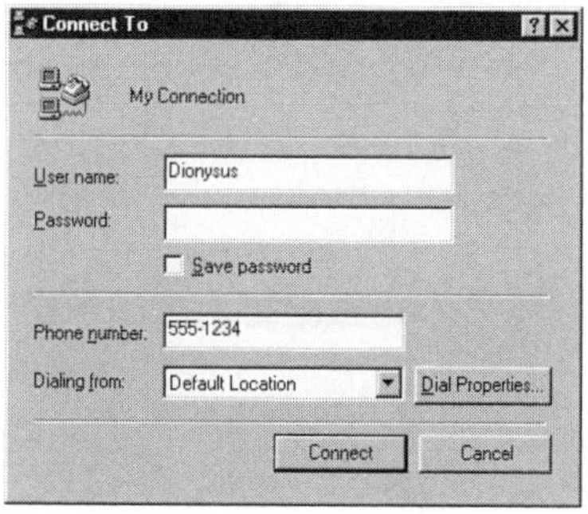

Use this dialog box to initiate the connection.

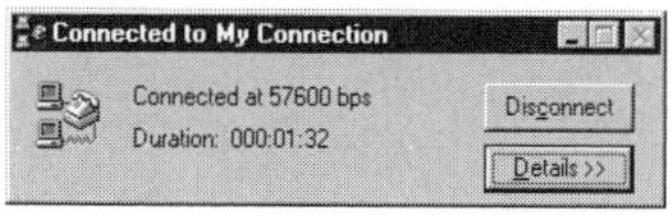

Once you connect, this dialog box tracks your connect time.

Once you connect, your computer becomes a full member of the network, so you can access network resources, browse the Network Neighborhood, and others on the network can see your computer, as well.

Disconnecting from the Remote Network

When you finish your online work, you need to remember to disconnect to clear the line and avoid running up long distance charges (if applicable).

To disconnect, display the "Connected" dialog box previously shown, and then click the **Disconnect** button.

Using Locations with Dial-Up Networking

You probably noticed that the Connect To dialog box has a Dialing Properties button. This button enables you to specify different dialing locations, which tell Windows 95 whether or not you use a calling card, the number to dial to get an outside line, and more. Locations are particularly useful for Dial-Up Networking because notebook computer users will often have to connect to their networks from different places:

➤ You may need to connect from home where you have call waiting, which you need to disable.

➤ You may need to connect from a client's office where you have to dial 9 to get an outside line.

➤ You may need to connect from out of town, and have to dial the number as long distance and use your corporate calling card.

For such situations, you can change these and other location parameters by selecting the **Dial Properties** button in the Connect To dialog box. The following figure shows the dialog box that appears.

Use the Dialing Properties dialog box to adjust the settings that Windows 95 uses to dial your modem.

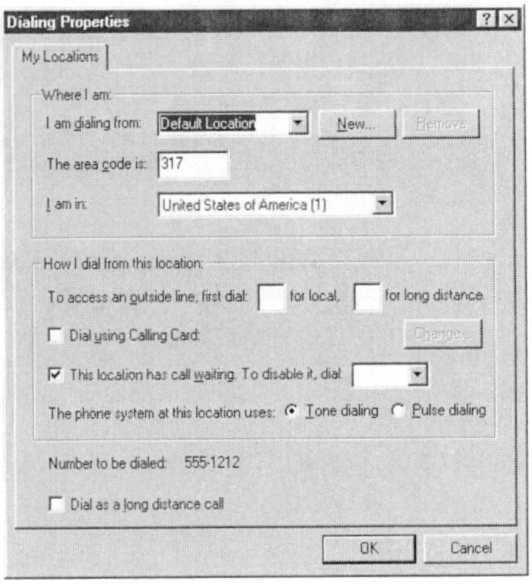

The controls in the Where I am group tell Windows 95 about your current location:

The area code is Use this text box to specify the area code at your current location.

I am in Use this text box to specify the country code at your current location.

The How I dial from this location group specifies a few extra dialing parameters:

To access an outside line Use these text boxes to enter the number you have to dial to access an outside line. Use the first text box for local calls and the second text box for long distance calls.

Dial using Calling Card Activate this check box to specify a calling card to use during the call. I'll explain how this works in more detail in the next section.

This location has call waiting To disable call waiting, activate this check box, and then use the **To disable it, dial** drop-down list to choose the appropriate dialing sequence for turning off call waiting.

The phone system at this location uses Select either **Tone dialing** or **Pulse dialing**.

Check This Out...

Caution: Always Disable Call Waiting

The extra beeps that call waiting uses to indicate an incoming call can play havoc on modem communications, so you should always disable call waiting before initiating a data call. The sequences *70, 70#, or 1170 (which are the ones listed in the To disable it, dial drop-down list) usually disable call waiting, but you should check with your local phone company to make sure. If another sequence is needed, type it in the text box.

Specifying a Calling Card or Long-Distance Carrier

Although most of your phone calls are likely to be free, there are times when this may not be the case, and you'll want to make some other arrangements for charging the call. Two situations, in particular, may crop up from time to time:

➤ You're dialing from a hotel and want to charge the call to your calling card.

➤ You need to make a long-distance connection, in which case you might want to first dial the number of a long-distance carrier.

Windows 95 can handle both situations. To specify either a calling card number or long-distance carrier phone number, activate the **Dial using Calling Card** check box, and then select the **Change** button. Windows 95 displays the Change Calling Card dialog box, as shown in the following figure. Use the **Calling Card to use** list to choose either your long distance carrier or the type of calling card you have. For the latter, enter the calling card number in the **Calling Card number** text box.

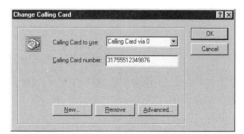

Use the Change Calling Card dialog box to enter a calling card number or select a long-distance carrier.

If your calling card or long-distance carrier doesn't appear in the list, follow these steps to add it:

1. Select the **New** button to display the Create New Calling Card dialog box.

2. Enter a descriptive name for the calling card or carrier, and then select **OK**.

3. Select **OK**. The Dialing Rules dialog box appears, as shown in the next figure. The dialing rules are codes that tell Windows 95 how to dial the phone in order to complete a calling card or long-distance carrier connection.

4. Fill in the three text boxes to define the rules Windows 95 should use for local calls, long distance calls, and international calls. The following table lists the various symbols you can use to construct these rules.

Symbols to Use When Constructing Dialing Rules

Symbol	Description
E	Dials the country code
F	Dials the area code
G	Dials the local number
H	Dials the calling card number
P	Switches to pulse dialing
T	Switches to tone dialing
W	Waits for a second dial tone
0-9	Dials the digits as entered
,	Pauses for two seconds
!	Hook flash (1/2 second on-hook, 1/2 second off-hook)
@	Waits for a ringing tone followed by five seconds of silence
$	Waits for a calling card prompt tone
?	Displays an on-screen prompt so you can continue dialing manually

5. Select **Close** to return to the Change Calling Card dialog box.

6. If you used the H (calling card number) symbol, the Calling Card number text box will be enabled. Enter your calling card number in this box.

7. Select **OK**.

For example, consider the rule 8,0FG$TH. This rule dials 8 for an outside line, pauses for two seconds (,), dials 0 followed by the area code (F) and local number (G), waits for the calling card tone ($), switches to tone dialing, and then sends your calling card number (H).

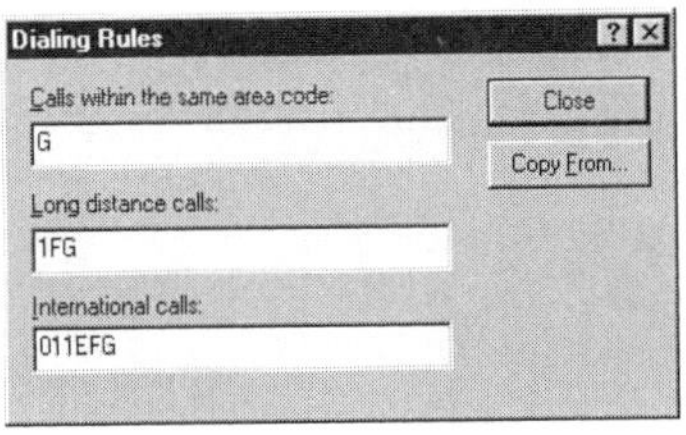

Dialing Rules

Calls within the same area code:
G

Long distance calls:
1FG

International calls:
011EFG

Close

Copy From...

Use the Dialing Rules dialog box to specify how Windows 95 dials a number with your new calling card or long-distance carrier.

Working with Different Dialing Locations

If you have a notebook computer, you can set up multiple dialing locations. For example, you can have one location for dialing from the office that uses extra digits to access an outside line and uses your corporate calling card. You can then have a second location for home that doesn't require anything extra to access an outside line and disables your call waiting service.

The location information you entered while installing your modem is stored in a location called New Location. To set up another location, select **New** in the Dialing Properties dialog box and select **OK**. Use the **I am dialing from** text box to change the name of the new location, and then enter your dialing properties for the new location.

To choose a different location, use the **I am dialing from** drop-down list.

The Least You Need to Know

This chapter showed you how to connect to remote networks by using Windows 95's Dial-Up Networking. I showed you how to create a new Dial-Up Networking connection and how to use this connection to dial in to a remote system. I also showed you how to work with different locations for maximum dialing flexibility when you're going mobile.

The next chapter shows you how to use Dial-Up Networking to connect to the Internet.

Chapter 28

Windows in Cyberspace: Getting on the Internet

In This Chapter

➤ Connecting to the Internet with Dial-Up Networking

➤ Connecting to the Internet via your network

➤ A complete list of all the info you need to establish a connection

➤ A tutorial on using Internet Explorer to get around the Net

➤ Your personal on-ramp to that information expressway thing

As you've no doubt figured out by now, computer nerds thrive on jargon and buzzwords. These terms range from the useful (such as *multimedia* and *drag-and-drop*) to the downright silly (*GUI* and *boot* come to mind). Fortunately, most jargon never makes it past the narrow confines of each nerd's subspecialty (which means the rest of us don't have to know about scary-sounding things like *bandwidth* and *client-server*).

Occasionally, however, the odd buzzword makes it into the mainstream where, tragically, it's quickly trampled to death by media overkill. (I call it the "cachet-to-cliché" syndrome.) The most spectacular example of this was the phrase *user friendly*, which appeared ad nauseam a few years back. The current champ in the overused-phrase category is *Information Superhighway*. Heck, the thing doesn't even exist yet, and we're already sick of hearing about it!

But just as *user friendly* was a good idea before it was knocked silly (after all, who'd want to use something that was *user hostile*?), so too is the Information Superhighway a good idea that's been obscured by hype. In this chapter, you'll ignore the hype, and I'll show you how to use Windows 95 to connect to the closest thing there is to a digital expressway: the Internet.

What's the Best Route to Take?

You have two routes you can take to set up an Internet connection:

➤ If you don't have an Internet account, use the Internet Connection Wizard to create and configure a new account automatically.

➤ If you have an existing Internet account, use the Internet Setup Wizard to do a step-by-step setup.

For the latter, here's a list of information you need to fill in as you go along (your ISP—Internet Service Provider—should have provided you with all of this data when you signed up for your Internet account):

➤ Whether or not your ISP uses something called *DHCP* (most don't).

➤ If DHCP isn't used, you need to know the *IP address* that has been assigned to your account and the appropriate *subnet mask* for your ISP.

➤ The address of your ISP's *DNS server*.

➤ The phone number to dial as well as your user name and password.

➤ Whether your connection is "PPP" or "SLIP."

Check This Out...

Don't Forget to Install a Modem

Before proceeding any further, you should install a modem in Windows 95, if you haven't done so already. I showed you how to do this back in Chapter 25, in the "Modem Installation Made Easy" section.

Creating a New Account with the Internet Connection Wizard

If you don't have an Internet account established, the easiest way to get your Windows 95 machine connected to the Internet is to use the Internet Connection Wizard. This wizard is available with later versions of Windows 95, known as Windows 95 B.

The Internet Connection Wizard helps you create the connection by leading you through all the necessary steps in typical wizard fashion.

There are a couple of ways to launch the Internet Connection Wizard:

➤ Double-click the **Internet** icon on your Windows 95 desktop. (Note that this method works only once. After you complete the wizard, double-clicking the Internet icon runs Internet Explorer, Microsoft's World Wide Web browser.)

➤ Open the **Start** menu, select **Programs**, **Accessories**, and then **Internet Tools**. In the submenu that appears, select **Get on the Internet**.

The initial wizard dialog box just gives you some introductory information, so click **Next>** to continue. The dialog box shown in the following figure presents you with your first choice. In this case, make sure to activate the **Automatic** option, and then click **Next >**.

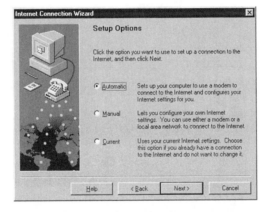

For easiest setup, use the Automatic option.

The dialog box that appears gives you an overview of the Automatic setup, so click **Next >** once again, and then click **OK** in the Installing Files dialog box. If you're asked to insert your Windows 95 CD-ROM or floppy disks, follow the instructions on the screen. When prompted to restart your computer, click **OK**.

When your computer restarts, the wizard will kick in once again and you'll see the dialog box shown in the first figure on the following page. Make sure your area code is correct, and then enter the first three digits of your phone number.

When you click **Next >**, the wizard dials your modem and proceeds to grab a list of the Internet service providers in your area. When that's done, the wizard displays a window similar to the second figure on the following page. This window lists a few providers and gives you a short description of each one. To find out more, click the **More Info** icon.

The wizard wants to know your area code and the first three digits of your phone number.

You'll eventually see a list of possible providers.

When you decide which one you want, click the Sign Me Up icon beside the provider. The wizard then connects you with the provider so you can complete the sign up procedure. (This varies from provider to provider.)

Setting Up an Existing Account with the Internet Setup Wizard

If you already have an Internet account, the Internet Setup Wizard makes it a breeze to set up a connection to the provider in Windows 95. This wizard is available via the Microsoft Plus! add-on, as a separate retail product, and with Windows 95 B. To start this wizard, use one of the following techniques:

➤ If you have Windows 95 B, launch the Internet Connection Wizard as described in the last section, and click **Next >** in the first dialog box. When you get to the Setup Options dialog box, activate the **Manual** option and then select **Next >**.

➤ If you have Microsoft Plus! or the Internet Explorer retail product, open the **Start** menu, select **Programs, Accessories, Internet Tools**, and then **Internet Setup Wizard**.

The first wizard dialog box gives you some introductory info, so just select **Next >**. The next dialog box (shown here) presents you with a choice:

Connect using my phone line: Activate this option if you'll use your modem to connect to the Internet.

Connect using my Local Area Network: Activate this option only if your computer is attached to a network and the network has an Internet connection.

Select **Next >** to continue.

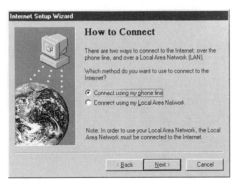

Use this dialog box to let the wizard know how you'll connect to the Internet.

The wizard now asks whether you want to use Windows Messaging (or possible Microsoft Exchange) to work with your Internet e-mail, as shown in the following figure. Activate the **Yes** option if you plan on using the Internet e-mail, and then click **Next >**.

Activate Yes if you want to do the Internet e-mail thing.

Now the wizard tells you that it's about to install a few files. Click **Next >** to proceed. You'll likely be prompted to enter your Windows 95 CD-ROM or a floppy disk or two. When that's done, the wizard prompts you to enter the name of your service provider, as shown next. This will actually be the name of the Dial-Up Networking connection that the wizard will create for your Internet access, so you can enter whatever you like. Click **Next >** when you're ready to move on.

Enter the name of your ISP or a description of the connection.

The next Wizard dialog box, shown in the following figure, asks for the Area code, Telephone number, and Country code of the ISP's dial-in phone number. In most cases, when connecting to the ISP, you need to enter your user name, your password, and other options by hand. To do this, activate the **Bring up terminal window after dialing** check box. When you're done, click **Next >**.

The next item on the Internet Setup Wizard's to-do list is to enter your user name and password. Enter the appropriate values in the **User name** and **Password** fields, and then click **Next >**.

Use this dialog box to enter your dial-in phone number.

The wizard next asks about your IP address. You have two choices:

My Internet Service Provider automatically assigns me one: Activate this option if your ISP doles out IP addresses on-the-fly.

Always use the following: Activate this option if your ISP has assigned you an IP address. Use the IP Address text box to enter the IP address.

Click **Next** > to proceed with the setup.

You're next asked to specify one or two DNS servers. Use the **DNS Server** text box to enter the IP address of your ISP's DNS server. If the ISP also has a secondary DNS server, enter its IP address in the **Alternate DNS Server** text box. Click **Next** >.

If you want to use Windows Messaging (or Microsoft Exchange) for your Internet e-mail, make sure to activate the **Use Internet Mail** check box in the next wizard dialog box that appears. (Note that you'll see this dialog box only if you told the wizard earlier that you'll use Windows Messaging to handle your Internet e-mail duties.) Enter your e-mail address in the **Your Email address** text box, and enter the name of your ISP's mail server in the **Internet mail server** text box. Click **Next** > to continue.

In the final Internet Setup Wizard dialog box, click **Finish**. If the wizard prompts you to restart your computer, click **Yes**. When you get back to Windows 95, you'll find a new connection in your Dial-Up Networking folder. To use this connection to establish an Internet session, see the next section.

Connecting to Your Service Provider

With your Internet connection set up and ready for action, you can establish your Net session at any time. If you access the Internet via your network, the connection is established automatically when you log on to the network. For dial-up connections, however, you need to run Dial-Up Networking, choose the appropriate connection for your ISP, and then select **Dial**.

When you're connecting to the ISP, you'll see the After Dial Terminal window in which you can enter your logon options. Depending on the ISP, you may have to enter some or all of the following (see the figure below):

➤ If you just see a blank terminal window, try pressing **Enter**.

➤ Your user name.

➤ Your password.

➤ The connection type. In some cases, you'll enter a command (such as **ppp**); in other cases, you'll select the connection type from a menu of choices.

When you've entered all of your options, select the terminal window's **Continue** button (or press **F7**).

Connecting to an ISP usually requires entering a few parameters in the terminal window.

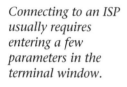

All right, you're on the Net and ready for some serious surfing! I'll show you how to wield Internet Explorer (Windows 95's built-in Web browser) in the next section. If you want to keep an eye on your connect time, double-click the **Dial-Up Networking** icon in the taskbar's system tray.

Starting Internet Explorer

The way some folks carry on, you'd think the World Wide Web and the Internet were synonymous. (The Web is, in fact, just a subset of the Internet.) Everywhere you turn, people are yakking about some cool Web site they visited or trading URLs (Uniform Resource Locators—the addresses of Net-based resources, especially Web pages) like nobody's business.

If you want to get in on the Web action, you'll need a Web browser. And since most of the Web's appeal lies in its graphical nature, you'll want to use a graphical browser that shows Web pages in their best light. The rest of this chapter shows you how to surf the Web using just such a browser: Internet Explorer. (Caveat emptor: Note that Microsoft is constantly updating Internet Explorer and making these updates available on its Web site (**www.microsoft.com**). This section describes the version of Internet Explorer that was available when I wrote this, but Microsoft may have moved on to an entirely different flavor of Explorer by the time you read this.)

To start (I'm assuming here that you've already established your connection to your service provider), double-click the desktop's **The Internet** icon. The Web page that appears depends on the version of Internet Explorer that you use. In the latest versions, you'll see the "Internet Start" page shown in the following figure.

Here's a summary of the main features of this screen:

Title   The top line of the screen shows you the title of the current Web page.

Toolbar   These buttons give you point-and-click access to some of Internet Explorer's main features. If you prefer to hide the toolbar (because, say, you'd like more screen real estate), deactivate the **View** menu's **Toolbar** command.

Address bar   This area shows you the address of the current page.

Links bar   This area gives you a few predefined "links," which are connections to other locations on the Web. Click one of these links (I explain each of them later) to head for that page.

Content area   This is the area below the Address bar and Links bar that takes up the bulk of the Internet Explorer screen. It's where the body of each Web page appears. You can use the vertical scroll bars to see more of the current document.

Image link/text link   The content area for most Web pages also boasts a link or two (or ten). These links come in two flavors: images and text (the latter appear underlined in a different color). You select a link by clicking it. When you point to a link, Internet Explorer does two things: it changes the mouse pointer to a hand with a pointing finger, and in the status bar, it displays **Shortcut to** and the name of the document to which the link will take you.

Status bar   This bar lets you know Internet Explorer's current status, displays a description of the links you point to, and it tells you the progress of the current Internet Explorer operation (such as downloading a file).

The Internet Explorer screen.

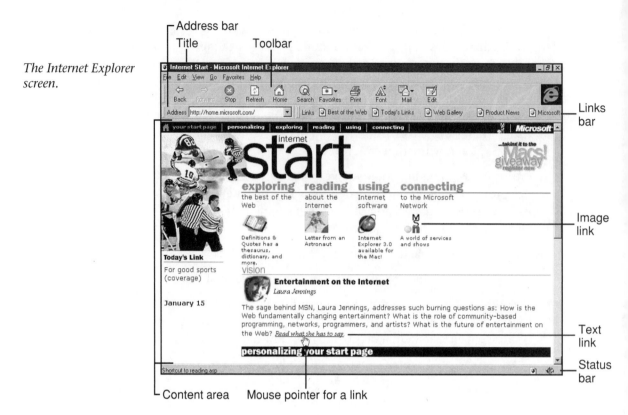

Navigating with Internet Explorer

Now that you're familiar with the lay of the Internet Explorer land, you can start using it to navigate sites. The next few sections take you through the various ways you can use Internet Explorer to weave your way through the Web.

Following the Links

As I've said, Internet Explorer displays links either as an image or as text in an underlined font that's a different color from the rest of the text. To follow one of these links, you have a couple of choices:

➤ Click it with your mouse.

➤ Right-click the link and then select **Open In New Window** from the menu that appears. This command spawns a new Internet Explorer window and opens the linked Web page in that window.

Some Images Are All Show and No Go

Just to keep you confused, not all of the images you see on a Web page are necessarily links. Some are there strictly for show, and you can click them until you're blue in the face and nothing will happen. How can you tell links from nonlinks? The only sure-fire way is to point your mouse at the picture. If the mouse pointer turns into the little hand with the pointing finger, then you know you're dealing with a link.

Using the Links Bar

If you're not sure where you want to go on the Web, Internet Explorer's Links bar contains five prefab sites that you can try out to get your feet wet. Here's a summary of each link:

Best of Web: This is a great place to start your Web explorations. Clicking this link takes you to the Start Exploring page, which contains even more links arranged by category: Entertainment, Finance, News, Sports, and much more.

Today's Links: This link connects you to the Internet Start page.

Web Gallery: This link takes you a site designed for Web site creators. It features an online gallery of images, sounds, and other tools used by Web weavers.

Product News: Click this link to get the latest Internet Explorer news and updates.

Microsoft: This link takes you to Microsoft's home page.

Entering a Web Page Address

If you want to strike out for a particular Web site, you can specify the address using any of the following methods:

➤ Click inside the Address bar, delete the current address, type in the one you want, and then press **Enter**.

➤ Select the **File** menu's **Open** command. In the Open dialog box that appears (see the following figure), type the address in the **Open** text box and then select **OK**.

*Use this dialog box
to specify the address
of the Internet site
you want to open.*

Retracing Your Steps

Once you start leaping and jumping through the Web's cyberspace, you'll often want to head back to a previous site, or even to your start page (the first page you see when you launch Internet Explorer). Here's a rundown of the various techniques you can use to move to and fro in Internet Explorer:

➤ To go back to the previous document, either click the **Back** toolbar button or select the **Go** menu's **Back** command.

➤ Once you go back to a previous document, you can move ahead to the next document either by clicking the toolbar's **Forward** button or by selecting the **Go** menu's **Forward** command.

➤ To return to the start page, either click the **Home** button or select **Start Page** from the **Go** menu.

➤ To return to a specific document you visited, pull down the **Go** menu and select the document's title from the list near the bottom of the menu. If you need to see the document's address or a larger list, select the **Go** menu's **Open History Folder** command. In the history folder that appears, double-click the document you want to open.

Using the Search Page

The navigation approaches you've tried so far have encompassed the two extremes of Web surfing: clicking links randomly to see what happens, and entering addresses to display specific sites. However, what if you want to look for information on a particular topic, but you don't know any appropriate addresses and you don't want to waste time clicking aimlessly around the Web? In this case, you can put the Web to work for you. That is, you can crank up one of the Web's search engines to track down sites that contain the data you want to find.

Conveniently, Internet Explorer contains a link that gives you easy access to five of the Web's best search engines (you can search the Microsoft Web site, as well). To view these links, either click the toolbar's **Search** button or select the **Go** menu's **Search the Web** command. You see the page shown in the following figure. To try a search, enter your search text in the text box provided, activate one of the search options, and then click the **Search** button. If you're not sure which search engine to try, select a search service link to see descriptions of each engine.

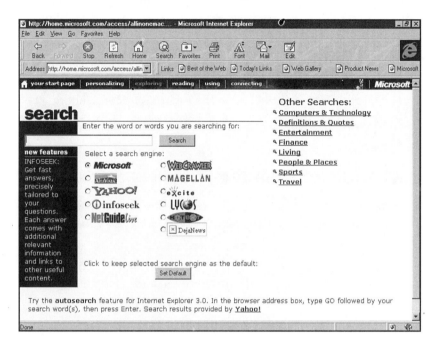

Internet Explorer displays this page when you select Search the Web.

Internet Explorer's Favorites Folder: Sites to Remember

The sad truth is that much of what you see on the Web is utterly forgettable and not worth a second surf. However, there are all kinds of gems out there waiting for you to uncover—sites that you'll want to visit regularly. Instead of memorizing the appropriate addresses, jotting them down on sticky notes, or plastering your desktop with shortcuts, you can use Internet Explorer's handy Favorites feature to keep track of your choice sites.

The Favorites feature is really just a folder (you'll find it in your main Windows 95 folder) that you use to store Internet shortcuts. The advantage of using the Favorites folder, as opposed to any other folder, is that you can add, view, and link to the Favorites folder shortcuts directly from Internet Explorer.

Adding a Shortcut in the Favorites Folder

When you find a site that you want to declare as a favorite, pull down the **Favorites** menu and select the **Add To Favorites** command. In the Add To Favorites dialog box that appears, the title of the Web page appears in the Name text box. Edit the name, if you like, and then select **OK**.

Viewing the Favorites Folder

If you want to work with the Favorites folder directly, pull down Internet Explorer's **Favorites** menu and select **Organize Favorites** to open the Favorites folder window.

From here, you can rename shortcuts, delete shortcuts, and create new subfolders to organize your shortcuts.

Opening an Internet Shortcut from the Favorites Folder

The purpose of the Favorites folder, of course, is to give you quick access to those sites you visit regularly. To link to one of the shortcuts in your Favorites folder, you have two choices:

➤ In Internet Explorer, the Favorites menu contains the complete list of your Favorites folder shortcuts. To link to a shortcut, pull down this menu and then select the shortcut you want.

➤ Open the Favorites folder and double-click a shortcut.

The Least You Need to Know

This chapter showed how Windows 95 and the Internet get along. As you saw, they get along just fine, thank you. I showed you how to use both the Internet Connection Wizard and the Internet Setup Wizard to get connected. With that done, I then showed you how to surf the Net using Internet Explorer.

Another Internet service that you'll want to use is e-mail. I'll show you how to set up Microsoft Exchange for Internet e-mail in the next chapter.

Chapter 29

Exchanging E-Mail with Microsoft Exchange

In This Chapter

➤ What's this Exchange thing all about?

➤ Sending and receiving e-mail

➤ Setting up Microsoft Exchange to suit yourself

➤ An excellent Exchange excursion that'll help you survive in the have-your-people-e-mail-my-people world

Online aficionados use the term *snail mail* as a snide reference to mail sent through the post office. Why "snail?" Well, regular mail has the nerve to actually take *days* to reach its destination, and that just won't cut it in our fast-paced, I-need-it-yesterday lives. No, in this wired world, communication times are measured in minutes thanks to e-mail systems and fax machines. So how's a body to keep up?

Well, if you have Windows 95, you can put the pedal to your communications metal by using Microsoft Exchange. Exchange is a sort of electronic post office box that you can use to both send and receive e-mail and faxes. It's a one-stop communications shop that lets you read and compose all your digital correspondence from the comfort of Windows 95. This chapter explains Exchange and takes you on a tour of its basic features.

Microsoft Exchange Versus Windows Messaging

Throughout this book, I've mentioned a later version of Windows 95 called Windows 95 B. In this chapter, you come across yet another difference between the original (version A) and version B. Namely, that in version B Microsoft Exchange is now called Windows Messaging. To avoid confusion, I'll use the term "Exchange" in this chapter.

Installing Microsoft Exchange

The best way to tell whether Microsoft Exchange is installed is to look for the Inbox icon on your desktop, or to select the **Start** button, open the **Programs** folder, and then look for the Microsoft Exchange icon. If you see either one, great: it means Microsoft Exchange is installed.

There are no worries, though, if Exchange is nowhere in sight. You can install Exchange using the Add/Remove Programs utility in the Control Panel. The "Adding Windows 95 Components" section in Chapter 23 gives you the full scoop on this.

Once you install Exchange, Windows 95 pushes the Inbox Setup Wizard on stage, as shown in the following figure. (In Windows 95 A, this is the Microsoft Exchange Setup Wizard.) This Wizard will lead you through the entire Exchange setup procedure.

The Inbox Setup Wizard shows up after you install Exchange.

This first dialog box wonders whether or not you've used Windows Messaging before. I'll assume you haven't, so make sure to activate the **No** option and then select **Next >**.

Setting Up Microsoft Exchange

Before you can send or receive e-mail missives with Exchange, you have to supply it with a few particulars about your e-mail account, which is what you'll do in this section. If you continue with the Exchange installation from the last section, you should now see the wizard dialog box shown in the following figure. If you start the Exchange setup from scratch, you can get to this dialog box by double-clicking the desktop's **Inbox** icon.

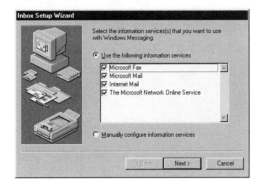

Use this wizard dialog box to choose the services you want to use.

In this dialog box, the wizard pesters you about which "information services" you want to use. What's the deal there? Well, there are all kinds of ways to send e-mail messages. For example, if your computer is part of a network, you might use a system called Microsoft Mail to correspond with your corporate colleagues. Similarly, you can also use the Internet to exchange notes with folks in the far-flung corners of the world. And if you signed up with the Microsoft Network, it has its own e-mail system.

Although most e-mail programs can only handle messages from a single type of e-mail system, Exchange is multitalented: it will gladly work with e-mail from Microsoft Mail, the Internet, and the Microsoft Network.

So the initial wizard dialog box just wants to know which of the e-mail services you'll use. (The services you see depend on which ones are installed on your system.) Make sure to activate the **Use the following information services** option, activate the appropriate check boxes for the services you want, and then select **Next >**.

Setting Up Microsoft Mail

If you activated the Microsoft Mail check box, you see the wizard dialog box shown in the following figure. This time, the wizard wants to know where it can find your network *postoffice*, which is the central location where your incoming messages are stored. (I'm assuming here that you plowed through Chapter 26, "An Introduction to Windows 95 Networking.") You have a couple of options for specifying the postoffice location:

➤ Enter the postoffice's network address in the text box provided.

➤ Select the **Browse** button to display the Browse for Postoffice dialog box, open the Network Neighborhood, find the computer that contains the postoffice, and then highlight the postoffice folder (called something like WGPO, or WGPO0000).

If you're not sure about any of this, your network administrator will be happy to give you the correct location. When you have it all sorted out, select **Next >** to continue.

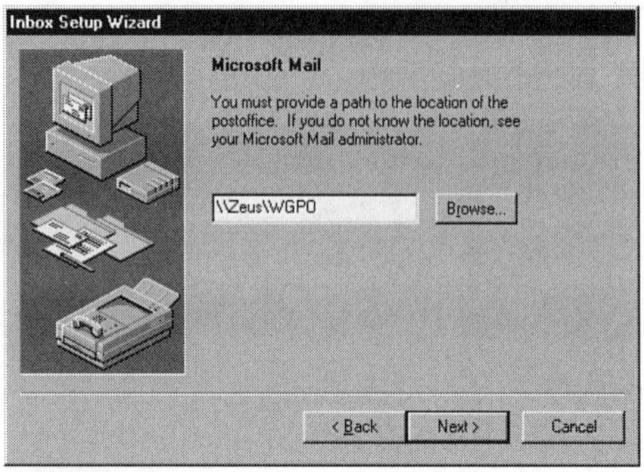

This wizard dialog box begs you for the location of your network Microsoft Mail postoffice.

As shown in the next figure, the Wizard presents you with a list of all the users that have accounts on the Microsoft Mail postoffice you chose in the last step. All you need to do is highlight your name and then select **Next >**. (Don't see your name? You'll need to chastise your network administrator.) The wizard then asks you to enter a password for your account. Type your password in the text box provided, and then select **Next >**. This ends the Microsoft Mail portion of our show.

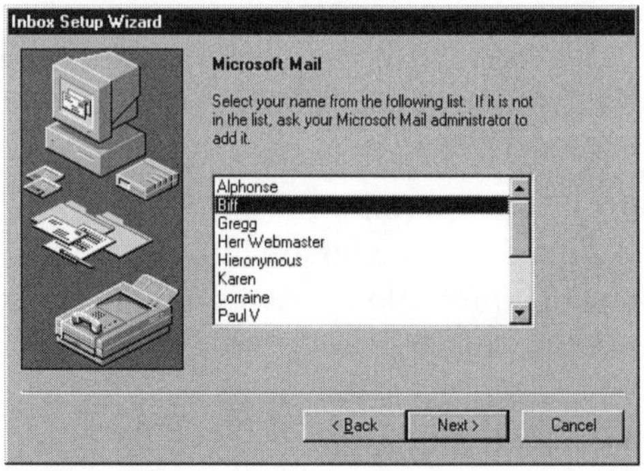

This wizard dialog box presents a list of the users in the selected postoffice.

Setting Up Internet Mail

If you activated the Internet Mail check box in the initial Inbox Setup Wizard dialog box, the wizard will run through the setup of your Internet e-mail particulars. (For simplicity's sake, I'll assume that you've already set up Windows 95 for your Internet connection. If not, check out Chapter 28 to get the full scoop.) The next figure shows the first of the wizard's Internet Mail dialog boxes. You have two choices here:

Modem Activate this option if you access your Internet account via your modem and Dial-Up Networking.

Network Activate this option if you access the Internet via your network connection.

Select **Next** > to move on.

You'll see this dialog box if you plan to use Exchange's Internet Mail service.

If you chose the Modem option, the Wizard asks you to select the Dial-Up Networking connection to use. Select the appropriate connection from the drop-down list provided, and then select **Next** >.

The next item on the wizard's agenda is the name or "IP address" of the "mail server" (see the next figure). A *mail server* is a computer that does two things:

➤ It stores your incoming e-mail messages in a special account. As you'll see later on, you can use Exchange to connect to this computer and transfer your waiting mail to your computer.

➤ It takes the e-mail you send out and forwards it to the appropriate destination.

In the vast majority of cases, the mail server you use will have a name (such as **mail.mcfedries.com**). Your network administrator or the administrator of your Internet service provider can tell you this. Make sure to activate the **Specify the name** option, and then enter the name in the text box provided. (If all you have is a bunch of numbers—such as 100.200.57.5—activate the **Specify the IP address** option and enter the numbers in the text box beside it.) Select **Next** > to carry on.

You're getting there (trust me). Now yet another wizard dialog box shows up, this one with two option buttons:

Off-line With this option, Exchange won't get or send your messages automatically. Instead, you need to use a separate Exchange feature called Remote Mail to send and receive messages. This is the option you should choose if you use Dial-Up Networking to connect to the Internet.

Automatic With this option, Exchange sends and receives your messages without any help from you. This is ideal if you use your network to connect to the Internet.

Once you make your choice, select **Next >**.

The wizard is wondering about the mail server that you use for your Internet e-mail.

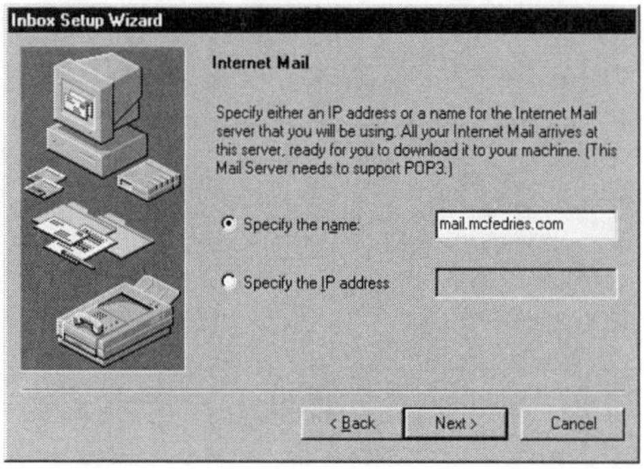

The wizard, ever curious, now asks you to enter your e-mail address (see the following figure). Your administrator will have provided this information to you, so enter it in the **E-mail address** text box. (The Your full name text box should show your name. If you like, you can also adjust this text, as required). As usual, select **Next >** to get on with it.

Use this wizard dialog box to enter your e-mail address.

The relentless wizard, showing us no mercy whatsoever, displays another dialog box. This time, it wants to know some stuff about your Internet mail account:

Mailbox name Use this text box to enter the name of your Internet mailbox. (Your administrator may refer to this as your "POP account.")

Password Use this text box to enter the password for your mailbox.

You know the drill by now: when you're done, select **Next >**.

If you activated the check box for the Microsoft Network, the wizard displays a dialog box with some information on this service. Select **Next >** to continue.

The next two dialog boxes are easy. In the first, the wizard asks for a "path to your personal address book." (The address book is where you'll store e-mail addresses you often use. I'll show you how it works later in this chapter.) Shrug your shoulders and select **Next >** to have the wizard create an address book for you.

The next dialog box asks for a "path to your personal folder file." (This is the file that Exchange uses to store your incoming messages.) Again, just select **Next >**.

Hallelujah, you're done! The last wizard dialog box reviews the information services set up for Exchange to use. Go ahead and select **Finish** to give the wizard the hook.

Okay, now that all that malarkey is over with and Exchange is pumped up and ready to roll, you can get right down to the nitty-gritty of reading and writing e-mail and fax messages. Your first chore is to wake Exchange from its hard disk slumbers by either double-clicking the desktop's **Inbox** icon, or by selecting the **Start** button, opening the **Programs** folder, and then selecting **Microsoft Exchange**. You'll begin in the next section by creating and shipping out an e-mail message.

Becoming a Composer: Creating a New Message

Composing a message isn't all that much different than composing a letter or memo in WordPad. You just need to add a few extra bits of information, such as the e-mail address of your recipient and a description of your message.

To start, pull down Exchange's **Compose** menu and select the **New Message** command (or press **Ctrl+N**). Exchange then displays the New Message window. Here are the basic steps to follow to compose your message:

1. In the **To** field, enter the e-mail address of recipient. If you want to send the message to multiple recipients, separate each address with a semi-colon (;).

2. In the **Cc** field, enter the addresses of any recipients that you want to receive copies of the message. Again, separate multiple addresses with semicolons.

3. In the **Subject** field, enter a brief description of the message. This description will appear in the Subject column of the recipient's mail program, so make sure it accurately describes your message.

4. Use the box below the Subject field to enter your message. (Feel free to use any of the formatting options found in the Format menu or the Formatting toolbar. Note, however, that not all systems will transfer the text formatting.) The following figure shows a complete message waiting to be shipped out.

5. To send your message, select the **File** menu's **Send** command, or press **Ctrl+Enter**.

Use the message composition window to compose your e-mail masterpieces.

Formatting toolbar—

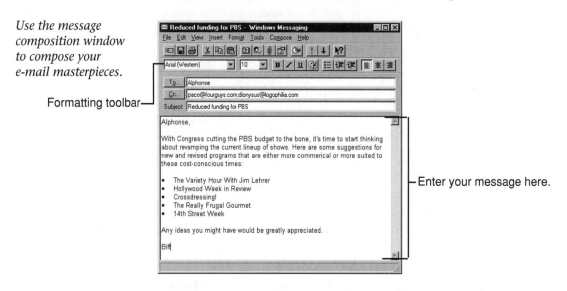

—Enter your message here.

Exchange then proceeds to deliver your missive to the recipient, right? Well, maybe. Remember earlier when the Microsoft Exchange Setup Wizard asked if you want to transfer messages "off-line" or "automatically"? If you selected the Automatic option, then, yes, Exchange delivers the message to the recipient's mailbox or to the remote system (depending on the address).

However, if you chose the Off-line option, Exchange *doesn't* deliver the message but, instead, stores it in a safe place. Why? Well, suppose you use the Internet to send e-mail and that you use Dial-Up Networking to establish an Internet connection via your modem. If you use Exchange off-line, you can first compose all your messages and *then* connect to the Internet to ship them out. This helps keep your connection time (and charges) to a minimum. Here's how it works:

1. Use the steps outlined earlier to compose and "send" all of your e-mail messages. (Remember: you're not actually sending the messages yet; you're just asking Exchange to store them for you temporarily. Where? Check out the Outbox folder.)

2. Pull down the **Tools** menu and select one of the following commands:

   Deliver Now   You see this command if you only chose to install one of the Exchange services (Microsoft Mail, Internet Mail, or The Microsoft Network).

   Deliver Now Using   You see this command if you installed Microsoft Mail, Internet Mail, and The Microsoft Network. In the new menu that appears, select **All Services** if you're sending messages to recipients in each service (or if your not sure what to do); select **Internet Mail** to send mail to just Internet recipients; or select **Microsoft Mail** to send mail to just Microsoft Mail recipients; select **The Microsoft Network** to send mail to just MSN members.

3. Exchange invokes the Dial-Up Networking connection that you specified during the Exchange setup procedure. You may see a dialog box asking you to enter your User name and Password. If so, enter the appropriate data and select **OK**.

Once you establish the connection, Exchange sends your messages (it will also look for any incoming messages) and then disconnect automatically.

Working with the Exchange Address Book

Exchange can store the addresses of your e-mail recipients in a handy address book. This is convenient because it saves you the drudgery of having to enter the address of a recipient every time you send them a message. To display the address book, pull down the **Tools** menu and select the **Address Book** command (or press **Ctrl+Shift+B**).

Populating Your Address Book

When the Address Book window appears, follow these steps to add an address:

1. Select the **File** menu's **New Entry** command. The New Entry dialog box appears.

2. Use the **Select the entry type** list to choose what kind of entry you want to add (Microsoft Mail Address or Internet Mail Address), and then select **OK**.

3. In the dialog box that appears, fill in the appropriate info (such as the Display Name and Email Address for an Internet user) and then select **OK**. Exchange returns you to the address book.

4. If you want to add more addresses, repeat steps 1–3. Otherwise, select the **File** menu's **Close** command to return to Exchange.

Using the Address Book to Specify Recipients

When you compose a message, you can use the Address Book to add recipients without having to type in their addresses manually. In the message composition window, first display the Address Book using either of the following methods:

➤ Select the **Tools** menu's **Address Book** command.

➤ Click either **To** or **Cc** (it doesn't matter which).

Use the **Show names from the** list to select the address list you want to work with. Highlight the recipient's name and then select either **To->** (if you want the name to appear in the To field) or **Cc->** (if you want the name to appear in the Cc field). After you add all the recipients for your message, select **OK**.

Retrieving and Reading Your Mail

If any of your friends or colleagues have sent some e-mail missives your way, the messages will wait patiently for you in your e-mail account. Before you can read these notes, you have to retrieve them to your Microsoft Exchange Inbox.

Again, how you go about this depends on whether you set up Exchange to transfer mail off-line or automatically:

➤ If you work off-line, pull down the **Tools** menu and select either **Deliver Now** (if you only use a single e-mail service) or **Deliver Now Using** (if you use two or more services). For the latter, select the appropriate service in the new menu that appears.

➤ If you work online, Exchange checks for incoming mail automatically: for Internet Mail, Exchange checks every 15 minutes; for Microsoft Mail, Exchange checks every 10 minutes. (Note, however, that you can check for messages any time by using the technique just outlined.)

Changing the Default Checking Intervals

If need be, you can force Exchange to check for new messages using a different time interval. Select the **Tools** menu's **Services** command, and then use these techniques:

➤ For Internet Mail, highlight **Internet Mail** and then select **Properties**. In the dialog box that appears, select the **Connection** tab, select the **Schedule** button, enter a new time interval, and select **OK**.

➤ For Microsoft Mail, highlight **Microsoft Mail** and then select **Properties**. In the dialog box that appears, select the **Delivery** tab, enter a new time in the **Check for new mail every** text box, and then select **OK**.

Once Exchange has retrieved your mail, it stores it in your Inbox folder, as shown in the following figure. As you can see, the Inbox consists of two panels. On the right side of the window is a list of mail you've received. On the left side are the folders into which you can file your mail. (If you don't see the folders, pull down the **View** menu and activate the **Folders** command.) As you see, some folders, such as the Sent Items folder, get stuff filed in them automatically. You'll learn about filing mail in the section "Moving and Deleting Messages" later in this chapter.

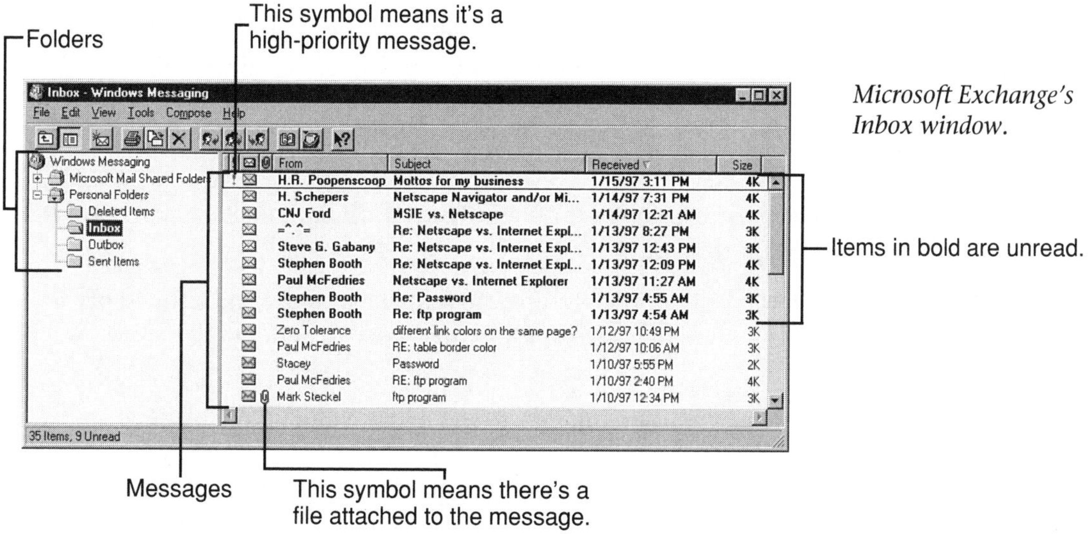

Microsoft Exchange's Inbox window.

Now that you have your stack of mail, you can read what your correspondents had to say by highlighting the message and selecting the **File** menu's **Open** command (or just double-click the message or press **Enter**).

A new window opens to display your message. The message area of the window has a scroll bar so you can view parts of your message that aren't visible at first.

What Do I Do with a Message After I've Read It?

When you get snail mail at the office, your assistant or somebody from the mailroom probably places it in your "In" basket. You then sort through and read the mail and farm out each message accordingly: some need to be responded to; some need to be forwarded; some get filed; and some get tossed in the garbage. Exchange gives you a similar range of choices after you peruse a message:

➤ You can send a reply to the author of the message.

➤ You can forward the message to someone else.

➤ You can save the message to a different folder.

➤ You can delete the message.

The next few sections give you the details for each task.

Holding Up Your End of the Conversation: Replying to a Message

One of the few negative consequences about e-mail's ease-of-use is that people aren't shy about asking you to send them information or to respond "ASAP" about one crisis or another. Hey, it was no sweat for them to send the message in the first place, so it should require even less sweat for you to respond, right? Well, luckily for them, that's usually the case, as you'll soon see.

To reply to a message, first use one of the following techniques to tell Exchange what kind of a reply you want to send:

 To send your retort only to the person who sent the message, click the **Reply to Sender** button, or select the **Compose** menu's **Reply to Sender** command.

 To send the reply to all the recipients of the original message, click the **Reply to All** button, or select the **Compose** menu's **Reply to All** command.

You'll use the Reply to Sender feature most often because the majority of messages have only one recipient (that's you!). However, the Reply to All option is useful for carrying on group discussions via e-mail. For instance, your boss might send a message to ten people asking for their opinions on the new product line. If you copy your reply to all recipients, you share your opinions not only with your boss, but with everyone else in the group.

Regardless of which option you choose, a reply window appears with the recipient(s) already filled in. Although the subject is also filled in (with **RE:** tacked onto the front), you can change it if you want.

In the reply window, the original message is automatically repeated for everyone's convenience. You can delete it or leave it as is. Type your response in the allotted space above the repeated message, and then send the message to the lucky recipient (who is no doubt waiting anxiously at his computer for your reply).

Psst! Pass It On: Forwarding a Message

Some messages just cry out to be shared with others. It can be a good joke, a brilliant argument, or some howler committed by a clueless correspondent. Whatever the reason, you can pass along a message to someone else by using Exchange's Forward feature.

Forwarding is a lot like replying, except that you have to fill in the To: line because Microsoft Exchange can't read your mind. (Although I hear the Microsoft programmers are working on it.) As with composing a new message, you'll either type in the address by hand or use the Address Book to pick out the recipient.

 To forward a message for someone else to take a look at, either select the **Forward** button from the toolbar, select the **Compose** menu's **Forward** command, or press **Ctrl+F.** Fill in the To: line and then send the message.

Deleting Messages You Don't Need

Some of the messages you'll receive will be the electronic equivalent of junk mail, and you won't want to bother with them again after you've read them. To keep the Inbox tidy, you should delete this detritus by highlighting the message and using one of the following techniques:

➤ Click the **Delete** button.

➤ Drag the message from the Inbox and drop it on the Deleted Items folder.

➤ Select the **File** menu's **Delete** command.

➤ Press **Ctrl+D.**

Whew! Recovering Accidentally Deleted Messages

When you delete a message, Exchange moves it to the Deleted Items folder. This is a precaution in case you change your mind about deleting a message, or if you delete a crucial message by accident. To recover a message, select the **Deleted Items** folder, highlight the message, and then move it back to its original folder. Keep in mind that Exchange cleans out the Deleted Items folder every time you quit the program. So if you're going to undelete a message, make sure you do it before ending your Exchange session.

Moving a Message to a Different Folder

Once you complete all your reading, replying, forwarding, and deleting, the messages left in your Inbox will be ones you intend to keep, just in case you need to refer to them later. But, just as you wouldn't keep all your opened snail mail in your office In basket, it doesn't make sense to have all those read messages cluttering Exchange's Inbox.

The solution is to create new folders to hold related types of messages. For example, if you and your boss exchange frequent e-mail notes, you can set up a folder just to hold her correspondence. Similarly, if you subscribe to an Internet mailing list, you can set up a folder to keep the regular mailings you get.

To create a folder in Exchange, highlight the **Personal Folders** folder, select the **File** menu's **New Folder** command, type the name of the folder in the New Folder dialog box that appears, and then select **OK**. The new folder appears on the left side of the Exchange window.

To move a message, you can either drag it from the Inbox and drop it on the folder, or you can pull down the **File** menu, select the **Move** command, choose the folder from the Move dialog box, and then select **OK**.

Reading More Messages

While you read a message, you can read the next or previous message in the same folder (in this case, your Inbox) just by using the following techniques:

 Select the **Previous** button, select the **View** menu's **Previous** command, or press **Ctrl+<**.

 Select the **Next** button, select the **View** menu's **Next** command, or press **Ctrl+>**.

Where's the Fax Stuff?

The proverbial space limitations meant I didn't have room to talk about Microsoft Fax in this chapter. If you'd like to get in on the faxing fun, I have an article that you can read that gives you just the fax facts. You can get this article using either of the following methods:

➤ To get a WordPad document via e-mail, send your request to the following address: **paul@mcfedries.com**.

➤ To view the article on my Web site, head for the home page of *The Complete Idiot's Guide to Windows 95*: **http://www.mcfedries.com/books/cigwin95/**.

The Least You Need to Know

If you're the kind of person who likes to stay in touch, Microsoft Exchange is the next best thing to being there. You can use it to send and receive e-mail both on your local network and over the vast reaches of the Internet.

Speak Like a Geek: The Complete Archive

386, 486   These are the aficionado's cool short forms for the *80386* and *80486* microprocessors. The microprocessor is the head honcho chip inside your computer that controls the whole shebang. Most people describe it as the "brain" of the computer, so you can think of these numbers as your computer's IQ. In that sense, a 486 machine is "smarter" than a 386 (although the high-end *Pentium* processor would have to be considered the genius of the group). To get the most out of Windows 95, you really should have a 486 or better microprocessor.

accessory   One of the mini-applications that comes free with Windows 95. Examples include WordPad (see Chapter 13), Paint (Chapter 14), and Microsoft Backup (Chapter 15).

active window   The window you're currently slaving away in. You can tell a window is active by looking at its title bar: if the bar shows white letters on a dark background, the window is active. (Inactive windows show light gray letters on a dark gray background.)

application   Software that accomplishes a specific practical task. It's the same thing as a *program*.

application window   A window that contains a running application, such as Explorer or WordPad.

ASCII text file   A file that uses only the American Standard Code for Information Interchange character set (techno-lingo for the characters you see on your keyboard).

background mode   A mode in which a program continues to perform a task "behind the scenes." Typical background tasks include spreadsheet recalculations, document printing, and modem file transfers.

boot   Computer geeks won't tell you to start your computer, they'll tell you to *boot* it. However, this doesn't mean you should punt your monitor across the room. The term *booting* comes from the phrase "pulling oneself up by one's own bootstraps," which refers to the fact that your computer can load everything it needs to operate properly without any help from the likes of you and me.

byte   Computerese for a single character of information. So, for example, the phrase *This phrase is 28 bytes long* is, yes, 28 bytes long (you count the spaces, too).

cascade   A cool way of arranging windows so that they overlap each other but you can still see each window's title bar.

cascade menu   A menu that appears when you select certain pull-down menu commands.

character formatting   Changing the look of text characters by altering their font, size, style, and more.

character spacing   The amount of space a font reserves for each character. In a *monospaced font*, every character gets the same amount of space regardless of its true width. In a *proportional font*, the space allotted to each letter varies according to the width of the letter.

check box   A square-shaped switch that toggles a dialog box option on or off. The option is toggled on when a check mark appears in the box.

click   To quickly press and release the left mouse button.

Clipboard   An area of memory that holds data temporarily during cut and paste operations.

command button   A rectangular doohickey (usually found in dialog boxes) that, when chosen, runs whatever command is spelled out on it.

commands   The options you see in a pull-down menu. You use these commands to tell the application what you want it to do next.

Control menu   A menu common to every Windows 95 window that you use to manipulate various features of the window. You activate the Control menu by clicking on the Control-menu box in the upper-left corner of the window or by pressing Alt+Spacebar (for an application window).

data files   The files used by you or your programs. See also *program files*.

delay   The amount of time it takes for a second character to appear when you press and hold down a key.

desktop   A metaphor for the Windows 95 screen. Starting a Windows 95 application is similar to putting a folder full of papers (the application window) on your desk. To do some work, you pull some papers out of the folder (the document windows) and place them on the desktop.

device driver   A small program that controls the way a device (such as a mouse) works with your system.

dialog boxes   Ubiquitous windows that pop up on the screen to ask you for information or to seek confirmation of an action you requested (or sometimes just to say "Hi").

directory   See *folder*.

diskette   See *floppy disk*.

document window   A window opened within an application. Document windows hold whatever you're working on in the application.

double-click   To quickly press and release the left mouse button *twice* in succession.

double-click speed   The maximum amount of time Windows 95 allows between the mouse clicks of a double-click.

drag   To press and hold down the left mouse button and then move the mouse.

drag-and-drop   Technique you can use to run commands or applications; you simply drag files or icons to strategic screen areas and drop them there.

drop-down list box   A list box that normally shows only a single item but, when selected, displays a list of options.

file   An organized unit of information inside your computer. If you think of your hard disk as a house, files can be either servants (your applications) or things you use (data used by you or by a program).

floppy disk   A portable storage medium that consists of a flexible disk protected by a plastic case. Floppy disks are available in a variety of sizes and capacities.

focus   The window that has the attention of the operating system (that is, Windows 95). See also *active window*.

folder   A storage location on your hard disk in which you keep related files together. If your hard disk is like a house, a folder is like a room inside the house.

font   A character set of a specific typeface, type style, and type size.

formatting   The process of setting up a disk so that a drive can read its information and write information to it. Not to be confused with *character formatting*.

fritterware   Any software that causes you to fritter away time fiddling with its various bells and whistles.

hard disk   The main storage area inside your computer. In the computer house analogy, the hard disk is equivalent to the inside of the house.

icons   The little pictures that Windows 95 uses to represent programs and files.

insertion point cursor   The blinking vertical bar you see inside a text box or in a word processing application, such as WordPad. It indicates where the next character you type will appear.

kilobyte   1,024 bytes. To be cool, always abbreviate this to "K."

list box   A small window that displays a list of items such as file names or directories.

maximize   To increase the size of a window to its largest extent. A maximized application window fills the entire screen (except for the taskbar). A maximized document window fills the entire application window.

megabyte   1,024 kilobytes or 1,048,576 bytes. The cognoscenti write this as "M" or "MB" and pronounce it "meg."

memory resident program   A program that stays in memory once it is loaded and works "behind the scenes." The program normally responds only to a specific event (such as the deletion of a file) or key combination. Also called a *terminate-and-stay-resident* (TSR) program.

menu bar   The horizontal bar on the second line of an application window. The menu bar contains the application's pull-down menus.

microprocessor   See *386, 486*.

minimize   To remove a program from the desktop without closing it. A button for the program remains on the taskbar.

multitasking   The capability to run several programs at the same time. Figuratively speaking, this simply means that Windows 95, unlike some people you may know, can walk and chew gum at the same time.

option buttons   Dialog box options that appear as small circles in groups of two or more. Only one option from a group can be chosen.

point   To place the mouse pointer so it rests on a specific screen location.

port   The connection into which you plug the cable from a device such as a mouse or printer.

program files   The files that run your programs. See also *data files*.

pull-down menus   Hidden menus that you open from an application's menu bar to access the commands and features of the application.

RAM   Stands for random-access memory. The memory in your computer that Windows 95 uses to run your programs.

repeat rate   After the initial delay, the rate at which characters appear when you press and hold down a key.

scalable font   A font in which each character exists as an outline that can be scaled to different sizes. Windows 95 includes such scalable fonts as Arial, Courier New, and Times New Roman. To use scalable fonts, you must have a software program called a *type manager* to do the scaling. Windows 95 comes with its own type manager: TrueType.

scroll bar   A bar that appears at the bottom or on the right of a window when the window is too small to display all of its contents.

system resources   Two memory areas that Windows 95 uses to keep track of things like the position and size of open windows, dialog boxes, and your desktop configuration (wallpaper and so on).

taskbar   The horizontal strip across the bottom of the Windows 95 screen. Each running application is given its own taskbar button, and you switch to an application by clicking on its button.

text box   A screen area into which you type text information, such as a description or a file name.

text editor   A program that lets you edit files that are text only. The Windows 95 text editor is called Notepad.

title bar   The area on the top line of a window that displays the window's title.

tracking speed   How quickly the mouse pointer moves across the screen when you move the mouse on its pad.

TrueType   A *font management program* that comes with Windows 95.

type size   A measure of the height of a font. Type size is measured in *points*; there are 72 points in an inch.

type style   Character attributes, such as regular, bold, and italic. Other type styles (often called type *effects*) are underlining and strikethru characters.

typeface   A distinctive graphic design of letters, numbers, and other symbols.

window   A rectangular screen area in which Windows 95 displays applications and documents.

word wrap   A word processor feature that automatically starts a new line when your typing reaches the end of the current line.

write-protection   Floppy disk safeguard that prevents you from changing any information on the disk. The 5¼-inch disks normally have a small notch on the side of the disk. If the notch is covered with tape, the disk is write-protected. Simply remove the tape to disable the write-protection. For a 3½-inch disk, the write-protection is controlled by a small movable tab on the back of the disk. If the tab is toward the edge of the disk, the disk is write-protected. To disable the write-protection, slide the tab away from the edge of the disk.

Index

385

W-Z